Printing on NetWare

Steve Whitaker

Stephen Kalman

Printing on NetWare

**Your Complete Guide to Managing and
Using NetWare's Most Powerful Utility**

M&T BOOKS

M&T Books
A Division of M & T Publishing, Inc.
411 Borel Avenue, Suite 100
San Mateo, CA 94402

© 1992 by M & T Publishing, Inc.

Printed in the United States of America

Library of Congress Cataloging-in-Publication Data

Kalman, Stephen
        p. cm.
    ISBN 1-55851-257-8 : $26.95
        1. Operating systems (Computers) 2. NetWare (Computer file)
I. Title
QA76.76.063K324   1992   91-44115
005.7'1369--dc20   CIP

Project Editor: Tova Fliegel   **Cover Design:** Lauren Smith Design
Copy Editor: Ken Neff   **Production Supervisor:** Cindy Williams
Technical Reviewer: Mickey Applebaum

95   94   93 92   4 3 2 1

For Gail,
who makes my failures bearable and my successes worthwhile

and for Jennifer and Sarah,
who give promise to a brighter future

Contents

SECTION III: ESTABLISHING A CUSTOM PRINTING ENVIRONMENT

SECTION IV: THIRD-PARTY PRINTING PRODUCTS

Acknowledgements

There is a long list of people and companies that have helped me create this book. I would like to give my thanks to:

Dennis Samuelson, and the staff at the MicroAge Learning Center. Dennis let me use his NAEC as a test site (guniea pig) whenever I needed a location with multiple printers, servers, routers or workstations; the staff had to put up with an often annoying "fluid" printing environment.

Tova Fliegel, acquisitions editor at M&T Books. This book would not exist but for her faith in the project. Her understanding and support did not go unnoticed.

Ken Neff, editor. I only expected Ken to correct punctuation and to revise some long-winded or wordy paragraphs. In addition to that he reworked major sections, created or suggested some key tables and charts, and added a large portion of much needed clarity and form. There isn't room for enough superlatives to adequately describe the quantity and quality of his work.

Mickey Applebaum, technical editor. As a NetWire Sysop, Mickey gives hundreds of hours a year to the NetWare user community with his support of the three printing sections on NetWire. It was my good fortune that he agreed to be the technical editor for this book. There are far fewer errors here now than there would have been without his efforts.

Kristin and Howard Marks, of Networks are Our Lives, Inc. Kristin and Howard have produced a seminar that covers Windows on NetWare; they were kind enough to give me permission to excerpt some of the printing related material, and even supplied it in machine readable form.

Hans Henderson, a fellow CNI (Certified NetWare Instructor) and NetWire addict. Hans gave me several megabytes of archived messages that I used in my research for the troubleshooting section.

Also, several companies supplied hardware and software for me to use as I wrote Section III (third party products). They are:

- Hewlett-Packard, for an HP3si (which I hope they forget about), and for a Lan I/O board.
- Pacific Page, for their Postscript Cartridge and PS-Print software.
- Intel, for a NetPort and for LanSpool software
- Castelle, for a JetPress and a Lanpress
- Insight, for their Mosaic print server, complete with the accounting module
- Fresh Technlogy, for Printer Assist and Queue Assist
- National Software Company, for PS-Manager
- Infinite Technologies, for IQueue
- POSTTE, written by Larry Armstrong while working for NdV Technica and placed into the public domain.

And last, to the programmers at WordPerfect Corporation, whose marvelous product made my job a little easier.

Why This Book is For You

If you have a NetWare LAN with at least one shared printer, this book is for you. It provides a wealth of information, starting with printing basics and going up to advanced printing concepts.

If you are an end user, this book will tell you how to make printing on a network printer easy and flexible. It will explain the NetWare commands and programs, and it will introduce some of the third-party products designed to assist you in setting up a custom printing environment.

If you are a LAN administrator in a small to medium sized network, this book will help you manage all the various printers spread around your network without having it become a full time job.

For LAN administrators of large networks, this book will help by providing troubleshooting and training tips, and by introducing third party packages that make better use of your system resources.

For consultants and installers, this book has the information you need to install or upgrade any common version of NetWare, plus installation hints and tips for many of the most useful third-party products.

If you are a network owner, you can use the information in this book to minimize your printing costs. You'll see how to you can create "floating" printers that can be moved to the area of heaviest need thus avoiding having to purchase extra printers that are usually idle.

Printing on NetWare provides a wealth of information for all users of Novell NetWare.

Introduction

How to Use This Book

Organization

This book is divided into three main parts. The first part, comprising Sections I through III, looks at Novell's solutions for NetWare printing.

- Section I is an overview of basic NetWare printing concepts. Case studies are used to give examples of practical situations and decision-making techniques.

- Section II examines each of the NetWare environments in common use today. These include NetWare 286 versions 2.15 and 2.20, and NetWare 386 version 3.11. The discussion of version 2.20 is divided into two chapters: one for those who choose "core" printing and one for those who prefer the print server approach.

    Each of these chapters begins with a discussion of the default printing environment, if there is one, for those who just want to get printing up and running with the least amount of fuss. A discussion of how to modify the defaults is also included for those who want a more customized printing setup. (Since most readers will be concerned with only one NetWare environment, some of the material is repeated from chapter to chapter.)

- Section III examines the NetWare print commands and utilities in detail. The main thrust of these chapters is to explore both the "how to" and the "whys" of using these programs to customize the NetWare printing environment. The explanation includes numerous examples from the case studies to show practical situations and decision-making techniques.

The middle part of the book—Section IV—looks at various third-party products for enhancing NetWare printing.

- Section IV explores other vendors' print servers, replacements for and supplements to the CAPTURE and NPRINT commands, and methods for attaching printers directly to the network cabling system.

    Our intent is not to compare one package or product to another. Given the speed at which these products are revised and reincarnated, the task of comparison is better suited to weekly or monthly trade magazines. Instead, this book focuses on the specific features and benefits offered by these alternate solutions. This section includes summarized instructions for installing and using these products in the NetWare environment.

The remainder of the book deals with troubleshooting and avoiding problems that can arise with NetWare printing.

- Section V is divided into two chapters: the first is organized by NetWare command; the second is organized by conceptual area (for example, upgrading or PostScript printing). This material is presented in question-and-answer format.

Lastly, three appendices provide supplemental information relating to NetWare printing.

- Appendix A lists all of NetWare's printing-related programs, their version numbers, and their date and time stamps. In those cases where an updated file is available on NetWire, the list gives the library and file names as well. (NetWire is a part of the CompuServe Information Service; Appendix A includes information on how to access NetWire.)

- Appendix B looks at the intricacies of using Microsoft Windows as part of the NetWare printing environment.

- Appendix C deals with NetWare Lite, Novell's new peer-to-peer networking product. Although NetWare Lite is not a third-party product per se, we treat it as a separate subject because the concepts behind printing on a peer-to-peer system are so fundamentally different from traditional printing on NetWare 286 and 386.

Section I:

Overview of Printing on NetWare

Printing to a network printer is only marginally the same as printing to your own dedicated printer. The two processes are similar in that, in both cases, you send something to the printer by using a command or by pressing the appropriate keys in your application program, and the output ultimately appears at the printer. The differences, however, are monumental.

When you print to a network printer, the data to be printed leaves your workstation and travels over the LAN to a file server, where it waits in line with print jobs sent by other users from their workstations. From there, the data is handed off to a program called a print server which is in charge of making sure it gets printed at the right printer. The print server might be a program running in the same machine as the file server, or it might be in a totally separate machine. The printer itself might be attached to the file server, or to the print server, or even to another user's workstation.

This section introduces some basic terms and concepts relating to the NetWare printing process. This elementary information will serve as a foundation for the remainder of the book.

CHAPTER 1

NetWare Printing Basics

When users share printers on a network, there has to be some mechanism to manage the process. Output has to be kept separate; users' printouts should be printed someplace convenient for the user; the waiting time should be kept to a minimum. Novell's solutions to these needs are the focus of most of this book; this chapter presents an overview of the basics of network printing.

Definitions and Terminology

Throughout this book, we'll use printing terms and phrases that have meanings specific to NetWare. To avoid having to define these terms every time they are used, we list them here along with their meanings.

Server (sometimes File Server). This is the computer that is running a version of NetWare. The versions discussed in this book are NetWare 286 versions 2.15 and 2.20, and NetWare 386 version 3.11.

Queue (sometimes Print Queue). This is where print jobs from network workstations are collected and held before they are printed.

Local Printer. This is a printer that is physically attached to the computer where the print server program is running.

Remote Printer. This is a shared printer that is managed by a print server, but is attached to a user's workstation.

Print Server. This is a program that controls both printers and print queues. It takes print jobs from the queues it manages and prints them on local and remote printers.

Print Job (sometimes Printout). The output from a user's workstation that is destined for a network printer.

The NetWare Printing Process

The NetWare printing process can be viewed as a series of links in a chain, as illustrated in Figure 1-1.

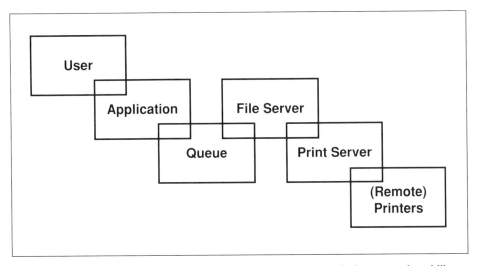

Figure 1-1: The various components involved in NetWare printing are related like links in a chain.

In NetWare, all printing is done by way of queues. Queues are merely subdirectories of SYS:SYSTEM. When you define a queue, its default set of users is the group EVERYONE, but you can easily change that.

The first three links of the chain represent how data arrives in a NetWare print queue. Typically, a user at a workstation running DOS (COMMAND.COM) initiates an application. The application might be a NetWare-aware program, such as WordPerfect, that can be set up to send data directly to a network print queue. Or, for applications that aren't designed for network printing, the user might run NetWare's CAPTURE command to redirect data destined for a local printer port to a network print queue. As another possibility, the user could use the NetWare NPRINT command to send a file that has already been formatted for printing to a print queue.

Once the data is in the queue, the other three links take over to finish the printing process. The file server takes the data from the queue and delivers it to the print server. (It's possible that the file server and print server reside within the same physical computer; in this case, one process is taking the data from the queue and giving it over to another process to handle.) Then, the print server sends the data to the printer, which might be attached to the file or print server itself, or to a remote workstation.

These links aren't necessarily separate physical devices. As mentioned, the file server might also be managing the printing; the printer might be physically attached to the file server or to the print server, or even to a remote workstation. Nevertheless, each link represents a separate logical step in the printing process.

Some third-party facilities available for NetWare bypass one or another of these links to provide a shorter, faster print path. However, they often do it at the expense of features or functions.

The purpose of this book is to examine each of the programs that make up these links and the relationships among them. Then we'll look at the variations and alternatives in a manner that will help you design the right printing environment for your needs.

Queue-to-Printer Relationships

When you establish the printing environment, you tell NetWare which printer(s) serve which queue(s). There are several possible combinations:

- One queue serving one printer
- One queue serving two or more printers
- Two or more queues serving one printer
- Multiple queues serving multiple printers

The details of establishing printer/queue relationships are discussed in two places later in this book: first in Chapters 8 and 9 which describe creating print queues and print servers via PCONSOLE, and second in Chapter 11 where the printing console commands are described.

One Queue-One Printer

Figure 1-2 is a representation of the default printing setup for NetWare version 2.15 and some version 2.20 installations. (For details on printing defaults, see Section II.) In this setup, there is only one print queue for each network printer. For example, jobs directed to PRINTQ_0 will be printed on Printer0.

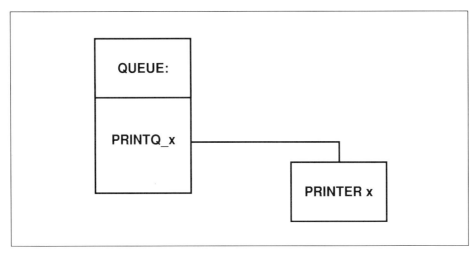

Figure 1-2: In this setup, one printer is servicing one queue.

For very small networks, having one queue for each printer attached to the file server is usually sufficient. But as networks grow in size and complexity, this default setup quickly becomes inadequate.

Many Queues-One Printer

NetWare also provides the ability to assign more than one queue to a single printer, as shown in Figure 1-3.

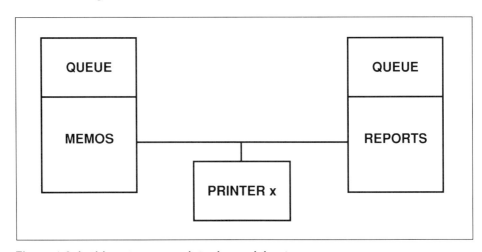

Figure 1-3: In this setup, one printer is servicing two queues.

When you have more than one queue for a printer, you can have each queue serviced at a different level of priority. Here's how the process works. Whenever the currently printing job ends, NetWare always checks the higher priority queue first. If it is empty, it checks the lower priority queue (and so on, if there are more than two queues) until it finds a job.

Network administrators can use these rules to better manage print output. For example, suppose management has decreed that all jobs up to three pages in length will be called "memos" and should be printed before longer jobs (called "reports"). To implement this system, the network administrator would create two queues and assign both of them to a single printer (as shown in Figure 1-3). In creating the queues, the administrator would give the MEMOS queue a higher priority than the REPORTS queue.

The steps required to implement this and other queue-printer assignments vary, depending on whether the file server is operating with core printing enabled or if there is a print server defined. We'll discuss the actual commands in detail in Section III.

One Queue-Many Printers

Another alternative is to have two or more printers assigned to service a single queue, as shown in Figure 1-4.

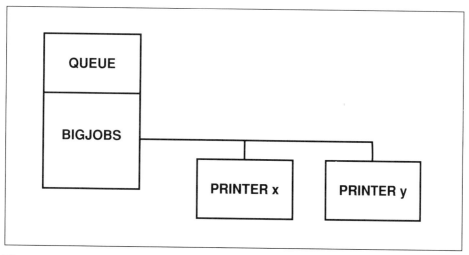

Figure 1-4: In this setup, two printers are servicing one queue.

Occasionally, the print jobs sent to a given queue are so large that they cause a severe backlog in print output. Even if the files contain just plain ASCII text to be printed (no fonts, graphics, or PostScript command strings), a single printer can quickly become overloaded when used on a network.

For example, one of the most popular network printers is the HP LaserJet Series II. This printer can print eight pages per minute. A little arithmetic shows that a single copy of a 150-page report would take almost twenty minutes to print. If multiple users are sending large reports (especially if they also request more than one copy), the printer could easily be backed up for hours.

One solution to this problem is to assign more than one printer to service the queue, as shown in Figure 1-4. With two printers, NetWare will send the first job in the queue to the first printer, then give the second job to the second printer. Whichever printer finishes first will then get the third job, and so on.

Combining Queue-Printer Configurations

The preceding queue-printer configuration options are not mutually exclusive. For example, combining the setups shown in Figures 1-3 and 1-4 might result in the setup shown in Figure 1-5.

PRINTER NUMBER	QUEUE NAME	PRIORITY
0	MEMOS	1
0	REPORTS	2
0	BIGJOBS	3
0	PRINTQ_0	4
1	MEMOS	1
1	BIGJOBS	2
1	PRINTQ_1	3
2	BIGJOBS	1
2	PRINTQ_2	2

Figure 1-5: Combining the previous examples results in a mixed setup to handle the needs of medium-sized networks.

This combined setup is typical for a medium-sized network. Printer 0 services four queues at different priorities. Most of the time, this printer will be busy with the memos and reports. But if neither of those queues had jobs pending, the printer would service the BIGJOBS queue rather than sit idle.

Similarly, Printer 1 will be used mostly for BIGJOBS. But it will always check the MEMOS queue first and handle those short printouts as its top priority. Printer 2 is dedicated to the BIGJOBS queue on a full-time basis.

Note that the default queues (PRINTQ_0, PRINTQ_1, and so on) are also assigned, but at the lowest priority. This assignment ensures that any output sent to those queues will be printed. However, making them low-priority discourages their use.

We'll use this combined setup as the basis for our discussions in Section II of the default environments and the techniques for modifying them.

Case Studies

To facilitate the introduction and description of various printing situations, and to emphasize some of the more important points of working with NetWare printing, we'll refer throughout this book to three representative case studies:

- Hirsch and Cabot, a small consulting partnership
- Allied Accounting Associates, a medium-sized accounting firm
- Southern Confederacy Insurance Company, a large regional insurance company

Each of these companies has a different type of Novell network and, as we'll see, each has different shared printing needs.

Hirsch and Cabot

Hirsch and Cabot is a small computer consulting partnership that employs the two principals, a secretary, and occasionally some temporary help. They run NetWare version 2.20 on a nondedicated file server, using core printing. Their application programs include Microsoft Word, Microsoft Excel, and FoxPro.

This small network has two printers: an Epson LQ-800 attached to the file server's LPT1 port, and a LaserJet Series II attached to the COM1 port. They use the Epson for printing program listings and spreadsheets; the LaserJet is for correspondence and final program printouts to be included in the formal documentation they give their clients.

Figure 1-6 illustrates Hirsch and Cabot's network environment.

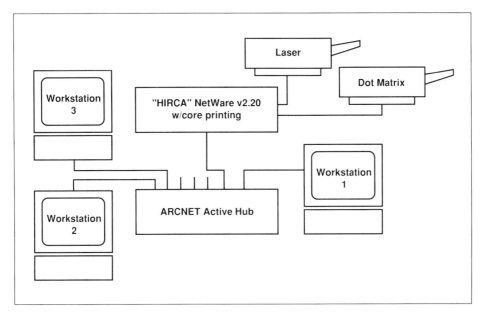

Figure 1-6: Hirsch and Cabot's network illustrates the typical printing needs of small LANs.

Allied Accounting Associates

Allied Accounting is a medium-sized firm employing fifty people. Its offices are in an old, converted Victorian mansion, where almost all the employees have work-stations on a NetWare version 2.20 network. They run several specialized application programs, including Docu-Tax (a database program that generates tax returns), Early Retirement (a modified spreadsheet that tracks investment portfolios), Pay-day (a payroll program that they use for their own in-house payroll as well as for some of their client's payrolls), and WordPerfect, for general word processing.

The flurry of everyday business activity keeps the single file server plenty busy. In addition, Allied Accounting's printing workload calls for twenty shared printers. These are all HP LaserJet Series II or Series III printers, except for two IBM Pro-Printers used for printing checks. Because of the number of printers and the load on the file server, they have moved the network print services to two standalone print servers, named according to their location: WEST_WING and EAST_WING.

Figure 1-7 illustrates Allied Accounting's network environment.

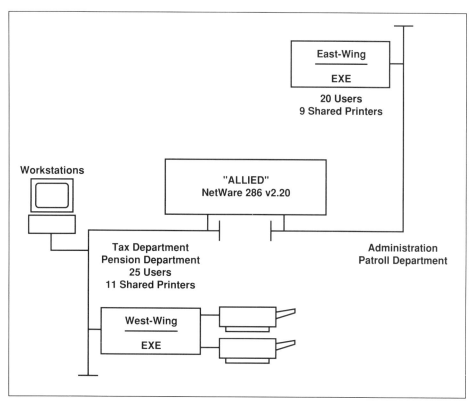

Figure 1-7: Allied Accounting's network represents the printing needs of typical medium-sized organizations.

Southern Confederacy Insurance Company

Southern Confederacy is a large regional insurance company with several offices in each of the six states where it does business. We'll look at one of their newest offices, located in a modern downtown office building.

Their network has four file servers: one running NetWare version 3.11, one running NetWare version 2.15 (with three attached, shared printers), and two servers running NetWare version 2.20 (one using core printing, the other using the print server VAP). In total, there are 175 users and 100 shared printers. To manage all these printers, they run PSERVER.NLM on the 3.11 server and two copies of PSERVER.VAP—one on the 2.20 file server and one on the router. They also have five standalone print servers running PSERVER.EXE.

In addition to the normal complement of 100 shared printers, Southern Confederacy has 35 more printers that generally are not shared. However, when printing backs up, or when the usual user of one of those printers is out of the office for the day, these additional printers are added to the shared pool.

Figure 1-8 illustrates Southern Confederacy Insurance's network environment.

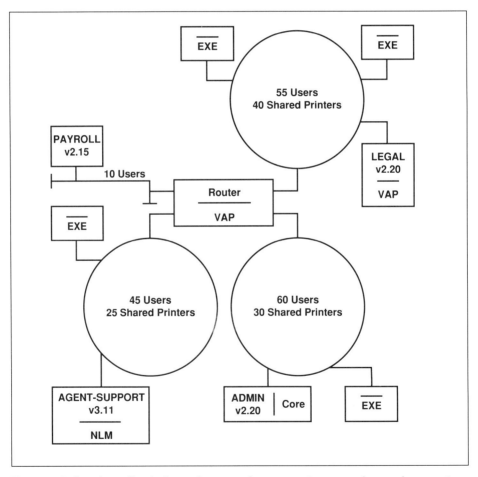

Figure 1-8: Southern Confederacy's network represents a complex environment that uses all of NetWare's print services.

We'll draw on these case studies for concrete examples in various sections of this book, when the point of discussion is of importance to an organization of a particular type or size.

Section II:

NetWare's Default Printing Environments

NetWare has always provided some sort of shared printing environment. However, as new versions are released, Novell has continually improved that environment. This section covers the default printing environments for the versions of NetWare currently in widespread use.

• Chapter 2 covers the default printing environments for NetWare 286 version 2.1x.

• Chapter 3 discusses the default environment for NetWare 286 version 2.20 with core printing.

• Chapter 4 covers the defaults for NetWare 286 version 2.20 when a print server is defined.

• Chapter 5 discusses the default environment for NetWare 386 version 3.11.

We define a default printing environment as: the combination of print facilities that are available to users immediately after the generation or installation of the file server, before any intervention on the part of the network supervisor.

As you will see, the more recent versions of NetWare have moved further and further away from the default environments that were in place after installing earlier versions of NetWare. In version 2.1x, printing worked immediately after the NETGEN process was completed, so long as the supervisor did nothing to change it. In version 2.20 with core printing, the supervisor has only a small amount of work to do to make the system ready to print. In both version 2.20 without core printing and in version 3.11, there is no default environment at all; the supervisor must set up printing facilities as one of the first tasks after installation.

Each of the chapters in this section starts out by describing the default environment (if any). From there, they explore the options available within NetWare to modify the default setup and maintain the NetWare printing environment.

CHAPTER 2

NetWare 286 Version 2.1x

NetWare version 2.1x is the last version of NetWare that provided a working print environment immediately after installation. The only prerequisite condition is that a printer be attached to the file server and "spooled," or defined as a network printer, during the NETGEN installation process. Once the operating system is generated and installed, users of any version from 2.10 to 2.15C can log in and print without any further intervention on the part of the network supervisor. The printer begins producing output as soon as a user sends a print job.

In this chapter, we'll look at how to establish this default environment and discuss some of the techniques for modifying it.

The NetWare Version 2.1x Defaults

With NetWare version 2.1x, a program called NETGEN is included with the basic software package. This is the program installers use to link and configure a custom NetWare operating system.

One of the final steps of the NETGEN installation process presents a screen like the one in Figure 2-1.

To provide users the ability to print to a printer attached to the file server, the installer must "SELECT" at least one of these ports. The first port selected corresponds to Printer 0, the next to Printer 1, and so on. If the installer wanted the parallel port to be the default printer (Printer 0), he or she had to be sure to select it first.

The NETGEN program is capable of looking at the computer on which NetWare is being installed and determining which of the five possible ports actually exist on that machine. On many computers (such as the one used for the screen in Figure 2-1), there is no LPT3 port.

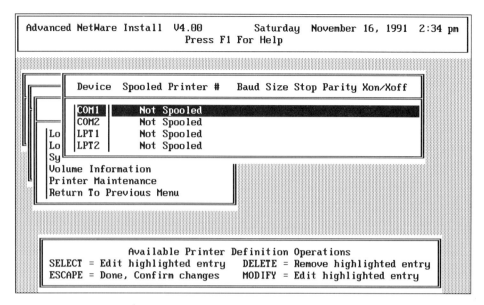

Figure 2-1: Near the end of the installation process, NETGEN presents this printer definition screen.

> **Note:** Occasionally, a port called "LPT4" will appear. This is most likely the mouse port. Since the NETGEN program predates built-in mouse ports, it mistakes them for an additional parallel port. Be careful not to select LPT4; it will prevent the file server from initializing.

When the installation process is complete and the file server is brought up, NetWare 2.1x automatically assigns Printer 0 to service entries in PRINTQ_0, Printer 1 to service PRINTQ_1, and so forth.

These default assignments remain in effect even after the file server is rebooted; you don't have to reinstate them each time. However, this is true only in the absence of an AUTOEXEC.SYS file on the server. Once the network supervisor creates an AUTOEXEC.SYS file (no matter what commands it contains), NetWare will ignore the default printing configuration the next time the server is rebooted. (See "Putting Defaults in the AUTOEXEC.SYS File" below for more information.)

Spooler Assignments

In addition to assigning the queues, NetWare also sets up default spooler assignments. Spooler assignments accommodate users who try to send print jobs directly to a printer, rather than to a queue. Sending jobs to a printer was a valid procedure in earlier versions of NetWare, but starting with NetWare 2.1x it is no longer the accepted method.

By setting up a spooler assignment, NetWare can trap any print jobs that users send to a particular printer and reroute them to a queue. For example, the command "SPOOL 0 TO PRINTQ_0" intercepts any print jobs sent to Printer 0 and submits them instead to the queue PRINTQ_0. If another command is entered to assign that queue to Printer 0, the output will still be printed where it is supposed to be, but via the preferred route (user to queue to printer).

Putting Defaults in the AUTOEXEC.SYS File

When a NetWare 2.1x file server is booted, the operating system looks for a file named AUTOEXEC.SYS in the SYS:SYSTEM directory. This file, if it exists, contains console commands that the supervisor wants to be issued every time the file server is restarted.

This file should also include the print setup commands. One of the most common causes of the complaint "My network suddenly stopped printing" is that someone created an AUTOEXEC.SYS file. The mere presence of this file, even if it had no printing-related commands, causes NetWare to stop establishing the default assignments between queues and printers.

Even though NetWare 2.1x establishes a default printing environment, the network supervisor should always create an AUTOEXEC.SYS file that includes the default printer-queue assignments. Figure 2-2 shows the commands to enter to duplicate the default assignments in the AUTOEXEC.SYS file. Of course, if you don't have five network printers, you would include only as many commands as there are printers.

```
PRINTER 0 ADD QUEUE PRINTQ_0 AT PRIORITY 1
PRINTER 1 ADD QUEUE PRINTQ_1 AT PRIORITY 1
PRINTER 2 ADD QUEUE PRINTQ_2 AT PRIORITY 1
PRINTER 3 ADD QUEUE PRINTQ_3 AT PRIORITY 1
PRINTER 4 ADD QUEUE PRINTQ_4 AT PRIORITY 1

SPOOL 0 TO PRINTQ_0
SPOOL 1 TO PRINTQ_1
SPOOL 2 TO PRINTQ_2
SPOOL 3 TO PRINTQ_3
SPOOL 4 TO PRINTQ_4

START PRINTER 0
START PRINTER 1
START PRINTER 2
START PRINTER 3
START PRINTER 4
```

Figure 2-2: To be safe, include these default-equivalent print commands in the AUTOEXEC.SYS file.

To underscore the importance of duplicating the defaults in the AUTOEXEC.SYS, consider this experience related by Ann Cabot, partner in Hirsch and Cabot.

I was working as a network administrator for a thirty-user network. An assistant administrator, Marty, was assigned to me just a week before I left on my honeymoon. I gave Marty the supervisor password for emergency use, showed him a few things he might need it for—such as changing a password and clearing an intruder detect—and told him I'd train him when I got back.

I was gone just three days when an urgent message for me arrived at the hotel. It seems that printing no longer worked. Jobs went to the queues all right, but they never printed out. They needed me to come back right away.

Well, my new husband wasn't very pleased, but we flew home and I went right in to the office. I asked Marty if he did anything to the print setup. He said, "No." It took me about an hour to find it, but it turns out that Marty was playing around in SYSCON and had created an AUTOEXEC.SYS that had the single command: MONITOR. He explained that he wanted to see the network usage as soon as it came up, and he didn't see any harm in doing so.

Exercising extreme self-control, I explained that the act of creating that file also killed the system's default print environment, so the printers were never assigned to service the queues. I added the proper commands to the AUTOEXEC.SYS file, brought the server down and back up, and printing resumed.

But that's not the end of the story. When I went to my boss to complain about Marty's actions having cost me the rest of a week in the sun, my boss told me it was my own fault for relying on a system default—especially one that was so easy to disable. He said I should have placed the proper commands into the AUTOEXEC.SYS long ago, and that if I had done so, I'd still be sipping daiquiris at the poolside. It took me a long time to admit that he was right.

Techniques for Modifying the Defaults

As mentioned in Chapter 1, the relationship between printers and queues is potentially a many-to-many relationship. However, it is always a good idea to start with a baseline, and in this case that baseline is the default environment. Figure 2-2 shows the commands that mimic the default.

The next two figures show the commands you can use to change those defaults. Figure 2-3 shows the commands necessary to assign two queues to a single printer, with one of them having a higher priority.

```
PRINTER 1 ADD QUEUE MEMOS   AT PRIORITY 1
PRINTER 1 ADD QUEUE REPORTS AT PRIORITY 2
```

Figure 2-3: These commands add queues to printers and assign priorities.

Figure 2-4 shows the opposite configuration—a single queue assigned to two printers.

```
PRINTER 2 ADD QUEUE BIGJOBS
PRINTER 3 ADD QUEUE BIGJOBS
```

Figure 2-4: These commands assign two printers to a queue.

As explained in Chapter 1, these options are not mutually exclusive. You might enhance the baseline shown in Figure 2-2 to produce the following setup, which is typical for a medium-sized network.

PRINTER NUMBER	QUEUE NAME	PRIORITY
0	MEMOS	1
0	REPORTS	2
0	BIGJOBS	
0	PRINTQ_0	4
1	MEMOS	1
1	BIGJOBS	2
1	PRINTQ_1	3
2	BIGJOBS	1
2	PRINTQ_2	2

Figure 2-5: This combination of printer and queue assignments is typical for a medium-sized network.

The commands in the AUTOEXEC.SYS file to produce this setup are shown in Figure 2-6.

In this arrangement, Printer 0 is assigned to four queues at different priorities. Most of the time, this printer will be busy with memos and reports. But if neither of those queues has any jobs pending, it can service the BIGJOBS queue rather than sit idle.

```
PRINTER 0 ADD MEMOS AT PRIORITY 1
PRINTER 0 ADD REPORTS AT PRIORITY 2
PRINTER 0 ADD BIGJOBS AT PRIORITY 3
PRINTER 0 ADD PRINTQ_0 AT PRIORITY 4
PRINTER 1 ADD MEMOS AT PRIORITY 1
PRINTER 1 ADD BIGJOBS AT PRIORITY 2
PRINTER 1 ADD PRINTQ_1 AT PRIORITY 3
PRINTER 2 ADD BIGJOBS AT PRIORITY 1
PRINTER 2 ADD PRINTQ_2 AT PRIORITY 2
```

Figure 2-6: These commands set up the combination printer-queue assignments shown in the previous figure.

Similarly, Printer 1 is used mainly for BIGJOBS, but it will always check the MEMOS queue first and handle those short printouts as its top priority. Printer 2 is dedicated to the BIGJOBS queue on a full-time basis.

Note the assignment of the default queues (PRINTQ_0, PRINTQ_1, and so on), at the lowest priority, to ensure that any output sent to those queues is printed. Using the low priority discourages the use of the default queues.

Printing Maintenance Options in NETGEN

If your printing needs or facilities change at a later date (for example, if you acquire a new printer that is to be hooked up to a previously-unused port), you can use the NETGEN program to effect the change. You use the same menu (accessed from the "Miscellaneous Maintenance" option) to spool another port.

Here are the steps required to add or remove a printer from the spooled list. Before you begin, have all users log out of the network, since you have to bring the file server down to rerun NETGEN.

1. Bring the server down and start NETGEN. Use your working copies of the NetWare system diskettes to restart NETGEN and have it recognize the existing configuration. (Refer to the NetWare 286 Maintenance manual for exact instructions on how to restart NETGEN.) NETGEN's main menu is shown in Figure 2-7.

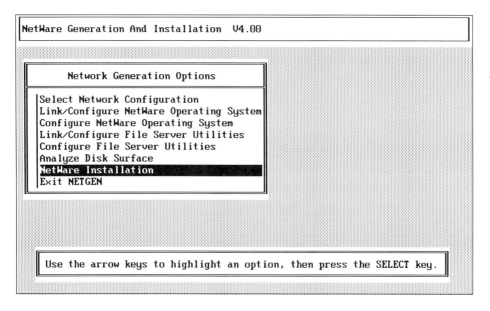

Figure 2-7: On an existing file server, NETGEN presents this main menu when you start the program.

2. Select "NetWare Installation" from the main menu to begin the maintenance process.

3. A screen like the one shown in Figure 2-8 will appear. Press <Esc> to indicate that you have examined the drive list and it is correct. (If it is not correct, refer to the NetWare 286 Maintenance manual for help.)

4. Press <Enter> (assuming the drive list is correct) when you see the screen shown in Figure 2-9.

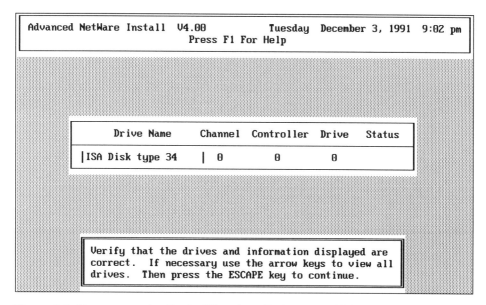

Figure 2-8: Once you enter the NetWare Installation part of NETGEN, it displays a list of network hard disks.

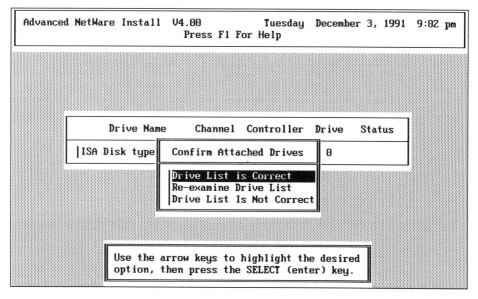

Figure 2-9: Once you have examined the drive list, select this option to confirm that the list is correct.

5. From the menu shown in Figure 2-10, choose "Select Custom Installation Options."

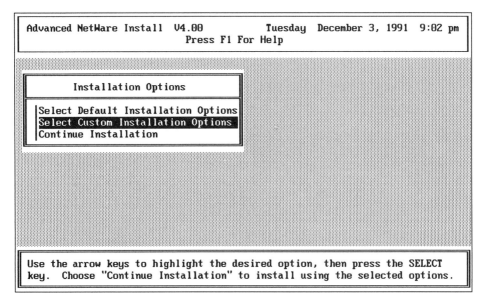

Figure 2-10: To access the printer maintenance options, you must selecting the custom installation option.

6. From the menu shown in Figure 2-11, choose "Miscellaneous Maintenance."

7. From the next menu, select "Printer Maintenance," as shown in Figure 2-12.

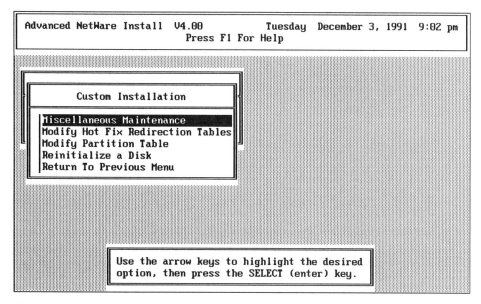

Figure 2-11: The printer maintenance options are found under NETGEN's "Miscellaneous Maintenance" option.

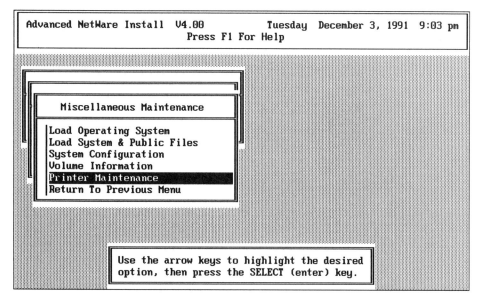

Figure 2-12: The "Printer Maintenance" option leads you to the screen for defining network printers.

8. Make the necessary changes in the screen shown in Figure 2-13. Press <Enter> to spool another printer, or press <Del> to unspool a previously spooled printer.

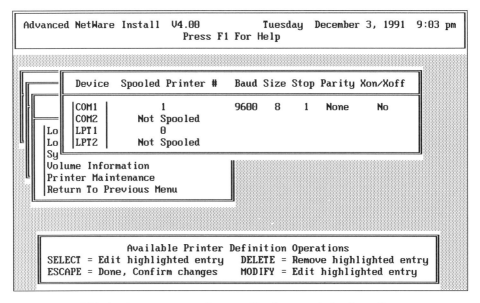

Figure 2-13: This is the screen used to modify the spooled printer list.

When you are finished making changes, press <Esc> to leave the spooled printer list and confirm your changes.

9. Select "Load Operating System" from the "Miscellaneous Maintenance" menu. Since your changes will only take effect if the operating system is reloaded, you must set the load flag as shown in Figure 2-14.

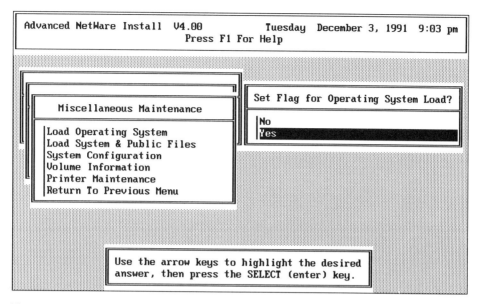

Figure 2-14: Before you exit NETGEN, set the operating system load flag.

As you exit NETGEN, the program will reload the updated operating system onto the server. Follow the program's prompts to insert the NetWare diskettes and exit. Your changes will be in effect when you bring the server back up.

CHAPTER 3

NetWare 286 Version 2.20 with Core Printing

The latest release of NetWare 286 is version 2.20. The installation program for this version is INSTALL.EXE (located on the SYSTEM-1 diskette).

When you start INSTALL, its first menu presents four choices, as shown in Figure 3-1.

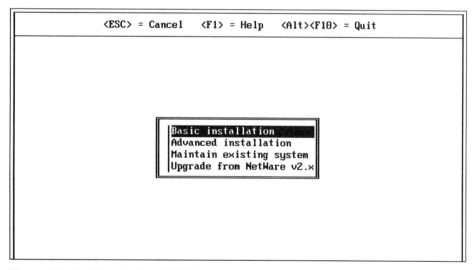

```
            <ESC> = Cancel    <F1> = Help    <Alt><F10> = Quit




                        ┌──────────────────────────┐
                        │ Basic installation       │
                        │ Advanced installation    │
                        │ Maintain existing system │
                        │ Upgrade from NetWare v2.x │
                        └──────────────────────────┘




```

Figure 3-1: NetWare 2.20's INSTALL program presents four initial choices.

Those users who choose "Basic Installation" will always have core printing enabled.

Only the users who choose "Advanced Installation" or "Upgrade from NetWare v2.*x*" will see the installation screen (Figure 3-2) where they get the initial opportunity to choose between including core printing or not including it. (This latter choice implies use of the print server software; either PSERVER.VAP at the file server or PSERVER.EXE at a dedicated workstation.) Those who have already made their choice and want to change it would select "Maintain existing system."

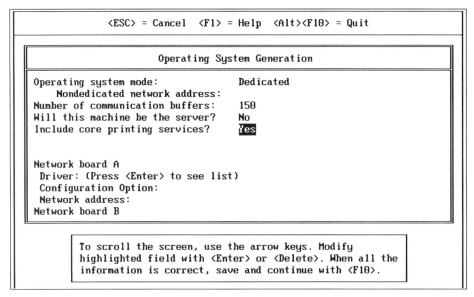

Figure 3-2: INSTALL's "Advanced Installation" option gives you the choice of including core printing services or not.

The default environment for a "Basic" installation is different from that of an "Advanced" one, and both are different from the "Maintenance" choice. The following sections in this chapter address these various options, but from the starting point of those who choose to enable core printing enabled.

The next chapter is for those who don't want core printing, preferring instead to use the print server VAP.

> **Note:** You can run the dedicated print server program (PSERVER.EXE) at a network workstation no matter which installation option you choose.

Basic Installation

"Basic Installation" is the option that is most similar to the prior release (NetWare version 2.1x). After the basic installation is completed, printing will automatically work. No further intervention is required of the network administrator.

The basic installation always includes core printing in the file server. It also creates a default print queue named PRINTQ_0. Additionally, it creates a default AUTOEXEC.SYS file that contains the following lines:

```
PRINTER 0 CREATE LPT1
PRINTER 0 ADD QUEUE PRINTQ_0
SPOOL 0 TO PRINTQ_0
```

Figure 3-3: The "Basic" installation creates this default AUTOEXEC.SYS file.

With the queue created by the installation program and the AUTOEXEC.SYS file ready to run when the server is started, all you need is a printer attached to the server's parallel port and you're ready to print.

After the server is brought up, the system administrator can create new queues and printer assignments. Detailed instructions for doing this are given in Section III.

Advanced Installation

Unlike the "Basic Installation" option, NetWare 2.20's "Advanced Installation" option provides no default printing environment at all. The only printing option to be concerned with at installation time is whether or not to include core printing. However, even if you include core printing, that merely provides the system with the capability of handling printers attached to the file server. It does not create any queues, nor does it define or configure any printers. No AUTOEXEC.SYS file is created by default either. These tasks are all left for the system administrator.

To establish a beginning print environment, the system administrator must complete at least two tasks.

- The first task is to create at least one (but usually several) queues. The best way to do this is through the PCONSOLE program. While it is also possible to create a queue by entering commands at the server's console (colon ":") prompt, queues created in this way cannot be managed by a dedicated print server. Therefore, for future convenience, it is best to define all new queues via the PCONSOLE program from the supervisor's workstation.

- The second task is to create and configure at least one printer and assign the queue(s) to the printer(s).

Print queues are permanent, in the sense that a subdirectory and its files are permanent—they'll still be there if the server is brought down and restarted. But anyone with the proper rights can intentionally delete them.

Printer assignments, on the other hand, are temporary. NetWare does not save the printer-queue assignments from one session to the next. Thus, the system administrator must either enter the commands at the console prompt every time the server is started, or place them in the server's AUTOEXEC.SYS file so they'll be automatically executed on every startup. Obviously, the latter is the preferred choice. Supervisors can access the AUTOEXEC.SYS file via the SYSCON program, under the "Supervisor Options" choice on the main menu.

Creating a Print Queue

To print on a core printer, you must first use the PCONSOLE program to create the queues that you need. Figure 3-4 summarizes the steps required to create a new print queue in PCONSOLE. More detailed instructions for creating print queues are given in Chapter 8.

1. Log in as SUPERVISOR or equivalent.
2. Start PCONSOLE.
3. Select "Print Queue Information."
4. Press <Ins>.
5. Type in the new queue name and press <Enter>.
6. Press <Enter> again.
7. Select "Queue Users."
8. Modify the queue user list as necessary, then press <Esc>.
9. Select "Queue Operators."
10. Modify the queue operator list as necessary, then press <Esc> three times.
11. Repeat from Step 3 for another queue, or press <Esc> to exit.

Figure 3-4: These are the steps for creating a print queue in PCONSOLE.

You can choose any names you want for your print queues. Bear in mind that prior versions of NetWare always created default queues named PRINTQ_0, PRINTQ_1, and so forth up to PRINTQ_4, and assigned them to Printer 0 through Printer 4, respectively. Since many veteran NetWare users have come to expect these default queues to exist, it is often a good idea to create queues with those names. (Other suggestions for naming queues are given in Chapter 8 under "Creating a Print Queue".)

Defining a Printer

Once you've created at least one print queue, go to the system console and define at least one printer for the server. The command to define a parallel printer is shown in Figure 3-5.

```
PRINTER n CREATE LPT1
```

Figure 3-5: Use this console command to define a parallel printer.

This command assumes that the printer is attached to the first parallel port. If the printer is attached to LPT2 or to LPT3, use these port designations in place of "LPT1" in the command.

To define a printer attached to a serial port, use a variation of the command as shown in Figure 3-6.

```
PRINTER n CREATE COM1
PRINTER n CONFIG BAUD=x WORDSIZE=x STOPBITS=x
        PARITY=x XONXOFF=x POLL=x
```

Figure 3-6: Use these console commands to define a serial printer.

Note that when you create a serial printer, you must establish its configuration (baud rate, word size, and so on) using the PRINTER CONFIG command. The default values for each parameter are shown in Figure 3-7. Uppercase letters indicate allowable abbreviations.

Parameter	Default	Valid values
Baud:	9600	300, 600, 1200, 2400, 4800, 9600
WordSize:	8	7, 8
StopBits:	1	1, 2
Parity:	NONE	None, Even, Odd
XonXoff:	NO	Yes, No
Poll:	15	1-60

Figure 3-7: These are the defaults for the serial printer configuration parameters.

If your serial printer is already set to match any of these defaults, you can omit those parameters from the command.

Assigning a Queue to a Printer

Once you have defined (and, if necessary, configured) a printer, the next task is to tell the printer what queue(s) to service. That command is shown in Figure 3-8.

```
PRINTER n ADD QueueName
```

Figure 3-8: Use this console command to assign a queue to a printer.

Entering a Default Spooler Assignment

Finally, you should enter a default spooler assignment. Although not absolutely necessary, this command may save you some frustrating debugging time later on. Older versions of NetWare had the ability to route print jobs directly to a printer. Programs that use that ability are still in circulation. If one of these programs is used on your network, the printouts will never find their way to a printer or a queue.

The solution is to use the SPOOL command to intercept the data aimed at a printer and place it into a queue. The syntax of the SPOOL command is shown in Figure 3-9.

```
SPOOL n TO QueueName
```

Figure 3-9: Use the SPOOL command to intercept data headed directly for a network printer and send it to a queue instead.

Once the data is in the queue, a command such as the one shown in Figure 3-8 will complete the process of getting it to the printer.

Entering the Commands in the AUTOEXEC.SYS File

To put all these pieces together into the AUTOEXEC.SYS file, start the SYSCON utility. Choose "Supervisor Options" and then "Edit System Autoexec File." Then type in the commands shown in Figure 3-10.

```
PRINTER 0 CREATE LPT1
PRINTER 1 CREATE LPT2
PRINTER 2 CREATE LPT3
PRINTER 3 CREATE COM1
PRINTER 3 CONFIG BAUD=9600, STOPBITS=1, WORDSIZE=8
        XONXOFF=OFF, PARITY=NONE
PRINTER 4 CREATE COM2
PRINTER 4 CONFIG BAUD=9600, STOPBITS=1, WORDSIZE=8
        XONXOFF=OFF, PARITY=NONE
PRINTER 0 ADD PRINTQ_0
PRINTER 1 ADD PRINTQ_1
PRINTER 2 ADD PRINTQ_2
PRINTER 3 ADD PRINTQ_3
PRINTER 4 ADD PRINTQ_4
PRINTER 0 ADD DEFAULT_Q
SPOOL 0 TO DEFAULT_Q
SPOOL 1 TO DEFAULT_Q
SPOOL 2 TO DEFAULT_Q
SPOOL 3 TO DEFAULT_Q
SPOOL 4 TO DEFAULT_Q
```

Figure 3-10: This sample AUTOEXEC.SYS file includes all the commands to set up the initial printing configuration.

Of course, your actual AUTOEXEC.SYS file will vary from this sample. You should only create printers for ports that actually exist, and you should add the queues that are appropriate to your network. In the example, the use of PRINTQ_0, PRINTQ_1, and so on is a throwback to older versions of NetWare; these were the queue names that NetWare created by default. It's still a good idea to use them, though, because people who have had experience using older NetWare versions have come to expect these default queues to exist.

In addition, you might choose to send spooled output to a different printer, or you might even choose to not use a SPOOL command at all. The reasoning here is that when users complain about not getting their printouts, you can easily make it print for them. But you will then know which users are trying to send jobs directly to a printer. Thus you'll know where to take the necessary steps to get the printouts sent to the proper queue without help from either you or from the SPOOL command.

Techniques for Modifying the Defaults

In Chapter 1, we discussed the potential many-to-many relationship between printers and queues. In this section, we'll present the commands to establish the printer-queue setup described there.

Before making any changes, it is important to define the starting point. For this discussion, the starting point will be the configuration shown in the sample AUTOEXEC.SYS in Figure 3-9.

The next two figures show the commands you can use to change this baseline configuration. Figure 3-11 shows the commands necessary to assign two queues to a single printer, with one of them having a higher priority.

```
PRINTER 1 ADD QUEUE MEMOS   AT PRIORITY 1
PRINTER 1 ADD QUEUE REPORTS AT PRIORITY 2
```

Figure 3-11: These commands add queues to printers and assign priorities.

Figure 3-12 shows the opposite configuration—a single queue assigned to two printers.

```
PRINTER 2 ADD QUEUE BIGJOBS
PRINTER 3 ADD QUEUE BIGJOBS
```

Figure 3-12: These commands assign two printers to a queue.

As explained in Chapter 1, these options are not mutually exclusive. Combining the baseline configuration shown in Figure 3-10 with the examples shown in Figures 3-11 and 3-12 might result in the following setup, which is typical for a medium-sized network.

PRINTER NUMBER	QUEUE NAME	PRIORITY
0	MEMOS	1
0	REPORTS	2
0	BIGJOBS	3
0	PRINTQ_0	4
1	MEMOS	1
1	BIGJOBS	2
1	PRINTQ_1	3
2	BIGJOBS	1
2	PRINTQ_2	2

Figure 3-13: This combination of printer and queue assignments is typical for a medium-sized network.

The commands in the AUTOEXEC.SYS file to produce this setup are shown in Figure 3-14.

```
PRINTER 0 CREATE LPT1
PRINTER 0 ADD MEMOS AT PRIORITY 1
PRINTER 0 ADD REPORTS AT PRIORITY 2
PRINTER 0 ADD BIGJOBS AT PRIORITY 3
PRINTER 0 ADD PRINTQ_0 AT PRIORITY 4
PRINTER 1 CREATE LPT2
PRINTER 1 ADD MEMOS AT PRIORITY 1
PRINTER 1 ADD BIGJOBS AT PRIORITY 2
PRINTER 1 ADD PRINTQ_1 AT PRIORITY 3
PRINTER 2 CREATE COM1
PRINTER 2 CONFIG BAUD=9600, STOPBITS=1, WORDSIZE=8,
         PARITY=NONE, XONXOFF=ON
PRINTER 2 ADD BIGJOBS AT PRIORITY 1
PRINTER 2 ADD PRINTQ_2 AT PRIORITY 2
```

Figure 3-14: These commands set up the combination printer-queue assignments shown in the previous figure.

In this arrangement, Printer 0 is assigned to four queues at different priorities. Most of the time, this printer will be busy with memos and reports. But if neither of those queues has any jobs pending, it can service the BIGJOBS queue rather than sit idle.

Similarly, Printer 1 is used mainly for BIGJOBS, but it will always check the MEMOS queue first and handle those short printouts as its top priority. Printer 2 is dedicated to the BIGJOBS queue on a full-time basis.

Note the assignment of the default queues (PRINTQ_0, PRINTQ_1, and so on), at the lowest priority, to ensure that any output sent to those queues is printed. Using the low priority discourages the use of the default queues.

Maintaining the Printing Environment

When your printing needs or facilities change (you acquire a new printer or retire an old one), there is no need to rerun the INSTALL program. Unless you must power off the server to add a parallel or serial card, you can perform printer maintenance without disturbing the system's active users.

You can make all software changes at the console prompt, using the console commands discussed above and in Chapter 11. Be sure to repeat any commands in the AUTOEXEC.SYS file so the new configuration will be permanent.

CHAPTER 4

NetWare 286 Version 2.20 Without Core Printing

The latest release of NetWare 286 is version 2.20. The installation program for this version is INSTALL.EXE (located on the SYSTEM-1 diskette).

When you start INSTALL, its first menu presents four choices, as shown in Figure 4-1.

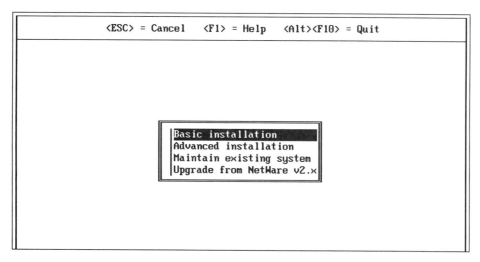

Figure 4-1: NetWare 2.20's INSTALL program presents four initial choices.

Those users who choose "Basic Installation" will always have core printing enabled.

Only the users who choose "Advanced Installation" or "Upgrade from NetWare v2.x" will see the installation screen (Figure 4-2) where they get the initial opportunity to choose between including core printing or not including it. (This latter choice implies use of the print server software; either PSERVER.VAP at the file server or PSERVER.EXE at a dedicated workstation.) Those who have already made their choice and want to change it would select "Maintain existing system."

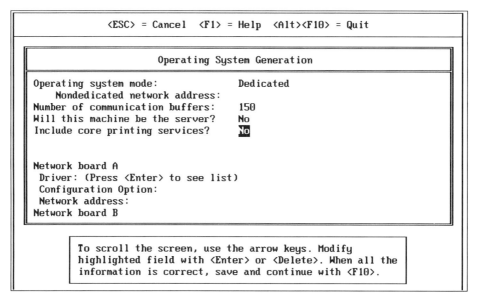

```
            <ESC> = Cancel   <F1> = Help   <Alt><F10> = Quit

        ┌─────────────────────────────────────────────────────┐
        │               Operating System Generation            │
        │ Operating system mode:          Dedicated            │
        │     Nondedicated network address:                    │
        │ Number of communication buffers:  150                │
        │ Will this machine be the server?  No                 │
        │ Include core printing services?  No                  │
        │                                                       │
        │                                                       │
        │ Network board A                                      │
        │  Driver: (Press <Enter> to see list)                 │
        │  Configuration Option:                               │
        │  Network address:                                    │
        │ Network board B                                      │
        └─────────────────────────────────────────────────────┘
          ┌─────────────────────────────────────────────────┐
          │ To scroll the screen, use the arrow keys. Modify │
          │ highlighted field with <Enter> or <Delete>. When all the │
          │ information is correct, save and continue with <F10>. │
          └─────────────────────────────────────────────────┘
```

Figure 4-2: INSTALL's "Advanced Installation" option gives you the choice of including core printing services or not.

This chapter is for those who choose any of the options on the initial installation screen (Figure 4-1) except the "Basic Installation" option, and who also choose to disable core printing.

Advanced Installation

Unlike the "Basic Installation" option, NetWare 2.20's "Advanced Installation" option provides no default printing environment at all. The only printing option to be concerned with at installation time is whether or not to include core printing. When you choose not to enable core printing, the NetWare operating system (NET$OS.EXE) itself will have no printing capabilities. You can still connect printers to the file server, but you must run PSERVER.VAP in order to work with them.

To establish a beginning print environment, the system administrator must perform at least two tasks:

- Create at least one print queue.
- Create at least one print server. Within the print server definition, the administrator must create at least one printer and assign that printer to service a queue.

All of these tasks can be done from within the PCONSOLE program. For detailed instructions for creating queues and print servers and for assigning printers, see Section III. The rest of this chapter gives a summary of the steps, incorporating the sample configuration we discussed in Chapter 1.

Setting Up the Sample Configuration

In Chapter 1, we described some sample printer-queue configurations. These examples showed the potential many-to-many relationships that can be established between printers and queues. The queues and printers defined in those examples are summarized in Figure 4-3.

PRINTER NUMBER	QUEUE NAME	PRIORITY
0	MEMOS	1
0	REPORTS	2
0	BIGJOBS	3
0	PRINTQ_0	4
1	MEMOS	1
1	BIGJOBS	2
1	PRINTQ_1	3
2	BIGJOBS	1
2	PRINTQ_2	2

Figure 4-3: This combination of printer and queue assignments is typical for a medium-sized network.

In this arrangement, Printer 0 is assigned to four queues at different priorities. Most of the time, this printer will be busy with memos and reports. But if neither of those queues has any jobs pending, it can service the BIGJOBS queue rather than sit idle.

Similarly, Printer 1 is used mainly for BIGJOBS, but it will always check the MEMOS queue first and handle those short printouts as its top priority. Printer 2 is dedicated to the BIGJOBS queue on a full-time basis.

Note the assignment of the default queues (PRINTQ_0, PRINTQ_1, and so on), at the lowest priority, to ensure that any output sent to those queues is printed. Using the low priority discourages the use of the default queues.

Creating Print Queues

Figure 4-4 summarizes the steps required to create new print queues in PCON-SOLE. More detailed steps are given in Chapter 8.

---

1. Log in as SUPERVISOR or equivalent.
2. Start PCONSOLE.
3. Select "Print Queue Information."
4. Press <Ins>.
5. Type in the new queue name and press <Enter>.
6. Press <Enter> (again).
7. Select "Queue Users."
8. Modify the queue user list as necessary, then press <Esc>.
9. Select "Queue Operators."
10. Modify the operator list as necessary, then press <Esc> three times.
11. Repeat from Step 3 for another queue, or press <Esc> to exit.

Figure 4-4: These are the steps for creating a print queue in PCONSOLE.

You can choose any names you want for your print queues. The sample configuration calls for queues named MEMOS, REPORTS, and BIGJOBS. (Other suggestions for naming queues are given in Chapter 8 under "Creating a Print Queue".)

Bear in mind that prior versions of NetWare always created default queues named PRINTQ_0, PRINTQ_1, and so forth up to PRINTQ_4, and assigned them to Printer 0 through Printer 4, respectively. Since many veteran NetWare users have come to expect these default queues to exist, it is often a good idea to create queues with those names as well.

To establish the print queues for the sample configuration described in Chapter 1, you would follow the steps shown in Figure 4-4 six times: for the queues MEMOS, REPORTS, BIGJOBS, PRINTQ_0, PRINTQ_1, and PRINTQ_2. When you are finished, selecting "Print Queue Information" from PCONSOLE's main menu will display the queues as shown in Figure 4-5.

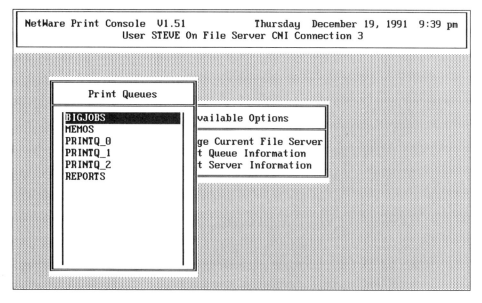

Figure 4-5: After you create the sample queues, PCONSOLE displays them in the "Print Queues" list.

Creating a Print Server

Next, you must create and configure a print server. The steps to take within PCONSOLE are summarized in Figure 4-6. More detailed steps are given in Chapter 9.

1. Log in as SUPERVISOR (or equivalent).
2. Start PCONSOLE.
3. Select "Print Server Information."
4. Press <Ins>.
5. Type in the new print server name and press <Enter>.
6. Press <Enter> (again).
7. Select "Server Users."
8. Modify the user list as necessary, then press <Esc>.
9. Select "Server Operators."
10. Modify the operator list as necessary, then press <Esc>.
11. Select "Print Server Configuration."
12. Select "Printer Configuration."
13. Configure the printers.
14. Press <Esc>, then select "Queues Serviced by Printers."
15. Assign one or more queues to each configured printer.
16. Press <Esc>, then choose "Notify List for Printer."
17. Set up notifications .
18. Press <Esc> twice to return to the "Print Server Information" menu.
19. Select "Change Password" and specify a password.
20. Enter a Full Name for the print server.
21. Repeat from Step 3 for another print server, or press <Esc> to exit.

Figure 4-6: These are the steps to create and configure a print server in PCONSOLE.

If you created a print server that works the way the sample configuration dictates, the list of configured printers would appear as in Figure 4-7.

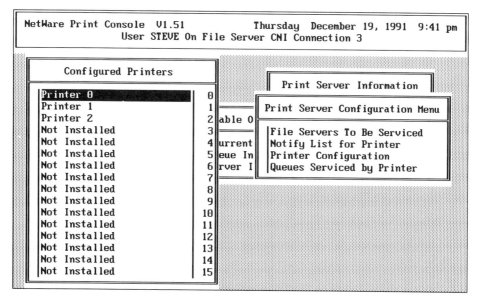

```
NetWare Print Console  V1.51              Thursday  December 19, 1991  9:41 pm
                  User STEVE On File Server CNI Connection 3

    ┌──────── Configured Printers ────────┐        ┌─ Print Server Information ─┐
    │ Printer 0                        0  │        │ Print Server Configuration Menu │
    │ Printer 1                        1  │═══      │                                 │
    │ Printer 2                        2  │able 0   │ File Servers To Be Serviced     │
    │ Not Installed                    3  │═══      │ Notify List for Printer         │
    │ Not Installed                    4  │urrent   │ Printer Configuration           │
    │ Not Installed                    5  │eue In   │ Queues Serviced by Printer      │
    │ Not Installed                    6  │rver I   │                                 │
    │ Not Installed                    7  │
    │ Not Installed                    8  │
    │ Not Installed                    9  │
    │ Not Installed                   10  │
    │ Not Installed                   11  │
    │ Not Installed                   12  │
    │ Not Installed                   13  │
    │ Not Installed                   14  │
    │ Not Installed                   15  │
    └─────────────────────────────────────┘
```

Figure 4-7: For the sample configuration, you would define three printers: Printer 0, Printer 1, and Printer 2.

To assign queues to these printers, you'd select "Queues Serviced by Printer" from the "Print Server Configuration Menu." Figure 4-8 shows the resulting screen.

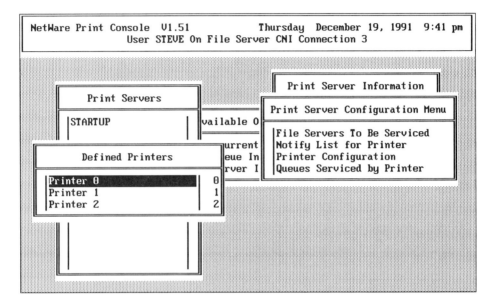

Figure 4-8: Select "Queues Serviced by Printer" to prepare to define queues for Printer 0.

Figure 4-9 shows the finished list of queues assigned to Printer 0, each with the appropriate priority.

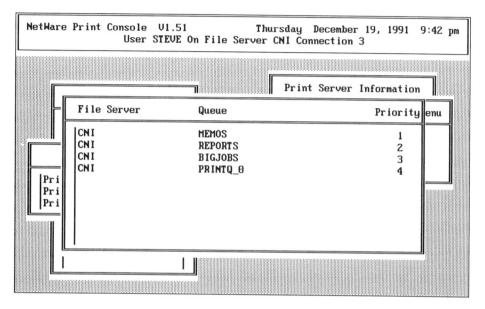

Figure 4-9: PCONSOLE displays the completed queue assignments and priorities for Printer 0.

Once created, both print servers and print queues are permanent, in the sense that a directory and its files are permanent. They will continue to exist even if the server is stopped and restarted again. But just as anyone with sufficient rights can delete the directory and its files, a supervisor-equivalent user can delete print queues and print server definitions.

Starting the Print Server VAP

Before you can load the print server VAP, you must copy the PSERVER.VAP file from the distribution diskette labelled "PRINT-1" into the SYS:SYSTEM directory.

To do this, log in as SUPERVISOR or equivalent from a workstation. Insert the PRINT-1 diskette into drive A and type:

```
NCOPY A:PRINT-1\SYSTEM\VAP\PSERVER.VAP SYS:SYSTEM
```

57

Once the .VAP file is in SYS:SYSTEM, the server will generate the following message when it is started:

```
Value Added Processes have been found.
Do you wish to load them?
```

The startup process will then pause, waiting for a reply. To proceed, you must type "Y" and press <Enter> at the server console.

If you want to be able to restart the server in an unattended mode, there are two things you must do. The first is to create a file called SERVER.CFG in the SYS:SYSTEM directory. You can use any text editor, or access the file from the "Supervisor Options" in SYSCON. Place the following line anywhere in the SERVER.CFG file:

```
VAP WAIT 10
```

With a SERVER.CFG containing this line, the startup message shown above will be replaced with:

```
PRESS ANY KEY TO ABORT VAP LOADING
```

This message is followed by a countdown timer starting at ten seconds. If no key is pressed before the time expires, the server will load any VAPs found in SYS:SYSTEM.

That brings us to the next step: loading the print server VAP. PSERVER.VAP version 1.2.1 was distributed with the first releases of NetWare 2.20. With this version of the VAP (as with all of its predecessors), you are always asked to supply the name of the print server whenever the file server was restarted. The presence of a SERVER.CFG file merely allowed the server to pass one of its stopping points (loading all VAPs) without intervention.

With the release of PSERVER.VAP version 1.2.2, completely unattended loading became possible. The first time the VAP is loaded, someone must type in the print server name. After that, however, the file server retains that print server name and uses it after each reboot. As long as there is no print server password, the file server startup and VAP loading process can proceed entirely without intervention. You can tell which version of the VAP you have by following these steps:

1. Start the print server.
2. Go into PCONSOLE.
3. Choose "Print Server Information."
4. Highlight the print server name, then press <Enter>.
5. Choose "Print Server Status/Control."
6. Choose "Server Info."

The resulting screen, shown in Figure 4-10, displays the version of the VAP and where it is running. If you don't have the current version, see Appendix A for information about obtaining the latest version from NetWire.

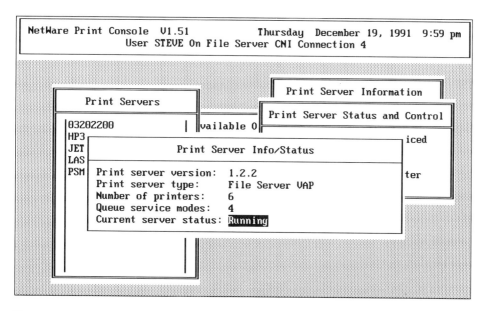

```
NetWare Print Console  V1.51              Thursday  December 19, 1991  9:59 pm
                  User STEVE On File Server CNI Connection 4
```

```
                                          Print Server  Information

        Print Servers                   Print Server Status and Control

   03202200              vailable 0                                        iced
   HP3
   JET               Print Server  Info/Status
   LAS
   PSM    Print server version:  1.2.2                                     ter
          Print server type:     File Server VAP
          Number of printers:    6
          Queue service modes:   4
          Current server status: Running
```

Figure 4-10: PCONSOLE shows the print server version in the "Print Server Info/Status" screen.

Starting the Print Server EXE

To start the PSERVER EXE, go to the workstation where it will be running and log in as any user (GUEST is fine). Then type

```
PSERVER PrintServerName
```

at the DOS prompt. (As a security measure, you will be logged out and the PSERVER will be logged in in your place.)

Maintaining the Print Environment

One of the advantages of using separate print server software is that it can be modified at any time via the PCONSOLE program. Minor, temporary changes (such as assigning another queue to an existing printer) can be made while the print server is up and running; these changes will take effect immediately.

Alternatively, you can make major changes (such as adding a new remote printer definition) to the print server definition of a currently running print server. However, before such a change takes effect, you must stop (down) the print server and restart it. In the NetWare 286 environment, you "down" a print server by going into PCONSOLE and using the "Print Server Status/Control" menu option.

If you are using the print server VAP, the next step is to go to the file server console and stop and restart PSERVER. The commands to do this are:

```
PSERVER STOP
PSERVER START
```

CHAPTER 5

NetWare 386 Version 3.11 Printing Environment

Unlike any version of NetWare 286, NetWare 386 provides no default print environment at all. The installation process doesn't even include any step where a decision about printing or printing services can be made.

To establish a beginning print environment, the system administrator must perform at least two tasks:

- Create at least one print queue.
- Create at least one print server. Within the print server definition, the administrator must create at least one printer and assign that printer to service a queue.

All of these tasks can be done from within the PCONSOLE program. For detailed instructions for creating queues and print servers and for assigning printers, see Section III. The next sections in this chapter give a summary of the steps, incorporating the sample configuration we discussed in Chapter 1.

Setting Up the Sample Configuration

In Chapter 1, we described some sample printer-queue configurations. These examples showed the potential many-to-many relationships that can be established between printers and queues. The queues and printers defined in those examples are summarized in Figure 5-1.

PRINTER NUMBER	QUEUENAME	PRIORITY
0	MEMOS	1
0	REPORTS	2
0	BIGJOBS	3
0	PRINTQ_0	4
1	MEMOS	1
1	BIGJOBS2	
1	PRINTQ_1	3
2	BIGJOBS	1
2	PRINTQ_2	2

Figure 5-1: This combination of printer and queue assignments is typical for a medium-sized network.

In this arrangement, Printer 0 is assigned to four queues at different priorities. Most of the time, this printer will be busy with memos and reports. But if neither of those queues has any jobs pending, it can service the BIGJOBS queue rather than sit idle.

Similarly, Printer 1 is used mainly for BIGJOBS, but it will always check the MEMOS queue first and handle those short printouts as its top priority. Printer 2 is dedicated to the BIGJOBS queue on a full-time basis.

Note the assignment of the default queues (PRINTQ_0, PRINTQ_1, and so on), at the lowest priority, to ensure that any output sent to those queues is printed. Using the low priority discourages the use of the default queues.

Creating Print Queues

Figure 5-2 summarizes the steps required to create new print queues in PCON-SOLE. More detailed steps are given in Chapter 8.

---

1. Log in as SUPERVISOR or equivalent.
2. Start PCONSOLE.
3. Select "Print Queue Information."
4. Press <Ins>.
5. Type in the new queue name and press <Enter>.
6. Press <Enter> (again).
7. Select "Queue Users."
8. Modify the queue user list as necessary, then press <Esc>.
9. Select "Queue Operators."
10. Modify the operator list as necessary, then press <Esc> three times.
11. Repeat from Step 3 for another queue, or press <Esc> to exit.

Figure 5-2: These are the steps for creating a print queue in PCONSOLE.

You can choose any names you want for your print queues. The sample configuration calls for queues named MEMOS, REPORTS, and BIGJOBS. (Other suggestions for naming queues are given in Chapter 8 under "Creating a Print Queue".)

Bear in mind that prior versions of NetWare always created default queues named PRINTQ_0, PRINTQ_1, and so forth up to PRINTQ_4, and assigned them to Printer 0 through Printer 4, respectively. Since many veteran NetWare users have come to expect these default queues to exist, it is often a good idea to create queues with those names as well.

To establish the print queues for the sample configuration described in Chapter 1, you would follow the steps shown in Figure 5-1 six times: for the queues MEMOS, REPORTS, BIGJOBS, PRINTQ_0, PRINTQ_1, and PRINTQ_2. When you are finished, selecting "Print Queue Information" from PCONSOLE's main menu will display the queues as shown in Figure 5-3.

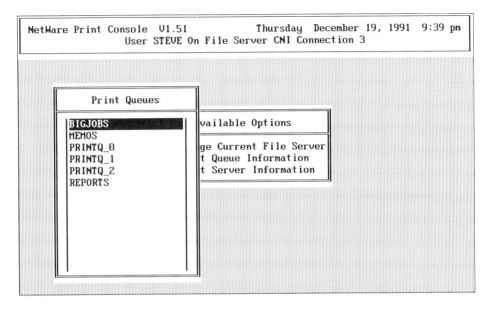

Figure 5-3: After you create the sample queues, PCONSOLE displays them in the "Print Queues" list.

Creating a Print Server

Next, you must create and configure a print server. The steps to take within PCON-SOLE are summarized in Figure 5-4. More detailed steps are given in Chapter 9.

1. Log in as SUPERVISOR (or equivalent).
2. Start PCONSOLE.
3. Select "Print Server Information."
4. Press <Ins>.
5. Type in the new print server name and press <Enter>.
6. Press <Enter> (again).
7. Select "Server Users."
8. Modify the user list as necessary, then press <Esc>.
9. Select "Server Operators."
10. Modify the operator list as necessary, then press <Esc>.
11. Select "Print Server Configuration."
12. Select "Printer Configuration."
13. Configure the printers.
14. Press <Esc>, then select "Queues Serviced by Printers."
15. Assign one or more queues to each configured printer.
16. Press <Esc>, then choose "Notify List for Printer."
17. Set up notifications.
18. Press <Esc> twice to return to the "Print Server Information" menu.
19. Select "Change Password" and specify a password.
20. Enter a Full Name for the print server.
21. Repeat from Step 3 for another print server, or press <Esc> to exit.

Figure 5-4: These are the steps to create and configure a print server in PCONSOLE.

If you created a print server that works the way the sample configuration dictates, the list of configured printers would appear as in Figure 5-5.

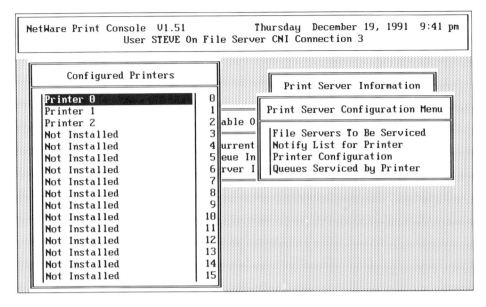

Figure 5-5: For the sample configuration, you would define three printers: Printer 0, Printer 1, and Printer 2.

To assign queues to these printers, you'd select "Queues Serviced by Printer" from the "Print Server Configuration Menu." Figure 5-6 shows the resulting screen.

Figure 5-7 shows the finished list of queues assigned to Printer 0, each with the appropriate priority.

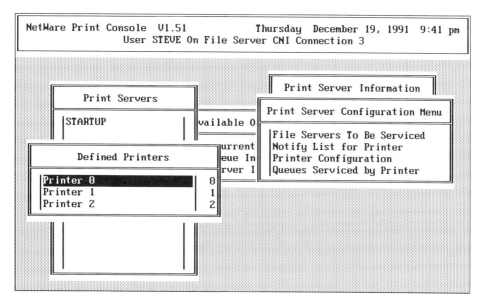

Figure 5-6: Select "Queues Serviced by Printer" to prepare to define queues for Printer 0.

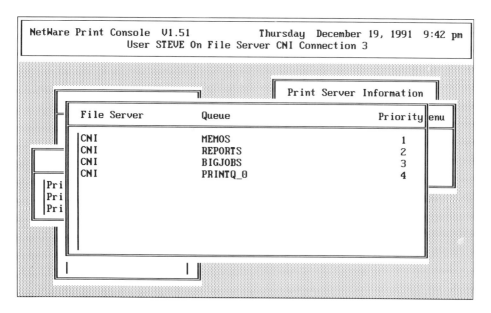

Figure 5-7: PCONSOLE displays the completed queue assignments and priorities for Printer 0.

Once created, both print servers and print queues are permanent, in the sense that a directory and its files are permanent. They will continue to exist even if the server is stopped and restarted again. But just as anyone with sufficient rights can delete the directory and its files, a supervisor-equivalent user can delete print queues and print server definitions.

To use the print server, the system administrator must decide whether to run it at the file server (as an NLM) or at a dedicated workstation (as an EXE).

Starting the Print Server NLM

To use the PSERVER NLM at the file server, the system administrator should log in as SUPERVISOR (or equivalent) and access the SYSCON utility's "Supervisor Options" to edit the AUTOEXEC.NCF file. (This file is created during the installation process.) You should add the line

```
LOAD PrintServerName
```

to the list of commands that will already be in the file. Once this line is added, the print server program will be loaded whenever the file server is brought up.

Starting the Print Server EXE

To start the PSERVER EXE, go to the workstation where it will be running and log in as any user (GUEST is fine). Then type

```
PSERVER PrintServerName
```

at the DOS prompt. (As a security measure, you will be logged out and the PSERVER will be logged in in your place.)

Maintaining the Print Environment

One of the advantages of using separate print server software is that it can be modified at any time via the PCONSOLE program. Minor, temporary changes (such as assigning another queue to an existing printer) can be made while the print server is up and running; these changes will take effect immediately.

Alternatively, you can make major changes (such as adding a new remote printer definition) to the print server definition of a currently running print server. However, before such a change takes effect, you must stop (down) the print server and restart it. In the NetWare 386 environment, you "down" a print server by going into PCONSOLE and using the "Print Server Status/Control" menu option.

If you are using the print server NLM it will be unloaded automatically when you down the print server. However, to make your changes effective, you still have to go to the file server console (or use RCONSOLE to operate the console remotely from a workstation) and then reload the print server. The command to do this is:

```
LOAD PrintServerName
```

If you are using PSERVER.EXE, you merely go to the print server machine, log in, and type:

```
PSERVER PrintServerName
```

Section III:

Establishing a Custom Printing Environment

This section discusses the NetWare programs and commands used to establish and facilitate network printing in a custom environment. The first three chapters describe the basics that apply to both "core" printing and print server-based environments. The latter three explain advanced procedures that apply in one environment or the other.

- Chapter 6 starts with the CAPTURE, ENDCAP and NPRINT commands, which are used to submit print jobs to network print queues comparing their parameters.

- Chapter 7 looks at PRINTDEF and PRINTCON, two programs that bring the full capacity of modern-day printers to the NetWare environment.

- Chapter 8 describes how to set up print queues through the PCONSOLE program, and how to manage the queues after print jobs are sent to them.

- Chapter 9 explains how to define a print server in PCONSOLE.

- Chapter 10 discusses how to run PSERVER (in all of its variations) and examines the RPRINTER and PSC commands.

- Chapter 11 covers the commands used only with "core" printing: PRINTER, QUEUE, and also discusses the console command, SPOOL, which is used in all three versions.

CHAPTER 6

CAPTURE, ENDCAP, and NPRINT

In this chapter we'll discuss the NetWare CAPTURE, ENDCAP, and NPRINT utilities. CAPTURE and NPRINT are the two commands that NetWare users use to send their print jobs to a queue for eventual printing. ENDCAP reverses the effect of the CAPTURE command. After we examine the various parameters and their combinations, we'll show how to make capturing automatic by including the command in the login script.

Most of the CAPTURE parameters are the same as those for NPRINT. The differences have a common thread; CAPTURE is for files that are about to be created, while NPRINT is for already existing files. In our discussion, we'll note which parameters apply to only one of the two commands.

Conceptual Overview

Figure 6-1 illustrates a moderately complex NetWare printing environment:

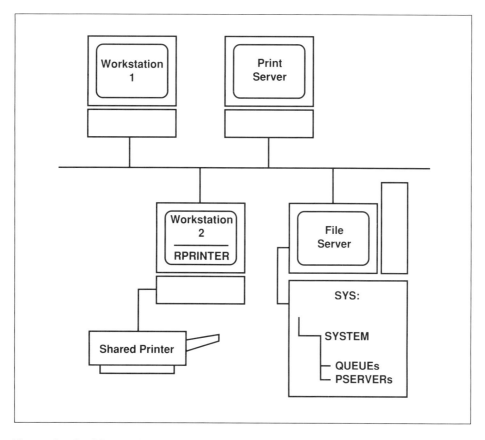

Figure 6-1: In this printing environment, users need the CAPTURE or NPRINT command to send jobs to a network printer.

In this environment, a user at Workstation 1 would use the CAPTURE or NPRINT command to send printouts to a queue on the server. As explained previously, queues are merely subdirectories of SYS:SYSTEM. From there, the print server software takes the print data and sends it to the workstation running RPRINTER, where it will print out.

As its name implies, the CAPTURE program is used to capture output destined for a local printer and divert it to a network print queue. When you issue a CAP-

TURE command, NETX (or whichever variation of the shell you use) modifies DOS so that it lets the shell monitor the printer port you are capturing. Anything sent to that port by DOS or an application program is intercepted and sent to the network queue you named in your CAPTURE command.

If you later decide to end capturing, you use the ENDCAP command. Once you enter this command, the shell stops monitoring the printer port and local printing resumes.

NPRINT, on the other hand, is a replacement for (and improvement on) DOS's PRINT command. You normally use NPRINT any time you want to print an existing file on a network printer.

Checking Versions and Getting Quick Help

As a starting point, it is important to identify the versions of CAPTURE and NPRINT you are using, because there are some slight differences in the allowable parameters. If you have access to a network, type the following command:

```
VERSION CAPTURE
```

The resulting output looks like this:

```
CAPTURE.EXE:
Version 3.50
© Copyright 1983-1990 Novell, Inc. All rights reserved
Checksum is 29D7D
```

Figure 6-2: The VERSION command displays the version number of any specified NetWare command.

In addition, you can get quick help (in the form of a list of possible parameters) by typing:

```
CAPTURE ?
```

For the version of CAPTURE shown above, the output from this command is:

```
USAGE: CAPTURE /SHow /Job=jobname /Server=fileserver
/Queue=queuename /Local=n /Form=form or n
/CReate=path /Copies=n (1-999) /TImeout=n
/Keep /Tabs=n (1-18) /No Tabs /Banner=bannername
/NAMe=name /No Banner /FormFeed /No FormFeed
/AUtoendcap /No Autoend /NOTIfy /No NOTIfy
/DOmain=domain
```

Figure 6-3: The "CAPTURE ?" command displays quick help information about its possible parameters.

> **Note:** If you have a CAPTURE.EXE that is older than version 2.0, it will contain a "Printer=" parameter. This parameter is obsolete. (Appendix A lists all the current print programs for the various versions of NetWare. Instructions for obtaining the latest releases are included at the end of that list.)

Similarly, you can obtain the version number for NPRINT.EXE by typing:

```
VERSION NPRINT
```

However, you cannot get help for NPRINT by typing

```
NPRINT ?
```

because the NPRINT program interprets the question mark as a wildcard character in a filename. Thus it presumes you want to print all files whose filename is a single letter or number. However, merely typing the command "NPRINT" displays the help screen shown in Figure 6-4.

Usage: NPRINT *path flaglist*

flaglist: /Banner=*bannername* /NAme=*name* /No Banner

/[No] FormFeed /[No] NOTIfy

/Tabs=*n* (1-18) /No Tabs

/Copies=*n* (1-999) /Delete /Form=*form* or *n*

/Job=*jobconfiguration* /PrintServer=*printserver*

/Queue=*queuename* /Server=*fileserver* /DOmain=*domain*

Figure 6-4: The "NPRINT" command by itself displays quick help information about its possible parameters.

CAPTURE and NPRINT Parameters

Between them, CAPTURE and NPRINT have over twenty parameters, which are summarized in Figure 6-5.

Parameter	Abbreviation	Possible Values for Variable	Default Value	Available to CAPTURE	NPRINT
Show	SH	None	None	Yes	No
Job=*JobName*	J=	Any print job configuration defined in PRINTCON	Default job	Yes	Yes
Queue=*QueueName*	Q=	Any valid print queue name	Queue for Spooler 0	Yes	Yes
Server=*ServerName*	S=	Any valid file server name	Default server	Yes	Yes
Local=*n*	L=	1, 2, or 3	1	Yes	No
Form=*FormName* or Form=*n*	F=	Any valid form name or number	0	Yes	Yes
Create=*Path*	CR=	Filename, including directory path	None	Yes	No
Copies=*n*	C=	1-999	1	Yes	Yes

(continued)

(continued)

Parameter	Abbreviation	Possible Values for Variable	Default Value	Available to CAPTURE	NPRINT
Timeout=*n*	TI=	0-1000 seconds	8	Yes	No
Autoendcap	A	None	On	Yes	No
No Autoendcap	NA	None	Off	Yes	No
Keep	K	None	Off	Yes	No
Tabs=*n*	T=	0-18	8	Yes	Yes
No Tabs	NT	None	Off	Yes	Yes
Banner=*BannerName*	B=	Any word/string up to 12 characters	LST:	Yes	Yes
Name=*Name*	NAM=	Any word/string up to 12 characters	Username	Yes	Yes
No Banner	NB	None	Off	Yes	Yes
Form Feed	FF	None	On	Yes	Yes
No Form Feed	NFF	None	Off	Yes	Yes
Notify	NOTI	None	Off	Yes	Yes
No Notify	NNOTI	None	On	Yes	Yes
Domain=*DomainName*	DO=	Any valid NNS domain name	None	Yes	Yes
Delete	D	None	Off	No	Yes

Figure 6-5: CAPTURE and NPRINT share many of the same parameters.

Many of these parameters are merely opposites (for example, Form Feed and No Form Feed). Others are mutually exclusive (for instance, if you declare No Banner, you cannot define a Banner Name). We'll describe the meaning and implications of the various parameters in sets when applicable, looking at the opposites, the pairs, and the exclusives, and comparing them to each other.

The "Show" Parameter

This parameter displays (shows) the current CAPTURE status of the three parallel ports. If capturing is active, you'll see the LPT port number, the file server and queue names, and several other status indicators. When you include this parameter in the command line, any other parameters are ignored.

The "Job=" Parameter

The "Job=" parameter will be discussed in detail in Chapter 7 when we talk about PRINTCON and PRINTDEF. Briefly, the PRINTCON database is a collection of records; each record contains a set of CAPTURE parameters appropriate to its purpose and is named with a job name.

By specifying the job name as the first CAPTURE or NPRINT parameter, you are saved the trouble of typing (and learning) all the parameters suitable for a specific need. For example, suppose a user regularly types the following CAPTURE command:

```
CAPTURE S=FS1 Q=LJ NB NT NFF NOTI
```

The user could easily store this set of parameters under the job name "TELLME" and then achieve the same effect by merely typing:

```
CAPTURE JOB=TELLME
```

To override or supplement a parameter in a print job configuration, you can use additional parameters along with the job name. Parameters listed along with the "Job=" parameter supplement or modify those specified in the PRINTCON record. For example, suppose you create a job named "MYJOB" that specifies, among other things, the No Form Feed parameter, but does not contain a Copies= parameter. If you type

```
CAPTURE JOB=MYJOB FF C=2
```

the Form Feed ("FF") parameter would override the stored value (No Form Feed), changing it to its opposite. The "C=2" parameter would change the number of copies from the default value of 1 to 2.

The "Queue=" Parameter

On a Novell LAN, print output must always be directed to a particular queue. The "Queue=" parameter merely names the queue. When we discuss the PCON-SOLE program in Chapter 8, we'll discuss the concept of queue users (users authorized to place jobs into a particular queue).

The "Server=" Parameter

This parameter names the server that contains the queue to which the user wants to direct the output. If the user is not currently attached to that server, CAPTURE will attach to that server using the following logic:

1. Attempt to attach as user GUEST with no password.
2. Prompt for a user ID and password.
3. If unsuccessful at attaching to the target file server, the CAPTURE command will fail.

> **Tip:** The default server can easily vary when you have drives mapped to different servers. For example, suppose you have mapped drive G: to SERVER-1 and drive K: to SERVER-2. When your current drive is G:, the default server is SERVER-1. But if you switch the current drive to K:, the default server becomes SERVER-2. Since it is possible to have print queues of the same name on both servers (many NetWare servers have a queue named "PRINTQ_0"), it is easy for print output to be accidentally directed to the wrong printer.
>
> For this reason, it is a good policy to always name the server (or the domain) as part of your CAPTURE parameters.

The "Local=" Parameter

This parameter refers to the parallel port number that will be captured. If you want to capture output directed to LPT1, enter a 1 for n; for LPT2, enter 2; for LPT3, enter 3.

> **Note:** This field has absolutely nothing to do with the physical port the printer is attached to, whether it is on the file server, a print server, or a remote printer.

The "Form=" Parameter

In NetWare, forms are both numbered and named. For this parameter, you can specify either the form name or the number. Forms are discussed in detail in Chapter 7.

The "AUTOendcap" Parameter

It's easy for NetWare to determine when a print job begins—a job starts with the arrival of the first character in the specified queue. Determining the end of the print job is not so easy. Three parameters help with this determination: Autoendcap, Noautoendcap, and Timeout. These parameters are defined briefly here. A more thorough description of their interaction is provided at the end of these parameter definitions.

Autoendcap tells NetWare that print jobs end whenever the user exits the application program that started sending the print job to the queue. This application might be a long-running database report program, or merely the output of a command that was redirected to the printer. As soon as the DOS prompt appears, the print job is closed.

The "TImeout=" Parameter

Sometimes users intend to stay in a single application program for a long period of time, yet they also intend to send several print jobs from that application. This is typically the case in a word processing program. By specifying a number of seconds in the Timeout parameter, you tell NetWare to automatically end the print job after the specified number of seconds has elapsed without receiving any additional incoming print characters. Output arriving later than the Timeout period becomes part of the next print job.

The "NOAUTOendcap" Parameter

Include the Noautoendcap parameter to tell NetWare not to make any determination as to the end of a print job. It then becomes the user's responsibility to issue an ENDCAP command when the output is complete.

The "CReate=" Parameter

Instead of sending output to a print queue (and from there to a printer), the user can elect to send the data to a filename. This process creates a file that can be saved, printed, or transmitted as appropriate. The "No Autoendcap" parameter should also be used with this parameter. No other parameters are valid. No print head or print tail (discussed later) will be generated.

The "Copies=" Parameter

By default, only one copy of each job is printed. However, you can use the "Copies=" parameter to make multiple copies of a print job.

The "Keep" Parameter

If a user loses his or her connection to the server without ending the currently accumulating print job, that job is usually lost—NetWare discards it. A loss of connection can occur due to catastrophic causes (such as if the network cable breaks), or for much more mundane reasons (such as when the user merely turns off his or her machine without logging out). By specifying the "Keep" parameter, you instruct NetWare to preserve the print job if the connection is lost. Rather than discarding the job, NetWare acts as if you had issued an ENDCAP command.

The "Tabs=" and "No Tabs" Parameters

If you enter a number for "Tabs" or just take the default of 8, NetWare will scan your output looking for ASCII "09" codes and change them into a number of spaces equal to the number you entered. However, if you choose "No Tabs," every character you send to the printer will be treated as a binary value and no modification will be made. (These values correspond exactly to the PCONSOLE "Byte Stream" and "Text" parameters discussed in Chapter 8.)

It is especially important to select "No Tabs" when working with laser printers. Failure to do so will cause any "09" code that happens to be in a downloaded font to be changed to a series of spaces, thus rendering the font unusable.

Banner-Related Parameters

The banner name (specified by the "Banner=" parameter) is any text string up to twelve characters long, with no embedded spaces. It will be printed in the middle of the banner page. Many organizations use the banner name to indicate delivery priority: for example, "Urgent," "Normal," "Overnight," and so on.

By default, the user's name will appear at the top of the banner page. You override the default by placing a text string up to twelve characters long in the "Name=" parameter. Changing the username is convenient if delivery of the printed copy is to be made to someone other than the originator.

Specifying the "No Banner" parameter suppresses the banner page altogether. This is important when special forms are mounted on the printer.

Form Feed Parameters

By default, a page eject (form feed) is issued at the end of every print job. If you experience a blank piece of paper being ejected between jobs, specify "No Form Feed" (NFF) to eliminate the extra page.

Notification Parameters

Normally, the user who sent the print job is not notified when the printout is finished (No NOTIfy). However, it is possible to request such notification by including the "NOTIfy" parameter. If you do, NetWare generates a SEND message to the user to indicate that the job has finished printing.

The NNS "Domain=" Parameter

If you are using the NetWare Name Service (NNS) product, use this parameter to specify the domain to which the queue belongs. Companies that have multiple servers and have installed NNS will instruct their users to log in to a particular domain. In any domain, a print queue created on one server is automatically created on every server in that domain. If you are printing to a printer in your domain, just name the queue. If you are printing to a queue in another domain, name the domain and the queue.

The "Delete" Parameter

This parameter, which is available only to NPRINT, causes the original file to be deleted after the printout is complete.

Note: This is a dangerous option, especially for NetWare 286 users. The Delete option does not ask for confirmation, even if all the files in a directory are to be printed and deleted. Also, if multiple files are specified, each file is deleted as it is sent to the queue. NetWare 286's SALVAGE command will only recover the results of the last delete command. In other words, if a directory contains five files, all ending in .BAT, the command

```
NPRINT *.BAT q=anyqueue DELETE
```

will delete all five BAT files. SALVAGE will only recover one of them. (NetWare 386's SALVAGE utility has more options, so it could recover them all.) It is a much better idea to manually delete the files after they've been successfully printed.

Interaction Between the Autoendcap and Timeout Parameters

The Autoendcap, No Autoendcap, and Timeout parameters must be closely coordinated. The allowable combinations are:

```
AUTOENDCAP        TIMEOUT=0
AUTOENDCAP        TIMEOUT=n (seconds)
NOAUTOENDCAP      (timeout disabled)
```

For examples of when to use these combinations, let's look at Hirsch and Cabot, one of our case studies.

Example 1

Hirsch and Cabot just received a consulting contract from the governor of their state. The governor wants to send a birthday card to every person in the state who is more than 100 years old. Upon learning that they can have access to the latest census bureau database, Hirsch takes on the job.

After doing some research, Hirsch learns that of the nearly ten million people in the state, approximately fifty are more than 100 years old. He writes a simple program to search the database and print a report listing all residents whose age is 100 or more.

The first time Hirsch runs the report, it takes an entire weekend. When he comes in on Monday, he is very disappointed with the output. The printer has put out ninety sheets of paper. Every other sheet contains one name, although occasionally a sheet has two names; the alternate sheets are banner pages.

Hirsch calls Cabot, who asks him what the CAPTURE parameters were. Hirsch types "CAPTURE SHOW" and sees that Autoendcap is on and the Timeout is set to 8 seconds.

Cabot tells Hirsch to run the report again, but this time set the CAPTURE parameters to "AUTOENDCAP TIMEOUT=0." Hirsch complies, but asks why. Cabot explains that when the timeout is set to a non-zero value, NetWare sets up a monitor on the file in the queue. As soon as a new character arrives, the timer is reset to the timeout value. If the timeout period elapses, NetWare closes out the print job and sends it off to be printed. When another character arrives, NetWare starts a new print file.

The timeout for Hirsch's report was initially set to 8 seconds. Since there was usually a long time between matches in the database, almost every match came out as a separate job (which explains the excess banner pages).

After resetting the parameters, Hirsch ran the report again. This time, the print job remained open until the database program finished all of its searching. Hirsch then exited the application and returned to the DOS prompt. This act signalled the shell that it was time to close out the print file and send it to be printed.

Example 2

Here's another example of how these parameters work. When Cabot first started consulting, she worked for a local law firm. Their word processing operators were frustrated because they always had to stop and exit their word processing program to get the memos to print out. One of Cabot's first assignments was to fix the printing setup so that the memos and reports would print a few seconds after the print keys were hit and the operators could continue working.

She accomplished this by adding the parameters "AUTOENDCAP TIME-OUT=10" to the CAPTURE command in their login scripts. With these parameters active, each memo or report became a separate print job. NetWare printed each one ten seconds after the last character of the job was sent to the queue.

Example 3

Hirsch asked Cabot if she had ever used the "No Autoendcap" parameter. She replied that this parameter is seldom used. The only time she had ever heard of it being used was when a programmer wanted to use CAPTURE to collect a group of print screens into a single file. Here's how he did it.

The programmer first ran CAPTURE with the "NA" parameter active. He then ran several different programs from one system, pressing the Print Screen key at appropriate times to send a screenful of information to the print queue. When he was finished, he typed the ENDCAP command to tell NetWare that the print job was ready for the printer. Of course, the programmer had to issue another CAPTURE command to prepare for sending the next job to the queue.

The ENDCAP Command

The opposite of CAPTURE is the ENDCAP (END CAPture) command. Issuing this command returns your captured LPT ports to local use. In other words, the NetWare shell stops monitoring them for output that it should send to a queue. ENDCAP has several parameters, which are described below.

ENDCAP With No Parameters

Issuing the "ENDCAP" command with no parameters will end the capturing of LPT1, since LPT1 is the default port for CAPTURE. It will also close out a "CAPTURE CReate=filename" command.

The "Local=" Parameter

Just as you can CAPTURE any one or more parallel ports, you can also end the capturing of any one of those ports. The default local port number is 1 (which matches the LPT1 default for CAPTURE).

The "ALL" Parameter

If you are capturing output for more than one port, include this parameter to end capturing for all of them at once.

The "Cancel" Parameter

This option ends capturing to LPT1 and discards any pending output without printing it.

The "CancelLocal=" Parameter

This form of the Cancel parameter allows the user to selectively end capturing and discard data from just one of the parallel ports. Note that "ENDCAP CL=1" is the same as "ENDCAP C."

The "Cancel ALL" Parameter

Use this parameter to abandon all captured output at once.

Note: It is not always necessary to issue an ENDCAP command. Logging out causes NetWare to issue it for you. Logging in to another server does the same thing. When you issue a LOGIN command while you already logged in, NetWare first logs you out of all servers before it processes the new LOGIN command.

In addition, issuing a new CAPTURE command causes NetWare to assume that you want to end the existing CAPTURE.

Rules for Conflicting Parameters

If you place multiple, conflicting parameters in the same CAPTURE command, the later parameters override the former ones. For example, consider the following CAPTURE statement:

```
CAPTURE S=fs1 Q=laser NB C=3 NAME=novice
```

Even though the "No Banner" (NB) parameter is included, this command will produce a banner page because the later parameter "NAME=Novice" turns it back on. (Remember that NAME is one of the fields printed on a banner page).

Here's another example:

```
CAPTURE S=fs1 Q=reports TI=8 NA
```

In this case, the "No Autoendcap" (NA) parameter will override the Timeout, which can only apply when Autoendcap is on. Thus the specified Timeout of 8 seconds will be turned off.

Automating CAPTURE in the Login Script

To automate the use of CAPTURE on your network, you can include a CAP-TURE command in the system login script or in users' personal login scripts. The syntax is:

```
#CAPTURE Q=QueueName S=ServerName
```

Note the "#" sign preceding the word CAPTURE. NetWare requires this symbol before any external command used in a login script. The "#" indicates that the following command is not one of the internal login script commands.

Here's another example of a login script CAPTURE command:

```
#CAPTURE J=printcon-def NAME=%LOGIN_NAME
```

Note the use of the %LOGIN_NAME variable. This variable substitutes the user's login ID for the user name on the banner page. While this is the default, you will see in the next chapter that when we use a global PRINTCON definition, the automatic banner name no longer works.

CHAPTER 7

PRINTDEF
and PRINTCON

One of the primary reasons for installing a network has been (and, to some extent, still is) the ability to share printers. In many cases, companies can still buy a single, full-featured printer for less than the total cost of purchasing a barely adequate printer for every user.

Once the shared printer is procured, the natural next step is to obtain one of the top word processing programs and use its functions to access all of the printer's features. However, many network administrators soon find that not all users print by way of a word processing program: programmers want to print out code listings; accountants want to print spreadsheets; managers want to use database programs to print reports. These users also want to take advantage of the printer's capabilities, but often don't know how.

This chapter discusses NetWare's PRINTDEF (PRINTer DEFinition) and PRINTCON (PRINT job CONfiguration) utilities. By using these two programs to define the capabilities of network printers and pre-set configurations for various types of print jobs, you can give users access to the full capacity of today's printers.

In this chapter, we will use as an example Melanie, a programmer working for Southern Insurance. Melanie wants to print her program code on an HP LaserJet Series II laser printer, with the left margin set at one inch (to accommodate three-hole punched paper), the lines per inch set at eight, and the font set to the built-in compressed font. She also wants to reset the printer back to normal after she is done.

Conceptual Overview

All printers have the ability to accept commands from a computer. These commands cause the printer to exercise one of its features or functions. For example, many dot matrix printers have the ability to switch to Near Letter Quality (NLQ) mode. Other printers can print double-high or double-wide characters. Some (especially laser printers) can switch into sideways, or landscape, mode.

To access these special features, printers must have a way to determine the difference between characters to be printed and commands to be followed. This differentiation between commands and characters is accomplished by the use of "escape codes."

Escape Codes

One of the characters that can be sent to a printer is the "Escape" character (ASCII code 27). Most printer manufacturers adhere to a loose standard that identifies command strings by starting them with the Escape character—hence the general name "escape codes." After the Escape character, the escape code contains a series of numbers, letters, or special characters that the printer interprets as a command.

Each escape code string makes only one change in the printer's status. If it's necessary to make multiple changes, you must send a separate escape code string for each change.

To take advantage of the full range of a network printer's functions, then, you first need to know what the escape codes are for all the functions you want to use. The actual command strings vary from one printer manufacturer to another, and even among different printers from the same manufacturer. The manual for most printers contains a section that describes each function and its corresponding escape code. Sometimes you must order this documentation separately from the manufacturer.

Once you find the escape codes, the next step is to put them into a table that can be accessed by anyone who wants to use them. After that, a user simply sends the correct series of codes from the table before sending the data to be printed. If one of the codes resets the printer to its normal state, that code should be sent after all the data is printed.

If this process is to be repeated often for the same type of print job, it makes sense to group relevant escape code strings together to form standard configurations. This makes complicated printer commands more easily accessible and helps ensure that none of them is inadvertently omitted.

To help you accomplish these tasks, Novell supplies the PRINTDEF and PRINT-CON utilities with NetWare. You use PRINTDEF to build the table of escape codes and escape code groupings (called printer definitions). Then you use PRINTCON to define a way for users to send those codes to the printer when they need them (by using print job configurations).

Technical Description

Printer definitions are files with .PDF extensions, usually found in SYS:PUB-LIC, that contain predefined modes and functions. A function is one escape code or sequence that a printer interprets as a command to affect its behavior, rather than as a series of characters to be printed. A mode is a collection of functions that, together, set the printer into a desired configuration.

NetWare comes with printer definitions for many of the most popular printers. These definitions contain a wide selection of modes and functions for your use. Nevertheless, there will be times when you will want to create new modes using the existing functions, or maybe add new functions and use them to make additional modes. This section explains how to accomplish these tasks.

Setting Up Printer Definitions in PRINTDEF

Figure 7-1 summarizes the steps necessary to establish printer definitions with the PRINTDEF utility.

---

1. Log in as SUPERVISOR (or equivalent).
2. Start the PRINTDEF program.
3. Select "Print Devices."
4. Select "Import Print Devices."
5. Select directory (probably SYS:PUBLIC).
6. Choose your printer from the list.
7. Repeat Steps 5 and 6 until you have selected all printers in use on your network.
8. Select "Edit Print Devices."
9. If you have selected more than one printer, choose the one you want to edit first.
10. Select "Device Functions."
11. Press <Ins> to add any necessary escape codes (functions) that might be missing.
12. Select "Device Modes."
13. Press <Ins> to begin a new mode, and choose an appropriate name.
14. Press <Ins> to bring up the list of functions, then select the functions you wish to be associated with that mode by repeatedly highlighting a function, pressing <Enter> and then pressing <Ins> again. Press <Esc> when finished.
15. Repeat Steps 13 and 14 as needed for each mode.
16. Repeat Steps 8 to 15 for each printer defined.

Figure 7-1: Steps for creating printer definitions in PRINTDEF.

The following comments describe each step in more detail.

1. Log in as SUPERVISOR (or equivalent).

NetWare comes with about 20 predefined printer definitions, contained in files with a .PDF extension. The definitions in these .PDF files can't be used until the SUPERVISOR (or a supervisor-equivalent user) imports them into the NET$PRN.DAT printer definition database file. This database file is located in the SYS:PUBLIC directory and is maintained via the PRINTDEF program. To update this file, you must have all rights in SYS:PUBLIC, a privilege that is normally reserved for network supervisors.

2. Start the PRINTDEF program.

Although you can start PRINTDEF from any directory, starting from a drive mapped to SYS:PUBLIC will make Step 5 automatic. Type "PRINTDEF" and press <Enter>.

3. Choose "Print Devices."

There are two possible selections at this point: "Print Devices" or "Forms." Choose "Print Devices." (The other option, "Forms," will be discussed later in this chapter.)

4. Select "Import Print Devices."

This option adds a definition to the NET$PRN.DAT database. If the database file does not yet exist, it will be created automatically.

5. Select the directory where the printer definition files (extension .PDF) exist.

When NetWare is installed, the .PDF files are copied into SYS:PUBLIC. However, they may have been moved since then, or you may have received an updated set of files. This option lets you specify the location of the PDF files you want to use. PRINTDEF prompts you with the current directory (SYS:PUBLIC, if you started PRINTDEF from a drive mapped to that directory).

6. Choose your printer from the list.

Figure 7-2 shows what the PRINTDEF screen should look like at this point. If your specific printer is not listed, choose the option closest to it. For example, if you have an HP LaserJet Series IID, you would choose the definition for HP LaserJet I/II printers.

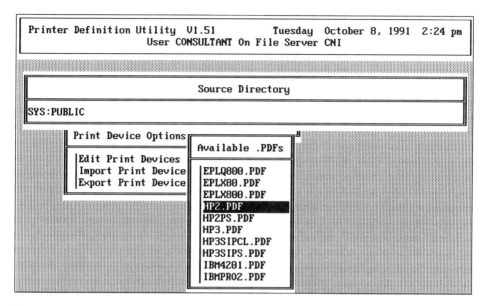

Figure 7-2: After you specify the source directory, PRINTDEF lists the .PDF files available for import into the NET$PRN.DAT database.

7. Repeat Steps 5 and 6 for all printer types.

If you have more than one kind of printer on your network, you should select printer definitions for all of them. Non-supervisors can create their own print job configurations, but they cannot add print definitions to the NET$PRN.DAT database.

8. Choose "Edit Print Devices" to continue.

9. Select the first print device to edit.

After you select all the printer definitions you want to import, choose the one you want to edit.

10. Select "Device Functions."

Since print modes are made up of functions, you must define the various functions first.

11. *Press <Ins> to add any necessary escape codes (functions) that might be missing.*

11a. When you are creating a new function, you must type a name for it after you press <Ins>. (Note that you can also edit an existing function by highlighting its name and pressing <F3>.)

For our example, Melanie wants to create a function that will contain the code to set a left margin of 10 characters. She types "LEFT-MARGIN" for the function name. Using all uppercase characters for user-defined function names is recommended so you can easily distinguish them from the functions that come with the NetWare-supplied PDFs (which use both uppercase and lowercase characters in their names).

11b. After typing in the name, enter the corresponding escape code for the function. To enter the ASCII Escape character, type the string "<ESC>".

For the HP LaserJet in our example, the code for a 10-character left margin is "<ESC>h10C". The PRINTDEF screen should now look like the one shown in Figure 7-3.

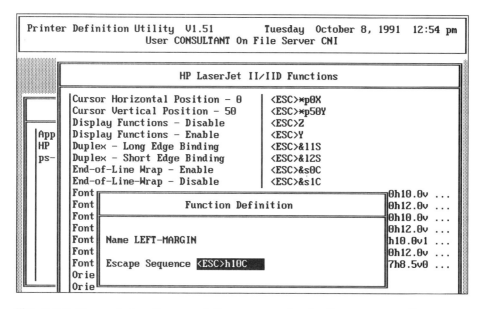

Figure 7-3: For each function you define, you must enter the corresponding escape code for the printer.

11c. Continue inserting functions until you have entered all the escape code strings you need. Press <Esc> to exit the list of functions. Answer "Yes" to the "Save Changes" prompt, then press <Esc> again.

The other codes Melanie needs (Compressed, 8 LPI, and Reset) are already defined for the HP LaserJet II. So she presses <Esc>.

12. Select "Device Modes."

A device mode is a group of related functions (escape codes) that together set up the printer to print a certain way. You define and name the modes now for later inclusion in print job configurations.

13. Press <Ins> to begin a new mode, and choose an appropriate name.

It's best to give each mode a mnemonic name so you can easily tell what it is for. In our example, Melanie types "PROGLIST" for the name of her mode.

14. Press <Ins> to bring up the list of functions, then select the functions you wish to be associated with that mode by repeatedly highlighting a function, pressing <Enter>, and then pressing <Ins> again. Press <Esc> when finished.

Melanie selects the following codes for her PROGLIST mode:

```
Printer Reset
Font - Courier 12 pt.
LEFT-MARGIN
Font - Lineprinter 8.5 pt.
VMI - 8 lpi
```

For some printers (LaserJets among them), it is important to select the codes in the proper order. Note that Melanie selected the "Courier 12 pt." font before selecting her LEFT-MARGIN function. This is necessary because the escape code she used called for a ten-character margin. At ten characters per inch, that makes a one-inch margin. But at 16.66 characters per inch (the size of the built-in compressed font), it's only about 5/8 of an inch (10/16.66).

When all the codes are selected, the PRINTDEF screen appears as in Figure 7-4.

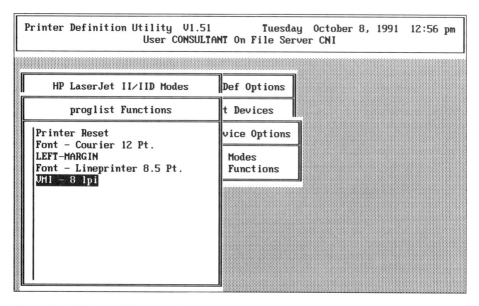

Figure 7-4: When adding functions to define a mode, you must be careful to insert the functions in the proper order.

15. Repeat Steps 13 and 14 as needed for each mode.

When you have defined all the modes you need for the current print device, press <Esc> until you return to the "Defined Print Devices" list.

16. Repeat Steps 8 through 15 for each printer you have defined.

When you are finished, press <Esc> until you see the "Exit PrintDef" prompt. When you answer "Yes," the "Exit Options" screen appears, as shown in Figure 7-5. Choose the "Save Database, then EXIT" option to leave the PRINT-DEF program.

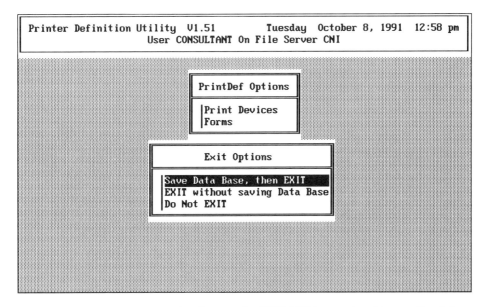

```
 Printer Definition Utility  V1.51        Tuesday  October 8, 1991  12:58 pm
                         User CONSULTANT On File Server CNI
```

```
                    ┌─────────────────────────┐
                    │  PrintDef Options        │
                    │ ┌───────────────────────┐│
                    │ │Print Devices          ││
                    │ │Forms                  ││
                    └─┴───────────────────────┴┘
              ┌─────────────────────────────────┐
              │        Exit Options             │
              │┌───────────────────────────────┐│
              ││Save Data Base, then EXIT      ││
              ││EXIT without saving Data Base  ││
              ││Do Not EXIT                    ││
              └┴───────────────────────────────┴┘
```

Figure 7-5: Whenever you make changes in PRINTDEF, you should save the database on exiting the program.

Defining Print Job Configurations in PRINTCON

Once you have defined all necessary modes (and their included functions), the next step is to define print job configurations that use these modes. The main steps for creating print job configurations are listed in Figure 7-6:

---

1. Log in as SUPERVISOR (or equivalent).
2. Start the PRINTCON program.
3. Select "Edit Print Job Configurations."
4. Press <Ins> and enter a name for the print job configuration.
5. Edit the print job configuration as necessary.
6. Repeat Steps 4 and 5 for each configuration.
7. Exit PRINTCON.

Figure 7-6: Steps for creating print job configurations in PRINTCON.

Here are some notes and comments about these steps:

1. Log in as SUPERVISOR (or equivalent).

Any user can enter PRINTCON and set up his or her own print job configurations. The resulting configurations are stored in a file named PRINTCON.DAT, which is placed in the user's mail directory on the server.

We suggest logging in as SUPERVISOR because on every NetWare network, the mail directory for the user SUPERVISOR is named SYS:MAIL/1. This directory is easy to find, and that will simplify the task of converting the supervisor's configurations into global configurations. If you are a supervisor equivalent user, you can still make your configurations global. However, you'll have to add an extra step. The exact procedure for making the PRINTCON.DAT file global is given under "Making Print Job Configurations Global" later in this chapter.

2. Start the PRINTCON program.

From any network drive, type "PRINTCON" and press <Enter>.

3. Select "Edit Print Job Configurations."

This is one of the items on the "Available Options" menu.

4. Press <Ins> and enter a name for your new print job configuration.

As always, the name you select should be easy to remember and descriptive of what the print job configuration is for. When you want to use the configuration you create here, you'll type a command similar to the following at the DOS prompt:

```
CAPTURE Job=JobName
```

where JobName is the name you select in this step.

For our example, Melanie chooses the name "Programs" for the configuration that incorporates the PROGLIST mode she has set up.

5. Edit the print job configuration as necessary.

At this point, you see a screenful of data items that can be defined as part of the print job configuration. Figure 7-7 shows an example of the PRINTCON edit configuration screen.

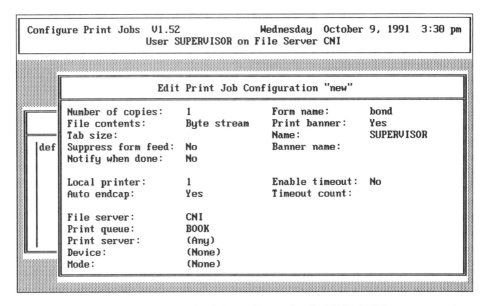

```
Configure Print Jobs  V1.52              Wednesday  October 9, 1991  3:30 pm
                         User SUPERVISOR on File Server CNI


                     ┌──────────────────────────────────────────────────────┐
                     │           Edit Print Job Configuration "new"          │
                     │                                                        │
                     │ Number of copies:    1          Form name:     bond    │
                     │ File contents:       Byte stream Print banner:  Yes     │
                     │ Tab size:                        Name:          SUPERVISOR
 │def│               │ Suppress form feed:  No         Banner name:           │
                     │ Notify when done:    No                                │
                     │                                                        │
                     │ Local printer:       1          Enable timeout:  No     │
                     │ Auto endcap:         Yes         Timeout count:         │
                     │                                                        │
                     │ File server:         CNI                               │
                     │ Print queue:         BOOK                              │
                     │ Print server:        (Any)                             │
                     │ Device:              (None)                            │
                     │ Mode:                (None)                            │
                     └──────────────────────────────────────────────────────┘
```

Figure 7-7: When you create a print job configuration in PRINTCON, you enter the necessary information in this edit configuration screen.

Guidelines for each of these settings are given below. When you are finished making changes, press <Esc> to save the configuration. Answer "Yes" to the "Save Changes" prompt.

6. Repeat Steps 4 and 5 for each print job configuration.

7. Exit PRINTCON.

Press <Esc> and answer "Yes" to the "Exit PrintCon" prompt. Then answer "Yes" to the subsequent "Save Print Job Configuration" prompt.

Guidelines for Print Job Configuration Settings

Below are some guidelines for making settings in the "Edit Print Job Configuration" screen shown above. The defaults, if any, are shown in square brackets. If you select other values, they will become the default values in effect when you use this configuration.

Number of Copies [1]

You will typically leave this field at its default value. You can always override it temporarily by specifying a different number of copies at the command line. (See "A Faster Way to Print Multiple Copies" at the end of this chapter for an alternate method of producing more than one copy of a print job.)

Form Name [The form name for form 0, or the word "Unknown" if none are defined]

Highlight this field and press <Enter> to see a pop-up list of all defined forms. If you haven't defined any forms in PRINTDEF for the current file server, this field will display "(None defined)."

File Contents [Byte Stream]

If you press <Enter> on this field, a submenu will pop up with two options: "Byte Stream" and "Text." If you choose "Byte Stream," every character sent to the printer will be treated as a binary value. NetWare makes no modification to the data as it goes to the printer. Use this option for sending files that have already been formatted for the particular printer within an application.

If you choose "Text," NetWare will scan your output for Tab characters (ASCII code 09) and change them into the number of spaces defined in the "Tab Size" field (described next). Use this option for printing straight DOS text files that contain no special formatting codes.

> **Note:** The "Byte Stream" and "Text" options correspond exactly to the "No Tabs" and "Tabs" CAPTURE parameters discussed in the previous chapter, except that in CAPTURE the default is "TABS" (equivalent to "Text").
>
> It is especially important to select "Byte Stream" when you are working with downloadable fonts on laser printers. Failure to do so will cause any "09" code that happens to occur in a downloaded font to be changed to a series of spaces, thus rendering the font unusable.

Tab Size [8]

If you chose "Text" in the "File contents" field, the "Tab size" field defaults to 8. You can change this number as you see fit. If you chose "Byte Stream," this field becomes blank and you can make no selection here (the cursor skips this field.)

Print Banner [Yes]

If you accept the default, NetWare prints a banner page before each print job. When this field is set to "Yes," you can fill in the "Name" and "Banner Name" fields below to change the information that is displayed on the banner page. To suppress banner pages, change this field to "No."

Name [Your User ID]

Normally, NetWare prints the user's login ID on the banner page to identify who sent the print job. However, if you follow the suggestions in the next section on making the print job configurations global, leaving this at the default setting would cause your username to be printed on everyone's banner pages. To prevent this, type in blanks in this field. (See "Getting the Right User ID on the Banner Page" later in this chapter for notes on how to insert the sending user's name on the banner page when using global print job configurations.)

Banner Name [blank]

If you leave this field blank, then this field will print as blanks. Some users prefer to put the print job configuration name in this field. Any text string up to 12 characters long is fine; it will not affect the rest of the output.

Suppress Form Feed [No]

By default, NetWare issues a page eject (form feed) at the end of every print job. If you find that a blank piece of paper is being ejected between print jobs, change this field to "Yes" to eliminate the extra page.

Notify when done [No]

By default, NetWare doesn't notify the user when a print job is finished. If you change this field to "Yes," a broadcast message will be sent to your workstation when the print job has finished printing. This message is not saved; if you are no longer logged in when the print job completes, NetWare discards the message.

Local Printer [1]

This setting refers to the number of the parallel port being captured. The default of 1 is for LPT1. If you want to capture output directed to LPT2, enter a "2" here; for LPT3, enter a "3" in the field.

> **Note:** This value has absolutely nothing to do with the physical port the printer is attached to, whether it is attached to the file server, to a print server, or to a remote printer.

Auto Endcap [Yes]

When enabled, Auto Endcap closes the print job when you exit your program and return to DOS (NetWare Automatically issues the Endcap command). If you select "No" here, you must issue the ENDCAP command yourself.

Enable Timeout [No]

By default, the Timeout feature is disabled. If you enable a timeout count by changing this field to "Yes," NetWare will issue an ENDCAP for you according to the following scheme. Whenever you start printing a job from within an application, NetWare waits until the stream of data to be printed stops. At this point, it waits a specified number of seconds (the "Timeout Count" described below). If no more data arrives during this time, NetWare assumes that all of the data has been sent, closes the print job, and sends it off to be printed. Of course, if you exit the program and return to DOS before the timeout count elapses (and you have Auto Endcap enabled), the ENDCAP will be sent at that time.

Timeout Count [blank] or [5]

The default Timeout Count depends on the choice you make in the previous field. If you choose not to enable a timeout, this field becomes blank and the cursor will skip over it. If you choose "Yes" in the Enable Timeout field, the default timeout count is 5 seconds. You can change the timeout count to any number of seconds from 1 to 1000.

Note: The concepts behind Timeout, Endcap, and Auto Endcap—and suggestions for their proper use—are discussed more fully in the previous chapter on CAPTURE command parameters.

File Server [Current Default File Server]

Since print queues are defined on NetWare file servers, your choice of file server in this field determines which queues you will be able to choose from in the "Print Queue" field below. If the print queue you want to print to is on another server, press <Enter> on this field to produce a list of all known file servers on the network. Choose the server you want from that list.

Print Queue [First Queue, Listed Alphabetically]

Pressing <Enter> on this field brings up a list of print queues from which you can make a selection. Only the queues defined on the file server specified in the field above are shown.

Print Server [Any]

If you have print servers defined and authorized to service your queues, it is best to leave this field set to the default of "Any." This setting allows any authorized print server to print the job. If you want a particular print server to handle your job, press <Enter> to display a list of available print servers. Choose the desired print server from this list.

Note: If you specify a particular print server, make sure the print queue you selected in the field above is being serviced by a printer defined on your selected print server. Otherwise, your print job will never be printed.

If you have no print servers defined, the field will say "(None defined)." Pressing <Enter> in this case generates an error message telling you that you cannot modify this field.

Device [None]

Press <Enter> to see a list of devices that have been entered into NET$PRN.DAT (that is, the devices defined in PRINTDEF). Then choose the device that you want this print job to print on. Remember, you are choosing the kind of printer (for instance, an HP LaserJet), not a specific printer attached to a particular computer.

For our example, Melanie chooses the HP LaserJet II/IID device.

Mode [None] or [Re-Initialize]

If you leave the Device field at its default of "None," this parameter defaults to "None" also. However, once you pick a print device, the default changes to "Re-initialize." Press <Enter> to see a pop-up list of all the modes you defined earlier in PRINTDEF. Select the mode that contains the escape codes you need to set up the printer the way you want it.

For our example, Melanie presses <Enter> and selects the "PROGLIST" mode.

Here is what the PRINTCON screen looks like when Melanie is finished editing her print job configuration:

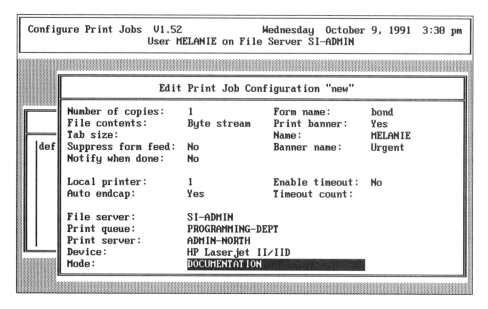

```
Configure Print Jobs  V1.52              Wednesday  October 9, 1991  3:30 pm
                      User MELANIE on File Server SI-ADMIN

                    ┌──────────────────────────────────────────────┐
                    │       Edit Print Job Configuration "new"       │
                    │                                                │
           │    │   │  Number of copies:   1        Form name:      bond     │
           │    │   │  File contents:      Byte stream  Print banner:   Yes      │
           │    │   │  Tab size:                    Name:          MELANIE  │
           │def │   │  Suppress form feed: No       Banner name:   Urgent   │
           │    │   │  Notify when done:   No                                │
                    │                                                │
                    │  Local printer:      1        Enable timeout: No       │
                    │  Auto endcap:        Yes      Timeout count:           │
                    │                                                │
                    │  File server:        SI-ADMIN                          │
                    │  Print queue:        PROGRAMMING-DEPT                   │
                    │  Print server:       ADMIN-NORTH                        │
                    │  Device:             HP LaserJet II/IID                 │
                    │  Mode:              [DOCUMENTATION]                     │
                    └──────────────────────────────────────────────┘
```

Figure 7-8: In PRINTCON, you can select the devices and modes you defined in PRINTDEF.

Specifying the Default Print Job Configuration

The first print job configuration you create automatically becomes the default configuration. The default configuration will be used whenever you enter the CAPTURE command without specifying any parameters. CAPTURE behaves as if you had entered the "JOB=" parameter on the command line to call for the default job configuration by name. Of course, you can override any or all of the default parameters by specifying other values in your CAPTURE command.

Because there are no system defaults, you cannot delete your default print job configuration unless you delete the entire PRINTCON.DAT file.

Once you have two or more configurations defined, you can change the default to another configuration. The "Select Default Job Configuration" option in PRINTCON's main menu allows you to specify which configuration you want to be the default.

Making Print Job Configurations Global

Normally, print job configurations are private—that is, only the user who created the configurations has access to them. However, it is possible to have a global print configuration database. Here are the main steps necessary to make the configurations you create available to all users on the network.

---

1. Log in as SUPERVISOR (or equivalent).
2. Type "NCOPY SYS:MAIL/1/PRINTCON.DAT SYS:PUBLIC."
3. Change to the SYS:PUBLIC directory (type "CD\PUBLIC").
4. Change the search mode of the following files to 5 by typing:

```
SMODE NPRINT.EXE 5
SMODE CAPTURE.EXE 5
SMODE PCONSOLE.EXE 5
SMODE PRINTCON.EXE 5
```

Figure 7-9: Steps for making print job configurations global.

Here are some notes on these steps:

1. Log in as SUPERVISOR (or equivalent).

Logging in as SUPERVISOR is necessary to have all rights in SYS:PUBLIC. (Normally, no one else has those rights).

2. Type "NCOPY SYS:MAIL/1/PRINTCON.DAT SYS:PUBLIC."

This step moves the PRINTCON.DAT file from the directory where it was created to the SYS:PUBLIC directory. If you created PRINTCON.DAT while logged in as SUPERVISOR, the file is in SYS:MAIL/1 because on every NetWare server the Supervisor's mailbox directory is "1."

If you were logged in as a supervisor-equivalent user, you will have to determine the mailbox directory for that user. The easiest way to find it is to go into SYSCON and select "User Information." Then select the user name you were logged in under and choose the "Trustee Directory Assignments" option. The list that comes up will contain a trustee assignment to that user's SYS:MAIL/userID directory.

3. Change to the SYS:PUBLIC directory.

A quick way to change to SYS:PUBLIC is to type "CD\PUBLIC." However, this DOS command works only if your current drive is mapped to any directory under the SYS volume.

4. Change the search mode of NPRINT.EXE, CAPTURE.EXE, PCONSOLE.EXE, and PRINTCON.EXE to 5.

These are the four programs that access PRINTCON.DAT. You change their search mode by using NetWare's SMODE command as follows:

```
SMODE NPRINT.EXE 5
SMODE CAPTURE.EXE 5
SMODE PCONSOLE.EXE 5
SMODE PRINTCON.EXE 5
```

In NetWare, the search mode describes the way a program looks for files (but not executables). SMODE 5 tells programs to look where they would normally look first (in this case, in the user's mail directory) and then to look in the directories named in the search path. The result is that any user can create his or her own PRINTCON.DAT (or copy and modify the general one you created). If they do so, that PRINTCON.DAT file will be the one that NPRINT, CAPTURE, PCONSOLE, and PRINTCON use. Any users who do not create their own PRINTCON.DAT files will default to the global database you copied into SYS:PUBLIC.

Editing Global Print Job Configurations

To edit the global print job configurations, just run PRINTCON again and make your changes. Having been set to search mode 5, the PRINTCON program will pick up the global PRINTCON.DAT file. However, when you exit the program, the updated file will be placed in your mailbox directory. You can then test the new configurations and modify them as necessary. When you are finished, copy the revised PRINT-CON.DAT file to SYS:PUBLIC to make the new configurations global.

For most users, the global definitions you create will be sufficient. However, you might find some users who require additional configurations or who want to change the global ones slightly to fit their individual needs. These users can follow the instructions in the previous paragraph to edit the global configurations, but they should not copy their modified PRINTCON.DAT back to SYS:PUBLIC.

Overcoming PRINTCON's Configuration Limit

The PRINTCON.DAT database can contain up to 31 print job configurations. When used non-globally—that is, a separate file for each user—this limit is rarely a problem. However, when used globally, there might be some large installations that require more than 31 configurations to handle all of the users' possible needs.

Fortunately, there is a relatively simple way to get around this limit. This solution is possible because search mode 5 calls for searching the path, and NetWare always searches these directories in the order in which they appear in the path. Here are the steps:

1. First, determine which users or groups of users need access to which print job configurations. No single user or group should require more than 31 configurations. For example, suppose your Pension department needs a different set of print job configurations than everybody else.
2. Create one or more subdirectories under SYS:PUBLIC (because you want all users to automatically have rights there). Each of these subdirectories will contain a different PRINTCON.DAT file. For the Pension department, you might name the subdirectory PENS_DEF.
3. Run PRINTCON several times, defining a different set of configurations each time. Move the resulting PRINTCON.DAT file into the appropriate subdirectory in SYS:PUBLIC before running PRINTCON again.

In our example, you would run PRINTCON once for the general users and place this PRINTCON.DAT file in SYS:PUBLIC. Then you would run PRINTCON again for the Pension department, placing this PRINTCON.DAT file in SYS:PUB-LIC/PENS_DEF.

4. In the system login script, test for some condition (such as group membership) that leads to a choice among those directories. If the condition is true, insert the appropriate directory as the first search drive mapping in the user's path.

For our example, a segment of the system login script might look like this:

```
IF MEMBER OF "PENSION"
MAP INSERT S1:=SYS:PUBLIC\PENS_DEF
```

Figure 7-10: By inserting a search drive into the path, you can have certain groups access a separate PRINTCON.DAT database.

This procedure puts the PENS_DEF subdirectory first in the path—ahead of SYS:PUBLIC, which is normally mapped as search drive S1. Thus, if a user is a member of the group PENSION, PRINTCON (set to search mode 5) will look first in PENS_DEF and find the PRINTCON.DAT file you created for the Pension department.

Getting the Right User ID on the Banner Page

In our earlier discussion of the print job configuration settings in PRINTCON, we advised you to put blanks in the "Name" field. If you choose not to do so, every banner page prints "SUPERVISOR" as the user ID. By changing this field to blanks, you cause nothing to be printed for the user ID on the banner page. The underlying assumption is that banner pages having the name "SUPERVISOR" (and the associated printout) will be distributed to the Supervisor, while printouts with no name on the banner page will be held for pickup at some central point.

While having nothing printed is an improvement over having SUPERVISOR printed on every banner page, it would be even better if the actual sender's name wound up on the banner page. To accomplish this, simply include the "BANNER=" parameter on the CAPTURE command line.

For example, Melanie could have the name "M-SMITH" printed on her jobs' banner pages by typing the following command:

```
CAPTURE Job=Programs BANNER=M-SMITH
```

If you issue the CAPTURE command from within a login script, you can use the "%login_name" login script variable to place the user's name on the banner. The syntax is:

```
#CAPTURE Job=Programs BANNER=%LOGIN_NAME
```

Note that even if you choose "No Banners" when defining the print job configuration, specifying a banner name in CAPTURE will override that choice. Therefore you need to specify the "BANNER=" parameter only when you have already decided that you want banners, but merely want to get the right name onto the banner page.

Batch File Example

For those users who use batch files (or menu programs that generate temporary batch files), there is another way to get the user's name onto the banner page. These users can take advantage of one of the facets of batch file processing. In a batch file, any variable surrounded by percent (%) signs will be replaced by the environment variable whose name matches the variable within the "%" signs.

An example will make this clearer. Create a DEMO.BAT file by typing the following at the DOS prompt:

```
SET NAME=ABCD
COPY CON DEMO.BAT
CAPTURE Q=queuename S=servername B=%NAME%
CAPTURE SHOW
^Z
```

Figure 7-11: This sample batch file demonstrates the use of a %name% environment variable for the banner name.

Now, type DEMO to trigger the batch file. The CAPTURE display will show you that the BANNER field has the value "ABCD."

To use this technique on your network, place the following command in the system login script:

```
DOS SET NAME="%LOGIN_NAME"
```

Then use the syntax from the DEMO.BAT example above in your batch files and menus.

NetWare MENU Example

Here is another example that shows how you could use this technique with the Novell MENU program. First create the following menu script, using any text editor:

```
BATTEST.MNU
%test
print options
     %print
done
     logout

%print,1,1
try-it
     Capture q=pension_wp b=%name%
     Capture show
     pause
```

Figure 7-12: This sample menu script demonstrates how to use the %name% environment variable with the Novell MENU program.

To execute this menu, type:

```
MENU BATTEST
```

This will result in a menu with only two items: a CAPTURE command, and the Logout command. While this exact menu would be useless in an everyday environment, the syntax serves as an example of how to use the DOS environment to supply parameters to NetWare commands.

Defining Forms in PRINTDEF

In NetWare, a form corresponds to a specific type of paper that you can mount in the printer. Forms are defined through PRINTDEF's "Forms" option. You must be logged in as SUPERVISOR or equivalent to define forms.

When you select the "Forms" option, PRINTDEF lists any forms you have already defined, as illustrated in Figure 7-13. Note that PRINTDEF always lists the known forms in form number sequence.

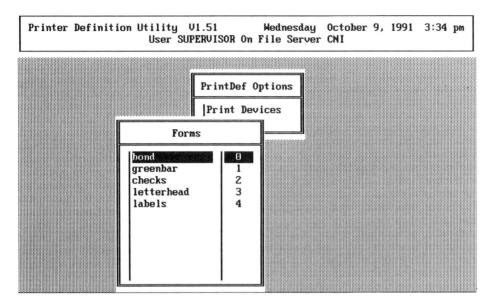

```
Printer Definition Utility  V1.51        Wednesday  October 9, 1991  3:34 pm
                           User SUPERVISOR On File Server CNI
```

```
                              PrintDef Options

                              |Print Devices

                    Forms
              bond              0
              greenbar          1
              checks            2
              letterhead        3
              labels            4
```

Figure 7-13: In PRINTDEF, you can define the types of paper, or forms, to be used on your network printers.

Press <Ins> to define a new form. You will see a window asking for a form name, number, length, and width.

While you can choose any name for your form, it is a good idea to choose as form 0 your most heavily used form. Whatever name you choose for form zero shows up in the PRINTCON and PCONSOLE definition pages, and is the default form for CAPTURE and NPRINT. Where possible, form names should be descriptive of their function. The sample screen above shows five form names that follow these suggestions.

> **Tip:** Be sure to choose form names that everyone can use to mean the same type of paper. Having one form called "Bond" and one called "Plain_Paper," when they are both used to represent the same paper stock, can be confusing. For example, suppose one user requests "Plain_Paper" as the form when everyone else is using "Bond." When that user's print job arrives, the print server will stop and wait for a form change, even though the user really wants to use the same paper that is currently loaded in the printer. Printing will not restart until someone

113

issues the proper command. (The actual commands for mounting forms will be discussed in detail in later chapters in this section.)

For the form number, be sure to enter the next available number in sequence (do not skip a number).

The values for the form length (in number of lines) and width (in number of characters) must both be greater than zero. These values are for your own information only; they are never checked by any other NetWare program or facility.

A Faster Way to Print Multiple Copies

From time to time, you might want to print multiple copies of a print job. There are several ways to do this. If you include the "Copies=n" parameter, NetWare will generate the specified number of copies for you. Or, if you are submitting the print job from a word processing program, you could command the word processor to send multiple copies to the queue.

Both of these cases involve extra data transmission overhead. If you use the parameter method, the print server will have more data to take from the queue; if you use your word processor, the size of the output will multiply.

Most laser printers provide another way to print multiple copies. Almost all laser printers have an escape code that sets the printer to make multiple copies. For example, the codes for the HP LaserJet family are:

```
For two copies    <ESC>&12X
For three copies  <ESC>&13X
For four copies   <ESC>&14X
```

(For more than four copies, just change the number before the "X" in the escape code.) By placing the desired code into a function, and then into a mode, you can cause the printer itself to generate additional copies. This eliminates the extra data transmission traffic on the network.

For graphics or PostScript output, this method also results in faster printing because the printer only has to generate the page image once. Thereafter, it can merely print the generated image multiple times, rather than having to regenerate the image for each copy.

There is one small catch to using this method. When you use it to print a multi-page document, the printer will print "n" copies of page 1, followed by "n" copies of page 2, and so forth, as opposed to the normally collated output. When the pages are all printed, you must collate the copies manually.

CHAPTER 8

Working with Queues in PCONSOLE

The NetWare PCONSOLE program is used for two main purposes: to define and manage print queues, and to define and manage print servers. This chapter deals with the first purpose, that of defining and managing print queues. We'll look at how queues are defined, how they're associated with printers, who has access to them, and who has the ability to manage them. The next chapter will discuss print servers.

Conceptual Overview

Starting with the release of NetWare v2.1, printing on a NetWare network is accomplished by sending print output (also called print streams or print jobs) to a print queue. This queue is merely a subdirectory of SYS:SYSTEM. Like any other subdirectory, it can contain a virtually unlimited number of files. Every time a user begins to send a printout to a queue, a new file is opened in the queue subdirectory and the print stream forms the file. When the user signals that the data stream has ended, the print file is then ready for printing.

Queue-to-Printer Relationships

Typically, a printer is set up so that it services a single queue. However, you can set up a "many-to-many" relationship between printers and queues. In other words, one or more printers can service a single queue, or a single printer can service multiple queues.

As an example of when you might want multiple printers servicing a single queue, suppose many users are submitting large print jobs to a single queue. At eight pages per minute (typical laser printer speed), a backlog can quickly grow. One way to alleviate the backlog is to assign another printer to service that queue. In that way, you effectively cut the printing time in half.

An example of having multiple queues directed to one printer might be a situation where management wants to give priority to small printouts. The network supervisor could create two queues: a MEMOS queue for short jobs, and a REPORTS queue for longer jobs. Both queues would be assigned to a single printer, but MEMOS would be given a higher priority. Whenever two or more queues are being serviced by the same printer, NetWare's print server checks the queues in priority order every time the current job completes.

Queue Users

When you create a print queue, NetWare makes the group EVERYONE a queue user by default. This allows every user on the server to submit print jobs to the queue. In some cases this default is appropriate and should be left as is. In other instances, the queue user list should be modified. For example, a queue that is to be directed to the executive secretary's printer should probably be restricted to top-level managers. We'll explain how to modify the queue user list under "Creating a Print Queue" below.

Queue Operators

For the most part, queues require little manual intervention. Print jobs are sent to queues by users (via CAPTURE or NPRINT commands) and NetWare takes them out of the queues and sends them to the network printers (via print servers or core print services). Occasionally, though, it is necessary to intervene: jobs sent in error need to be deleted; jobs already in the queue sometimes need to have a parameter changed (changing the banner name, for example); rush jobs need to be moved to the top of a busy queue; and so forth.

All users can modify or delete jobs that they themselves send to a queue. A special class of user, known as a "queue operator," can modify any of the parameters of all jobs in the queue. Other functions are also available to the queue operator that aren't available to users.

By default, SUPERVISOR and all supervisor-equivalent users are automatically assigned as queue operators for all queues on the server. Furthermore, these users can assign any other user to be a queue operator by adding that user's name to the list of queue operators in PCONSOLE. (See Steps 9 and 10 in Figure 8-1 for details on making someone a queue operator.)

Print Sequence

The print sequence of jobs in a queue is determined by a number of factors. The default sequence is first in, first out. However, there are a number of ways to override the default.

- Both the user and a queue operator have the ability to defer a printout to a future date and time, or place the job on hold.

- One particular job might use a different form than the others. While this doesn't usually cause the sequence of the printouts to change, it is possible to set remote printers to ignore form changes or to give priority to jobs of the same form type before changing paper.

- When two or more queues are routed to the same printer, you can give one queue a higher priority than the other.

Creating a Print Queue

In NetWare version 2.2, the installer chooses whether to include or exclude core printing. For those who include core printing (and for all users of NetWare 286 version 2.1x and earlier), it is possible to define a queue at the server console. (The commands for doing that are presented in Chapter 11.)

In all versions of NetWare from 2.1x to 3.1x, you can create a queue via the PCONSOLE program. Figure 8-1 shows the steps for creating a print queue in PCONSOLE.

1. Log in as SUPERVISOR (or equivalent).
2. Start the PCONSOLE program.
3. Select "Print Queue Information."
4. Press <Ins>.
5. Type a name for the new queue.
6. Press <Enter> twice.
7. Select "Queue Users."
8. Modify the queue user list as necessary, then press <Esc>.
9. Select "Queue Operators."
10. Modify the queue operator list as necessary, then press <Esc> three times.
11. Repeat Steps 3 through 10 to create another queue, or press <Esc> to exit.

Figure 8-1: Steps for creating a print queue in PCONSOLE.

The following comments describe each step in more detail.

1. Log in as SUPERVISOR (or equivalent).

You must be SUPERVISOR or equivalent to create print queues. Those users named as queue operators in Step 10 will be able to manage the newly-defined queue, but not create new queues.

2. Start the PCONSOLE program.

NetWare's queue management program, PCONSOLE.EXE, is located in SYS:PUBLIC so you can run it from any network drive.

3. Select "Print Queue Information."

This is the option you use to create or manage a queue.

4. Press <Ins>.

As with all NetWare menu utilities, pressing the <Ins> key lets you add a new item.

5. Type a name for the new queue and press <Enter>.

You can use any name you like for a print queue. The following Note gives some suggestions as to appropriate naming conventions.

> **Note:** Versions of NetWare 286 prior to 2.2 created default queues named PRINTQ_0, PRINTQ_1, and so on—up to PRINTQ_4. Users of NetWare version 2.2 or 3.x who upgraded from version 2.15 or earlier will have queues with these names as well. Many users have grown accustomed to having a PRINTQ_0 as the default queue, usually routed to a machine loaded with plain paper (such as a laser printer or a tractor-fed printer).
>
> Since so many systems have that queue name present, it is still a practical idea to create a queue named PRINTQ_0 and set it up as your default queue. Once you've done that, you can give other queues names that are suggestive of their purpose or the kind of printer to which they are routed. Possible queue names might include: Labels, Managers, Accounting, Postscript, LJ2D, Proprinter, and Plotter.

When you have typed the queue name, your screen should look something like Figure 8-2:

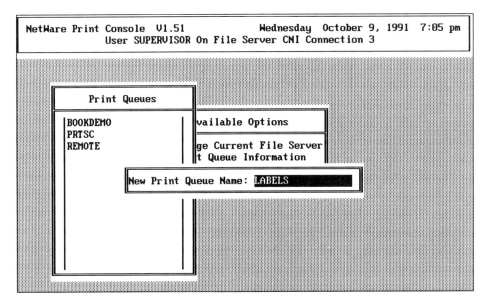

```
NetWare Print Console  V1.51              Wednesday  October 9,  1991   7:05 pm
                  User SUPERVISOR On File Server CNI Connection 3
```

```
    Print Queues

  BOOKDEMO              vailable Options
  PRTSC
  REMOTE               ge Current File Server
                       t Queue Information

             New Print Queue Name: LABELS
```

Figure 8-2: Pressing <Ins> in the list of print queues lets you add a new print queue and give it a name.

6. Press <Enter> twice.

The first <Enter> signals your acceptance of the queue name. (If you notice a typographical error, press <F3> to modify the name.)

Press <Enter> again to select the new queue and bring up the "Print Queue Information" menu. This menu has several options, as shown in Figure 8-3.

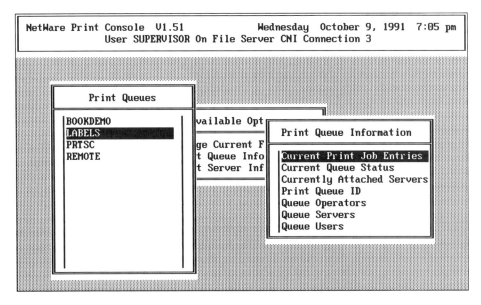

Figure 8-3: When you select a queue, you see the "Print Queue Information" menu.

Only two of the options—"Queue Users" and "Queue Operators"—are described here; the others will be described later in this chapter under "Managing the Print Queue."

7. Select "Queue Users."

You will see a list of users or groups who are currently allowed to submit jobs to the queue.

8. Modify the queue user list as necessary, then press <Esc>.

Press <Ins> to bring up a list of all users and groups not currently included as queue users. Initially, this list includes every user and group except the default group EVERYONE. Highlight the entry of your choice and press <Enter>.

If you want to select several users and groups, repeat this step several times. Or, you can mark the ones you want by highlighting each entry and pressing <F5>. Then press <Enter> to add them all at once.

In either case, you should then delete the group EVERYONE from the queue users list. When you are finished, press <Esc> to go back to the "Print Queue Information" menu.

9. Select "Queue Operators."

You will see a list of users or groups who are currently allowed to manage the queue. (The next section gives more details on performing queue management functions.)

10. Modify the queue operator list as necessary, then press <Esc> three times.

You can modify this list in the same manner as the list of queue users (described in Step 8). When you are finished, press <Esc> three times to return to PCONSOLE's main menu.

11. Repeat Steps 3 through 10 to create another queue, or press <Esc> to exit.

Managing the Print Queue

Before proceeding with the tasks described in this section, perform the following steps to place some jobs in the queue:

1. In PCONSOLE, create a new queue called "bookdemo" for your exclusive use. (See the preceding section if you need instructions.)
2. Type "CAPTURE q=bookdemo" at the network prompt.
3. Type "DIR > LPT1" to send the current directory list to the queue.
4. Type "WHOAMI > LPT1" to send information about your network identity to the queue.
5. Type "NPRINT C:*.BAT q=bookdemo" to send all batch files in your hard disk's root directory to the queue.

Now that there are several entries in the queue, we can practice some queue management tasks. PCONSOLE has two main queue management options—"Current Print Job Entries" and "Current Queue Status."

Controlling Jobs Currently in the Queue

The instructions in Figure 8-4 describe the steps necessary to view and control jobs that are already in a NetWare print queue.

1. Start the PCONSOLE program.
2. Select "Print Queue Information."
3. Select the desired print queue.
4. Select "Current Print Job Entries."
5. Select the entry you want to work with and change parameters as necessary. (See "Changing the Queue Entry Information" below for an explanation of the various fields.)
6. Press <Esc> to save your changes.
7. Press <Esc> four times to exit the program.

Figure 8-4: Steps involved in controlling a print job entry in the queue.

The following discussion takes you through these steps in more detail. When we get to Step 5, we'll explicitly examine the various management options available.

1. Start the PCONSOLE program.

You should be SUPERVISOR, supervisor-equivalent, or a queue operator for the queue you want to manage.

2. Select "Print Queue Information."

This is the second option in PCONSOLE's main menu.

3. Select the desired print queue.

For our example queue, highlight "BOOKDEMO" in the list of queues and press <Enter>. PCONSOLE displays the "Print Queue Information" menu.

4. Select "Current Print Job Entries."

The highlight bar will already be on the "Current Print Job Entries" option. Press <Enter> to see a screen displaying the queue entries, along with some basic identifying information about each entry. Figure 8-5 shows an example of a queue entries list.

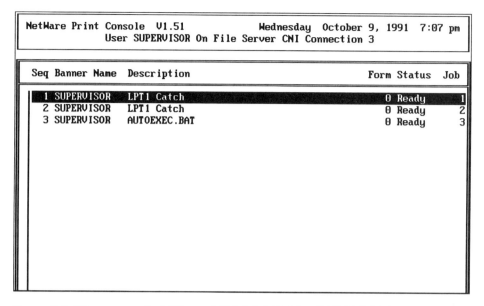

```
NetWare Print Console  V1.51              Wednesday  October 9, 1991  7:07 pm
                    User SUPERVISOR On File Server CNI Connection 3
```

```
 Seq Banner Name  Description                              Form Status  Job

   1 SUPERVISOR   LPT1 Catch                                  0 Ready      1
   2 SUPERVISOR   LPT1 Catch                                  0 Ready      2
   3 SUPERVISOR   AUTOEXEC.BAT                                0 Ready      3
```

Figure 8-5: When you select "Current Print Job Entries," PCONSOLE shows all the jobs currently in the queue.

Here is a brief explanation of the column headings on this screen.

Seq The service sequence number of the job. This reflects the order in which the jobs will be printed.

Banner Name The login name of the user who submitted the job. (If "no banners" was selected as part of the print job configuration, nothing appears here.)

Description The phrase "LPT1 Catch" if the print job was the result of a CAPTURE command, or the filename if the job was sent via the NPRINT command.

Form The form number (even if the CAPTURE or NPRINT command called for a form by name).

Status Legitimate values are: Active (currently printing), Ready (will print in its turn), Held (won't print until released), and Waiting (will print at the appointed day and time).

Job The job number. This is an arbitrary number assigned to each print stream as it enters the queue. It also forms part of the filename in the subdirectory for that queue. (Remember, queues are merely subdirectories and print jobs are files that NetWare prints and then deletes.)

As you make the changes described in Step 5, you will be able to see some of them reflected on this screen.

> **Note:** If you have another computer nearby on the network, you might want to log in there also and perform Steps 1 to 4. You will then be able to watch that screen change dynamically as you make some of these modifications.

5. Select the entry you want to work with and change parameters as necessary.

You can see the parameters on any queue entry, including the one currently printing, by highlighting it and pressing <Enter>. PCONSOLE displays a "Print Queue Entry Information" screen that shows the parameters that were in effect when this print stream was submitted to the queue. We'll explain how to modify the various fields under "Changing the Queue Entry Information" below.

6. Press <Esc> to save your changes.

If you've changed one or more of the fields that appear on the summary screen, the changes will be immediately evident.

7. Press <Esc> four times to exit the program.

A quicker way to exit any NetWare menu utility is to press <Alt>-<F10>. This keystroke takes you directly to the exit prompt.

Changing the Queue Entry Information

When you select an entry in the queue, PCONSOLE displays a "Print Queue Entry Information" screen like the one shown in Figure 8-6.

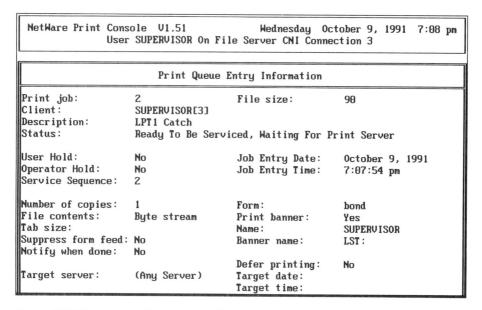

```
NetWare Print Console  V1.51            Wednesday  October 9, 1991  7:08 pm
                  User SUPERVISOR On File Server CNI Connection 3
```

```
                        Print Queue Entry Information

Print job:          2               File size:       90
Client:             SUPERVISOR[3]
Description:        LPT1 Catch
Status:             Ready To Be Serviced, Waiting For Print Server

User Hold:          No              Job Entry Date:  October 9, 1991
Operator Hold:      No              Job Entry Time:  7:07:54 pm
Service Sequence:   2

Number of copies:   1               Form:            bond
File contents:      Byte stream     Print banner:    Yes
Tab size:                           Name:            SUPERVISOR
Suppress form feed: No              Banner name:     LST:
Notify when done:   No
                                    Defer printing:  No
Target server:      (Any Server)    Target date:
                                    Target time:
```

Figure 8-6: When you select an entry in the queue, PCONSOLE displays this "Print Queue Entry Information" screen.

This screen has almost two dozen fields. Some of them just display information and are not changeable. Some are changeable only by queue operators; others can be changed by both queue operators and the job owner (submitter). In the following discussion, we'll indicate the category that each field falls into as follows:

[D] For information Display only

[O] Changeable only by a queue Operator

[S] Both operator and Submitter can change

Print job [D]

This is the same as the job number shown in the rightmost column in the previous screen. It is an arbitrary number assigned when the first character of that job arrives in the queue. It also forms part of the print stream's filename in the queue's subdirectory.

File size [D]

The file size is the number of bytes in the print stream. It is the same file size that would be shown in a DIR or NDIR listing.

After you've had a chance to examine a large number of jobs passing through the queue, you can use the file size to estimate the number of pages in the printout. Bear in mind that print streams generated by a word processor and destined for a dot matrix printer will contain very few escape (control) codes. The same output destined for a laser printer might be much larger due to the inclusion of downloadable fonts. On a PostScript printer it will be the largest of all. Of course, embedded page ejects in a print stream can distort the estimates.

Client [D]

The name in this field is the login name of the user who submitted the job, and the connection number of the station where they are logged in. If the user has asked to be notified when the job finishes printing, this field will be used to determine where to send the message.

Description [S]

Usually, this field shows either "LPTn Catch" (for jobs submitted via CAPTURE) or the filename (for jobs submitted via NPRINT). It is a changeable field, though, and it is often a good idea to use it for comments when a job is held or deferred. The contents of this field are also displayed in the Description column on the previous screen.

Status [D]

The following table lists the possible values in the Status field. The one-word summary of the status is also shown on the previous screen.

"Being Serviced by Print Server [name]"	Active
"Being Added to the Queue"	Adding
"Ready to be Serviced, Waiting for Server"	Ready
"Operator Hold on Job"	Held
"User Hold on Job"	Held
"Waiting for Target Execution Date & Time"	Waiting

Although this field is marked as Display only, some of the changes that Operators and Submitters can make will change the status of the job. The status change will be reflected by the contents of this field.

User Hold [S]

This field is usually set to "No", but the job owner can change it to "Yes" (just type "Y"). Putting a hold on a job keeps it in the queue until either the hold is removed or the job is deleted. (See the related field, "Defer Printing," for an alternative to placing a job on hold.)

Operator Hold [O]

This field also defaults to "No," but like the User Hold parameter, it can be set to "Yes." A queue operator can set and clear a user hold, but a user can neither set nor clear an operator hold.

Service Sequence [O]

This number represents the order in which the job will be serviced. The sequence number reflects how many jobs must be printed before the particular job is done (in other words, the currently printing job is number1). Queue operators can change the service sequence number, thus changing the job's print sequence.

Job Entry Date and Job Entry Time [D]

These two fields show the date and time the job first entered the queue.

Number of Copies [S]

Usually one, the value displayed in this field is based on the choice the user made in the CAPTURE or NPRINT command used to submit the job. The number of copies can be changed at any time until the job has finished printing.

File Contents [S]

This field is based on the Tabs/No Tabs parameter used in CAPTURE or NPRINT (Tabs = Text, No Tabs = Byte Stream). For laser printers, this setting should always be "Byte Stream."

Tab Size [S]

When the preceding field is "Byte Stream," the Tab Size field is bypassed, since it has no meaning in that context. When the preceding field is "Text," the Tab Size represents the number of spaces that NetWare will send when it encounters a Tab character.

Suppress Form Feed [S]

At the end of every print job, NetWare normally sends a form feed character. This automatic form feed can be suppressed by changing this field to "Yes." In CAPTURE and NPRINT commands, this setting is represented by the "Form Feed" and "No Form Feed" parameters.

Most word processors generate a form feed at the end of every file prepared for printing. When the print stream includes its own form feed, including another one merely wastes paper.

Notify when done [S]

This field is based on the "Notify" and "No Notify" parameters from the CAPTURE and NPRINT commands. The default is to not notify users when their jobs are finished printing. When notify is turned on, NetWare sends a broadcast message to the job owner (or to the person specified in the Client field) when the file finishes printing.

Form [S]

The default form is form 0. However, this field displays the form name rather than its number. Forms are named and numbered via the PRINTDEF program. This is an optional task that NetWare supervisors can perform when setting up the printing environment. If no forms have been defined in PRINTDEF, this field displays "Unknown."

Print Banner [S]

A setting of "Yes" in the Print Banner field indicates that a banner page will be printed. As explained previously, a banner page is a sheet of paper printed before the print job itself to identify the job and its sender. The banner page contains information such as the date and time printed, the print server, and the printer number.

Underneath that are the username and print stream name (see Name and Banner Name below) printed in large block letters.

Name [S]

The Submitter's login name is the default for this field. However, this default can be overridden by the "Name=" parameter in CAPTURE and NPRINT.

Banner Name [S]

The default for this field depends on the method used to submit the print stream. If the job is submitted via NPRINT, this field contains the filename. If the job is submitted via CAPTURE, this field contains the string "LST:". As with the preceding field, the default banner name can be overridden by using the "Banner=" command line parameter.

Target Server [S]

The default for this field is "Any Server," which means that any print server authorized to service this queue can handle the print job. Highlighting this field and pressing <Enter> brings up a list of all print servers that can possibly service this queue. If you select one of these, then that print server will be the only one that can service this particular job.

> **Note:** Be careful when you specify a target print server. All print servers, including any NetWare 286 file server that uses core printing services (and thus acts as a print server) will be included in the list of print servers—even if this queue has not been added to any of its printers. Therefore, it is possible to select a print server that is not currently servicing your queue, effectively closing off access to any other print servers that could normally handle the job.

Defer Printing [S]

The purpose of this field is to allow you to defer large or low-priority printouts to a time when the printer will not be busy with other work. Choosing "Yes" automatically sets the Target Date to tomorrow and the Target Time to 2:00am. By choosing the same deferred printing time for all jobs, you can have the jobs print out in job number order. However, it is very simple to defer printing to any future date and time by setting the Target Date and Target Time fields individually.

Target Date [S]

This field will be available for selection only if Deferred Printing is set to "Yes." To change the date shown, simply type in a new date or any part of a date. (Net-Ware allows you to abbreviate almost any way you want; for example, "d 25" is enough to select next Christmas.)

Target Time [S]

Like Target Date, this field is available only if Deferred Printing is set to "Yes." NetWare allows a wide range of abbreviations here also (for example, "3" or "3a" for 3:00 am, "21" or "9p" for 9pm).

Controlling a Print Queue's Status

The instructions in Figure 8-7 describe the steps for changing the status of a Net-Ware print queue.

---

1. Start the PCONSOLE program.
2. Select "Print Queue Information."
3. Select the desired print queue.
4. Select "Current Queue Status." (See the explanation in the text for the meaning and functions of the various fields.)
5. Press <Esc> four times to exit the program.

Figure 8-7: Steps involved in managing a print queue's status.

1. Start the PCONSOLE program.

You should be SUPERVISOR, supervisor-equivalent, or a queue operator for the queue you want to manage.

2. Select "Print Queue Information."

3. Select the desired print queue.

Again, select "BOOKDEMO" if you want to follow along with the subsequent instructions.

4. Select "Current Queue Status."

This brings up a screen like the one in Figure 8-8 that tells you about the status of the queue and gives you some further management choices. A description of the various settings follows Step 5.

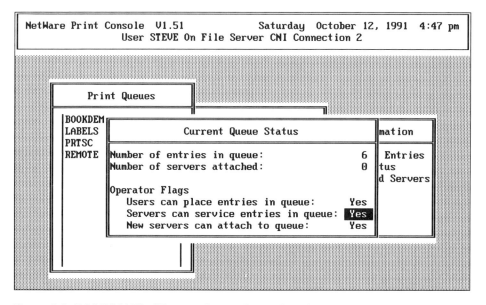

Figure 8-8: PCONSOLE's "Current Queue Status" option lets you monitor a queue's service status.

5. Press <Esc> four times to exit the program.

When you are finished viewing or changing the queue status options, press <Esc> repeatedly to exit (or press <Alt>-<F10> to exit immediately).

The default value for all the Operator Flags is "Yes." As each of the items on this screen is discussed, the implications of answering "No" will be explained.

Number of entries in queue:

This field shows the total number of jobs in the queue, no matter what their status is (Held, Waiting, and so on).

Number of servers attached:

This field shows how many print servers are logically attached to the queue (authorized to service it). As additional servers are added, the number increments. Note that even if a particular server can service the queue via several printers, the server is only counted once. If this number is zero, no printing can occur.

Users can place entries in the queue:

This flag must be set to "Yes" for queue users to be able to submit print jobs to the queue. If you set this flag to "No," a user can issue a CAPTURE to the queue, but attempting to send any characters will result in the following DOS error message:

```
Not ready writing LPTn
Abort/Retry/Ignore
```

Subsequent retries will continue to fail until this flag's setting is changed.

Servers can service entries in queue:

This flag must be set to "Yes" for print servers to be able to service the jobs in the queue. If this field is set to "No" when the print server is started, any printers that service only this queue will show "Waiting for Job" as their status even if there are jobs in the queue. If a job is already printing when the operator changes the setting to "No," the current job will be allowed to complete, but then printing will halt.

A common use of this setting is for a queue that is used to hold print jobs that will print later (for example, during the night). By changing this flag to "No," jobs can be submitted to the queue but won't be printed until it is changed back to "Yes." This is easier than trying to place an operator hold on every job as it comes in, and eliminates the possibility of missing some.

New servers can attach to queue:

This flag allows new print servers (besides the ones currently attached to the queue) to service the queue. Setting this flag to "No" prevents any other print servers from attaching to the queue.

If you try to authorize new print servers to service the queue, NetWare generates different error messages depending on how you attempt to attach.

1. If core printing is in place, then the console command

   ```
   Printer n ADD queuename
   ```

   will generate the following error message:

   ```
   Command Failed
   ```

   on the console. (Most console operators interpret this as a syntax error and waste a lot of time trying to find their mistake.)

2. If the queue is permanently assigned to one or more printers managed by a print server, and the server is brought up, the following error message is displayed:

   ```
   Print Queue FSNAME/QNAME cannot be serviced by printer
   n, because a queue operator has disabled print servers
   from attaching to the queue.
   ```

3. If the print server is already running and the print server operator attempts to add the queue to a printer on a temporary basis, the attempt will fail with this message:

   ```
   ERROR:
   "PSADDQUEUETOPRINTER" returned error 2

   DESCRIPTION:
   Description is not available
   ```

Note that the error is properly diagnosed and explained only in the second situation. Because of the potential for confusion, we advise you to avoid setting this flag to "No."

Adding Jobs to the Queue from PCONSOLE

CAPTURE and NPRINT allow you to submit jobs to NetWare print queues from the command line. Most network-aware applications allow you to submit jobs directly to a queue as well. There is also another way to get a file into the queue to be printed: by adding the job directly from PCONSOLE.

Figure 8-9 summarizes the steps required to add files directly into the queue from within PCONSOLE.

---

1. Start the PCONSOLE program.
2. Select "Print Queue Information."
3. Select the desired print queue.
4. Select "Current Print Job Entries."
5. Press <Ins>.
6. Specify the directory that contains the file(s) you want to add to the queue.
7. Press <Enter>.
8. Select the file(s) to be added and press <Enter>.
9. Select the print job configuration (or the PCONSOLE defaults).
10. Modify the fields as necessary, then press <Esc>.
11. Press <Enter> to confirm.

Figure 8-9: Steps for adding files to a queue from within PCONSOLE.

By now you should be familiar with Steps 1 through 4. Here is a more detailed explanation of Steps 5 through 11.

5. Press <Ins>.

Pressing <Ins> begins the process of adding an entry to the queue. PCONSOLE will display a box containing the current directory name.

137

6. Select the directory that contains the file(s) you want to add to the queue.

You can use the normal editing keys (Backspace, arrow keys, Delete, and so forth) to change the displayed directory path (including the server and volume names, if necessary).

Pressing <Ins> again will activate the NetWare menu program directory prompt function. (If you are unfamiliar with this method of specifying a directory path, refer to your NetWare manuals.)

7. Press <Enter>.

Pressing <Enter> after you specify the directory displays a list of all the files in that directory. Your screen should be similar to the one shown in Figure 8-10.

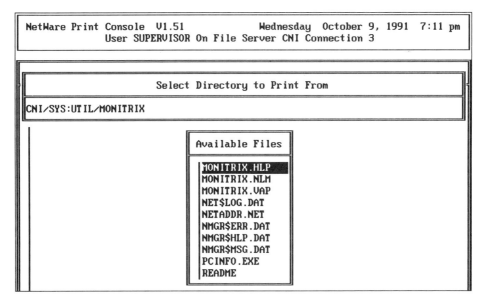

Figure 8-10: Once you select the directory to print from, PCONSOLE displays a list of files in that directory.

8. Select the file(s) to be added and press <Enter>.

To add a single file, simply highlight it and press <Enter>. If you want to add multiple files, highlight each one in turn and press <F5>. When you have highlighted all the files you want to add, press <Enter>.

9. Select the print job configuration (or the PCONSOLE defaults).

Once you select the file(s) to print, you will see a list of all the print job configuration defined in PRINTCON, plus one called "PConsole Defaults." (If no PRINT-CON.DAT file is available, only the "Pconsole Defaults" entry will be listed.) Figure 8-11 shows an example of what your screen should look like at this point.

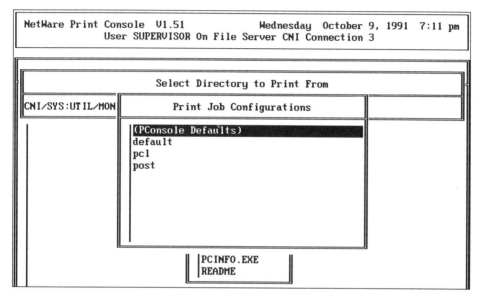

```
NetWare Print Console  V1.51           Wednesday  October 9, 1991  7:11 pm
               User SUPERVISOR On File Server CNI Connection 3

                      Select Directory to Print From
CNI/SYS:UTIL/MON           Print Job Configurations

                   (PConsole Defaults)
                   default
                   pcl
                   post




                       PCINFO.EXE
                       README
```

Figure 8-11: PCONSOLE lets you choose its own defaults or one of the print job configurations defined in PRINTCON.

Highlight the configuration most appropriate to the file(s) being printed and press <Enter>.

10. Modify the fields as necessary, then press <Esc>.

At this point, PCONSOLE displays the same screen as shown in Figure 8-6. However, this time some of the fields will be blank. Modify the field values as you see fit. When you are finished, press <Esc>.

11. Press <Enter> to confirm.

The "Yes" option is already highlighted. Pressing <Enter> confirms your intent to add the job to the queue.

Moving Data from One Queue to Another

From time to time, you might want to move print jobs from one queue to another. For example, maybe a long file is being printed and you want to move the other jobs in the queue, or perhaps a print job has been inadvertently misdirected.

The steps to move jobs between queues are relatively straightforward. They are listed in Figure 8-12.

---

1. Start PCONSOLE and select the queue containing the job(s) you want to move.
2. From the "Print Queue Information" menu, select "Print Queue ID" and make a note of the queue's object ID. Press <Esc>.
3. Select "Current Print Job Entries."
4. Find the job (not sequence) number of the print job(s) you want to move.
5. Press <Esc> until you return to the "Print Queues" list. Highlight the target print queue name, press <Enter> to bring up the "Print Queue Information" menu, and press <Enter> again to show the "Current Print Job Entries" screen.
6. Press <Ins>. Change the directory path in the "Select Directory to Print From" box to SYS:SYSTEM, then press <Ins> again.
7. Highlight the name of the subdirectory that matches the object ID you found in Step 2. (Leading zeroes are sometimes omitted). Then press <Enter>, <Esc>, and <Enter> to see an "Available Files" list.
8. Highlight the file whose name has the job number you identified in Step 4 and press <Enter>. Or, to move several jobs, mark them with the <F5> key and then press <Enter>.
9. A new list, called "Print Job Configurations," will appear. Select the proper configuration, make any necessary changes, then press <Esc> and <Enter>.

Figure 8-12: Steps for moving print jobs from one queue to another.

The method described here builds on the technique previously described under "Adding Jobs to the Queue from PCONSOLE." It is basically a matter of choosing the queue that currently holds the job as the source directory while positioned to add jobs to the queue you want to move the job into.

Here are some notes and comments about the process:

1. Start PCONSOLE and select the queue containing the job(s) you want to move.

First we must get to the source queue via PCONSOLE to find out the bindery object ID of the queue.

2. From the "Print Queue Information" menu, select "Print Queue ID" and make a note of the queue's object ID. Press <Esc>.

The print queue ID is the bindery object ID for the selected queue. It is also the name of the subdirectory in SYS:SYSTEM that holds the queue's files. We'll need this directory name in Step 7. Figure 8-13 shows the ID number for our sample "BOOKDEMO" queue.

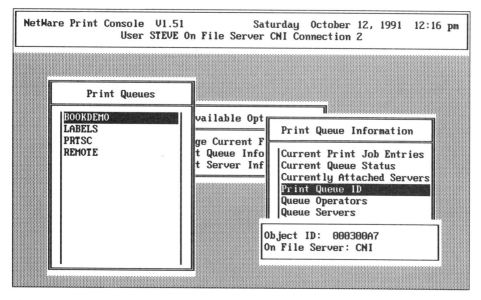

Figure 8-13: The object ID displayed when you select "Print Queue ID" in PCON-SOLE is also the name of the print queue's subdirectory.

3. Select "Current Print Job Entries."

Once you have noted the print queue ID, you need to switch to the list of print job entries so you can select the job(s) you want to move.

4. Find the job (not sequence) number of the print job(s) you want to move.

Remember, "Job" is in the rightmost column. The job number forms part of the print stream's filename. You might want to write the job numbers down if you are moving several jobs at once.

5. Press <Esc> until you return to the "Print Queues" list. Highlight the target print queue name, press <Enter> to bring up the "Print Queue Information" menu, and press <Enter> again to show the "Current Print Job Entries" screen.

Once you know the subdirectory name and the filename(s), you need to switch back to the "Print Queues" list and select the target queue.

6. Press <Ins>. In the "Select Directory to Print From" box, change the directory path to SYS:SYSTEM, then press <Ins> again.

As before, pressing <Ins> brings up a box in which you can type the name of the directory. When you change it to SYS:SYSTEM and press <Ins> again, PCON-SOLE displays a pop-up list of all the subdirectories to SYS:SYSTEM. Figure 8-14 shows what this list looks like:

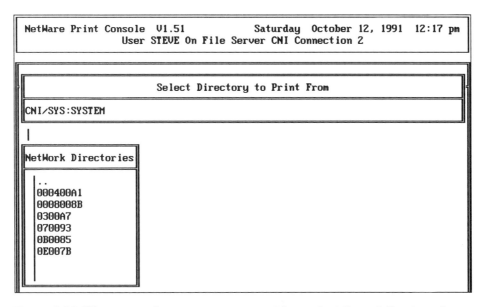

```
NetWare Print Console  V1.51          Saturday  October 12, 1991  12:17 pm
                  User STEVE On File Server CNI Connection 2


┌──────────────────────────────────────────────────────────────────────┐
│                   Select Directory to Print From                       │
│ CNI/SYS:SYSTEM                                                          │
├──────────────────────────────────────────────────────────────────────┤
│ │                                                                      │
│ ┌─────────────────┐                                                    │
│ │NetWork Directories│                                                  │
│ ├─────────────────┤                                                    │
│ │ ..              │                                                    │
│ │ 000400A1        │                                                    │
│ │ 0008008B        │                                                    │
│ │ 0300A7          │                                                    │
│ │ 070093          │                                                    │
│ │ 0B0085          │                                                    │
│ │ 0E007B          │                                                    │
│ └─────────────────┘                                                    │
└──────────────────────────────────────────────────────────────────────┘
```

Figure 8-14: When preparing to move queue entries, select the subdirectory that corresponds to the source print queue.

7. Highlight the name of the subdirectory that matches the object ID you found in Step 2. (Leading zeroes are sometimes omitted). Then press <Enter>, <Esc>, and <Enter> to see an "Available Files" list.

Once you select the correct queue subdirectory, pressing <Esc> automatically appends the subdirectory name to the directory path you typed in the box above. Pressing <Enter> again generates a new pop-up list called "Available Files." This is a list of all the files in the source queue.

Note: In NetWare 386, print queue subdirectory names may have a .QDR extension.

8. Highlight the file whose extension matches the job number you identified in Step 4 and press <Enter>. Or, to move several jobs, mark them with the <F5> key and then press <Enter>.

Note: You cannot move the active print job in any queue, because the active job is open and is flagged non-shareable.

143

9. A new list, called "Print Job Configurations," will appear. Select the proper configuration, make any necessary changes, then press <Esc> and <Enter>.

You can select any configuration defined in PRINTCON, or PCONSOLE's default configuration. Once you've made any changes, pressing <Esc> and <Enter> confirms your changes.

> **Note:** Any changes made to the job's configuration while it was in the source queue (such as number of copies, hold status, and so on) will not be carried over to the new queue.

You have now successfully copied the job(s) from one queue to another. To make the move complete, go back to the source queue and delete the print job(s) that you've moved.

Deleting a Print Queue

Deleting a print queue is easier than creating it. Simply follow the steps shown in Figure 8-15.

---

1. Start PCONSOLE.
2. Choose "Print Queue Information."
3. Select the queue to delete.
4. Press <Del>.
5. Confirm the deletion.

Figure 8-15: Steps for deleting a print queue.

These steps will successfully delete the queue and all of its contents. However, deleting a queue can create problems for any print server that might be servicing that queue.

When you restart any print server that expects to manage a queue you have deleted, you will see the following message:

```
PSERVER Warning
    Print Queue FSNAME/QNAME is unknown. Queue will
    not be serviced by printer n, printername
```

Figure 8-16: The print server issues this warning message when you delete a queue it is set up to service.

Do not try to re-create the queue in an attempt to fix the situation. If you do, the print server issues a different warning message:

```
PSERVER Warning
    Not authorized to service FSNAME/QNAME. Queue
    will not be serviced by printer n, printername
```

Figure 8-17: If you try to re-create the deleted queue, the print server issues this warning message.

This problem arises because NetWare doesn't re-use the same bindery object ID number when you re-create a queue with the same name as one you have deleted. (The bindery is NetWare's database of users, queues, print servers, and their rights. For example, the bindery keeps track of your password and whether you are a console operator. It assigns each user, group, print server, and print queue an "object ID.") The bindery also tracks which queues a print server is authorized to service, and by which printers. As far as NetWare is concerned, when you delete a queue and create another with the same name, you have created an entirely different print queue.

Personnel departments face a similar situation when an employee leaves the company and then returns. If they assign a new employee ID number, the system treats the employee as a new hire. Trying to merge the employee's previous records with the new information is difficult.

To avoid problems when you delete a print queue and want to re-create the queue later, follow these steps:

1. In the print server definition, delete all references to that queue (the next chapter gives details on how to modify the print server definition).
2. Delete the queue as described above.
3. Run the NetWare BINDFIX utility (located in SYS:SYSTEM). This utility removes all traces of the old queue and its old object ID from the bindery.
4. Re-create the queue in PCONSOLE.
5. Add the queue to the print server definition (as explained in the next chapter).

To be safe, it is a good idea to always perform the first step for every print server that services a queue before you delete that queue. Someone might come along after you and try to create a queue with the same name as one you have deleted.

CHAPTER 9

Working with Print Servers in PCONSOLE

In this chapter, we will learn how to create and maintain a NetWare print server. First we'll look at how to set up the print server to service queues on one file server. Then we'll modify the print server definition to handle queues on multiple file servers. The following chapter discusses the PSERVER program and the NetWare facilities for managing the print server while it is up and running.

Conceptual Overview

The concept of using a print server is relatively new to NetWare. As shipped from Novell, NetWare version 2.15C and its predecessors could only print on printers that were directly connected to a file server. Thus print management was an integral part of the file server's duties. If a company needed to print at a remote location away from the file server, the only answer Novell provided was to install a second file server. This inadequate solution opened the door for many successful third-party software packages to provide remote printing facilities in one form or another.

With the release of Netware 386, Novell changed its position on print services. NetWare 386 does not support (and never has supported) printing as a part of the built-in file server capabilities. Instead, it provides three versions of a print server program, named PSERVER.*xxx*, where *xxx* is the file extension that differentiates between the versions. The table in Figure 9-1 shows the different print server versions and the place where they were originally intended to be used:

extension	meaning	load location
.NLM	Netware Loadable Module	at the file server
.VAP	Value Added Process	at a router (bridge)
.EXE	DOS Executable	at a DOS workstation

Figure 9-1: NetWare 386 provides three version of the PSERVER program. Each version loads at a different place on the network.

With these three types of print servers, network administrators can choose the most convenient location for their network printers.

- Those who still want to connect printers to parallel or serial ports on the file server can use the NLM.

- Those who want to run the print server at a NetWare router (formerly called a NetWare bridge) can use the VAP. As an added bonus, anyone on a multiserver network that includes NetWare 286 software can run the print server VAP on a NetWare 286 file server.

- Those who want to use a standalone workstation to manage the printing function (thus either replacing or supplementing the equivalent function at the file server) can use the EXE.

The only difference between the print server versions is the control information at the beginning of the program that allows it to load on top of NetWare 386, NetWare 286 (or the router software), or DOS.

Before you can load the PSERVER.*xxx* software, you must first define a print server. Print servers are defined and configured as part of the PCONSOLE program, and that is the subject of this chapter. The next chapter focuses on the PSERVER software, including a section on the factors to be weighed in deciding when to use which version of the print server software.

Print Servers

A NetWare print server can manage a maximum of 16 printers and 32 print queues. Of these 16 printers, up to five can be attached to the computer running PSERVER (either a standalone machine, a router, or a file server). The remaining printers (16 less the number of printers physically attached) can be defined as remote printers.

The reason for the limit of five directly-attached printers is that the machines we use for print servers have, at most, three parallel ports and two serial ports. If some computer or board manufacturer ever makes more ports available on a single machine, the existing PSERVER program will be able to handle them.

Print Server Users

By default, NetWare assigns the group EVERYONE as print server users when you first create a print server. This ensures that every user who sends jobs to a queue managed by the print server will get their jobs printed.

Oddly enough, it is possible to be a queue user and be able to send jobs to a queue managed by a print server for which you are not an authorized print server user. (This is analogous to a manager who has keys to her own private office, but whose badge does not provide access to her department's floor.) However, the job will not print unless that queue is also being serviced by another print server to which you have been given access as a print server user. Since this kind of problem is difficult to track down, we strongly advise that you leave the default of EVERYONE in place and control access to printers via the queues.

Print Server Operators

A print server operator is a user or group of users who can manage the print server. By default, the user SUPERVISOR is the only print server operator when you first create a print server.

> **Note:** This is different than the default for print queue operators. SUPERVISOR and supervisor-equivalent users are automatically assigned as print queue operators. For print servers, supervisor-equivalents are not automatically assigned as print server operators, although they do have the power to add themselves to the list.

Deciding How Many Print Servers You Need

Before you start defining print servers, you should take some time to consider the users' needs. The best way to perform this needs analysis is to decide where you want the permanently shared printers to be located, and to find out which of the private printers on the network will occasionally be shared by a group or department.

Let's look at Allied Accounting as an example. They have twenty shared printers to be spread among their users. While twenty printers could be handled using core printing and a single print server, that configuration would leave no room for growth. It would also put a heavy burden on the file server itself—something we want to avoid.

To meet Allied Accounting's needs, it is much better to define two print servers. The physical layout of the two LANs—a file server near the receptionist's desk, with one cable running to the east wing and another to the west wing—suggests appropriate names and locations for these print servers. In the print server definitions, we'd assign ten remote printers to each, according to the specifications of the printers.

On the other hand, Southern Confederacy has a much more complex printing configuration. They have four LANs, each with its own server, connected by a router. The servers represent all four common NetWare configurations: version 2.15 with core printing, version 2.20 with core printing, version 2.20 without core printing, and version 3.11. Both servers with core printing have printers attached to them; all servers have print servers defined.

The key to success here is to minimize the confusion. Whenever possible, each print server will specialize in printers servicing queues on the same file server. We'd define one print server (the one to be loaded as a VAP on the router) to be capable of managing any queue on any file server.

This is the print server we would use to handle the temporarily shared printers.

Defining a Print Server in PCONSOLE

Defining a print server is accomplished via the PCONSOLE program. Figure 9-2 summarizes the instructions for creating a print server.

1. Log in as SUPERVISOR (or equivalent).
2. Start PCONSOLE.
3. Select "Print Server Information."
4. Press <Ins>.
5. Type the new print server name.
6. Press <Enter>.
7. Press <Enter> (again).
8. Select "Server Users."
9. Modify the list as necessary, then press <Esc>.
10. Select "Server Operators."
11. Modify the list as necessary, then press <Esc>.
12. Select "Print Server Configuration."
13. Select "Printer Configuration."
14. Configure the printers (see text for details).
15. Press <Esc>, then select "Queues Serviced by Printers."
16. Assign one or more queues to each configured printer, then press <Esc>.
17. Choose "Notify List for Printer" and set up the notification list (optional).
18. Press <Esc> twice to return to "Print Server Information" menu.
19. Select "Change Password" (optional).
20. Enter a "Full Name" for the print server (optional).
21. Repeat from Step 3 for another print server, or press <Esc> repeatedly to exit.

Figure 9-2: Steps for creating a print server in PCONSOLE.

Here is a more detailed explanation of each step.

1. *Log in as SUPERVISOR (or equivalent).*

You must be SUPERVISOR or supervisor equivalent to create print servers. Those users named as Print Server Operators in Step 10 will have the ability to manage the print server after it has been created, but they cannot create new print servers.

151

2. Start PCONSOLE.

PCONSOLE.EXE, the print server management program, is located in SYS:PUB-LIC so you can access it from any network drive.

3. Select "Print Server Information."

This is the option used to create or manage a print server.

4. Press <Ins>.

As with all NetWare menus, pressing <Ins> lets you add a new item.

5. Type in the new print server name.

You can use any name you like. Figure 9-3 shows the pending addition of the print server "WEST_WING" for our Allied Accounting example.

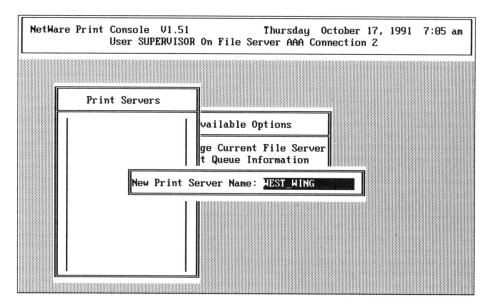

```
NetWare Print Console  V1.51            Thursday  October 17, 1991   7:05 am
                 User SUPERVISOR On File Server AAA Connection 2


        Print Servers

                               vailable Options
                               ge Current File Server
                               t Queue Information

                  New Print Server Name: WEST_WING
```

Figure 9-3: When creating a new print server, you must assign it a name.

6. Press <Enter>.

This signals your acceptance of the name. (If you notice a typographical error at this point, press <F3> to modify the name.)

7. Press <Enter> (again).

This selects the newly-named print server. PCONSOLE displays the "Print Server Information" menu. This menu has several options, only two of which will be described here: "Server Users" and "Server Operators." The other options will be described in subsequent sections in this chapter.

8. Select "Server Users."

Again, we recommend that you leave the default group EVERYONE in place as print server users. If you decide to change the list of users who can be served by this print server, follow the instructions in Step 9.

9. Modify the list as necessary, then press <Esc>.

To change the list of print server users, press <Ins> to bring up the list of all users and groups not currently included as server users. Highlight the entry of your choice and press <Enter>.

If you have several users or groups to select, repeat this step several times, or mark the ones you want by highlighting each entry in turn and pressing <F5>, then press <Enter> to add them all at once.

In either case, you should then delete the group EVERYONE from the list. When you are finished, press <Esc> to go back to the "Print Server Information" menu.

10. Select "Server Operators."

By default, the only user listed as a print server operator is SUPERVISOR, even if you are logged in as a supervisor-equivalent user when you create the print server. Figure 9-4 shows the default "Print Server Operators" list.

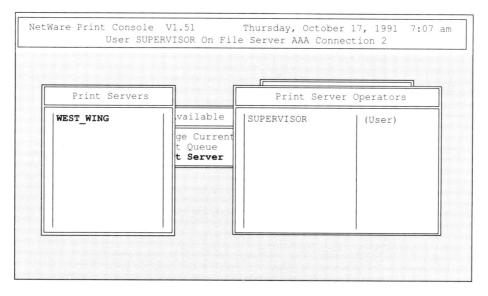

```
NetWare Print Console  V1.51        Thursday, October 17, 1991  7:07 am
                  User SUPERVISOR On File Server AAA Connection 2
```

```
        Print Servers                    Print Server Operators

    WEST_WING          vailable    SUPERVISOR          (User)

                       ge Current
                       t Queue
                       t Server
```

Figure 9-4: You can assign print server operators when you create a print server.

11. Modify the list as necessary, then press <Esc>.

Although supervisor-equivalent users can create a print server and perform most of the management tasks, there is one task that only users on this list can perform. That task is to "down" the print server. (The method for doing this is described under "Managing the Print Server" in the next chapter.) This seems to be a bug—it is the only place in NetWare where a supervisor-equivalent user is not really equivalent to SUPERVISOR. Nevertheless, if you want to have the ability to down the print server as a supervisor-equivalent user, you must add yourself to the list.

You can modify this list in the same manner as the list of server users, described in Step 9. When you are finished, press <Esc> to return to the previous menu.

12. Select "Print Server Configuration."

The next step is to define the print server configuration. When you select "Print Server Configuration" from the "Print Server Information" menu, PCONSOLE displays the "Print Server Configuration Menu" as shown in Figure 9-5.

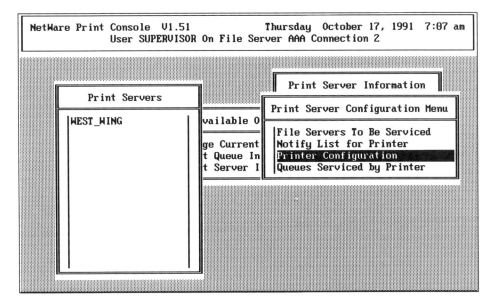

Figure 9-5: The "Printer Configuration" option is the first step in configuring a new print server.

13. Select "Printer Configuration."

The first step in configuring a print server is to define the printers it will service. To do this, highlight "Printer Configuration" and press <Enter>. PCONSOLE displays a list with sixteen entries, numbered 0 to 15, all with the label "Not Installed" (shown following).

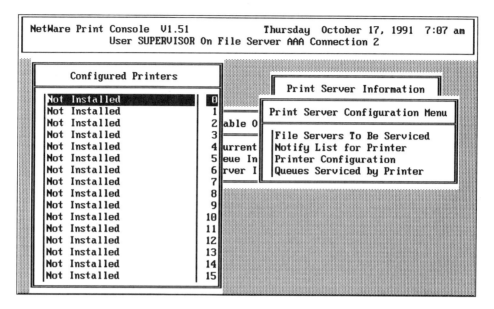

Figure 9-6: Initially, the sixteen possible printers are all listed as "Not Installed."

14. Configure the printers.

To configure a printer, highlight any printer number labelled "Not Installed."

Note: There is no preferred order in which to configure printers, nor are any printer numbers reserved for locally attached printers. However, it makes practical sense to configure the first eight printers before moving on to the last eight. When running the NLM or EXE versions of PSERVER, the program displays a print server management screen that shows the status of the sixteen printers, eight per screenful. If you configure the first eight printers consecutively, you'll be able to see them all on the first management screen and you won't have to constantly switch screens.

Configuring a Printer for the Print Server

Figure 9-7 shows the general steps to follow to configure a printer for the print server.

14a. Type a new name for the printer and press <Enter>.

14b. Press <Enter> again for a list of printer types and select the appropriate entry. (See the text for an explanation of the types.)

14c. Select the IRQ number.

14d. Modify the buffer size as necessary.

14e. Choose a starting form number.

14f. Press <Enter> to bring up the possible "Queue Service Modes" and select the appropriate one.

14g. For serial printers, set the bottom five fields to match the suggestions in the printer's manual.

14h. Press <Esc>, then confirm by selecting "Yes."

14i. Repeat Step 14 for another printer number, or press <Esc> to continue.

Figure 9-7: Steps for configuring printers for the print server.

The exact procedure varies slightly depending on what type of printer you choose: serial or parallel, local or remote. The detailed steps below describe what happens when you select "Remote Serial, COM1" as the printer type. After that, we'll explain what is different for the remote parallel and local parallel printer types.

14a. Type a new name for the printer and press <Enter>.

After you choose the printer number and press <Enter>, you'll see a screen entitled "Printer *n* Configuration" with the "Name:" field highlighted. The default value for the name is "Printer *n*." However, printer management is easier if you use a more descriptive printer name—for example, Label Printer, Kathy's Laser, Postscript Printer, and soon. As an example, type "Local Labels" as shown in Figure 9-8.

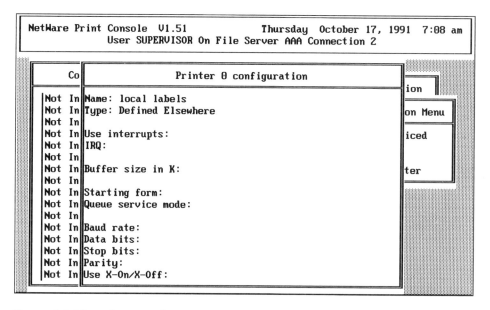

```
NetWare Print Console  V1.51          Thursday  October 17, 1991  7:08 am
                       User SUPERVISOR On File Server AAA Connection 2
```

```
       Co            Printer 0 configuration                    
                                                        ion
Not In Name: local labels
Not In Type: Defined Elsewhere                          on Menu
Not In
Not In Use interrupts:                                  iced
Not In IRQ:
Not In
Not In Buffer size in K:                                ter
Not In
Not In Starting form:
Not In Queue service mode:
Not In
Not In Baud rate:
Not In Data bits:
Not In Stop bits:
Not In Parity:
Not In Use X-On/X-Off:
```

Figure 9-8: The printer configuration form contains the fields for configuring a specific printer in PCONSOLE.

14b. Press <Enter> again for a list of printer types and select the appropriate entry.

After you select the name, the cursor will be in the "Type:" field. Pressing <Enter> brings up a list of sixteen printer types, as shown in Figure 9-9.

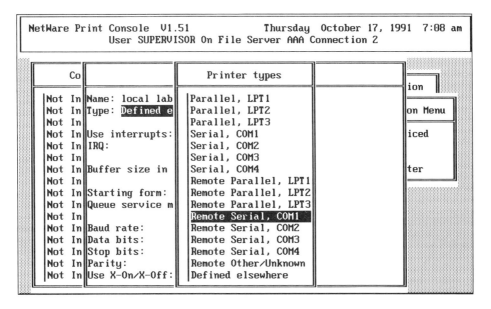

Figure 9-9: PCONSOLE offers sixteen different printer types.

The first seven printer types are for parallel and serial printers that are phys-ically attached to the computer running PSERVER (local printers). The next seven types are for printers attached to computers that will run the RPRINTER (remote printer) program. (The "Remote Other/Unknown" entry is for remote printers whose connection (parallel or serial) will be determined when the RPRINTER program is started. This option, along with the "Defined elsewhere" option, are described in detail at the end of this chapter.) Highlight the printer type you want and press <Enter>.

For our first example, highlight "Remote Serial, COM1" and press <Enter>. This selection changes the underlying screen to the one shown in Figure 9-10.

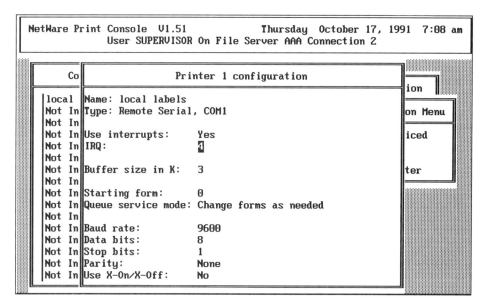

Figure 9-10: The printer configuration fields change depending on the type of printer you select. These are the fields for a remote serial printer.

14c. Select the IRQ number.

The default IRQ (Interrupt Request) for the COM1 port is 4. It is highly unlikely that you will have a COM1 that uses a different IRQ. Nevertheless, this field is changeable, in the event your COM1 port is configured differently. Figure 9-11 contains the list of default IRQ assignments:

IRQ Number	Standard Use
0	Clock (cannot be changed)
1	Keyboard (cannot be changed)
2	Cascade (Available)
3	COM2
4	COM1
5	LPT2
6	Floppy (also, XT-disk)
7	LPT1
13	Math Coprocessor (not on PC)
14	AT-Disk (not on PC)

Figure 9-11: These are the standard IRQ assignments for PCs and ATs.

14d. *Modify the buffer size as necessary.*

For most uses, the default buffer size of 3KB is appropriate. Increasing the buffer size will improve printing throughput slightly for files with a much higher than normal amount of data per page, such as graphics, or for printers with a very high print speed.

> **Note:** For the vast majority of printers, the slowest operation is moving the paper through the print mechanism. On a laser printer rated at eight pages per minute (the most common speed on the market), it takes less than a second to copy the data to the printer and almost eight seconds for the paper to travel from the input tray to the output stack. Since a page of single-spaced text is typically 2KB or less in size, a 3KB buffer can hold more than one page of data. Thus, there is plenty of time for the print server to supply the second page's data while the first page is printing.
>
> Exceptions to this are printers that handle PostScript output and printers that are sent large graphic files. For these printers, a larger buffer size (5-7KB) is more appropriate.

161

14e. Choose a starting form number.

Generally, it's best to use the default form number of zero. However, for printers that always have a special form mounted (such as labels or checks), the form number should match the form name defined in the PRINTDEF program. (See Chapter 7 for more information about defining forms.)

14f. Select the appropriate queue service mode.

NetWare provides four queue service modes. Before discussing them, remember that it is possible to have a printer service more than one queue. In this case, you can assign priorities to the queues being serviced by a printer. (Assigning queue priorities is discussed in more detail in Step 15.) The definitions for the queue service modes take both of these facts into account.

Figure 9-12 shows the service mode selection list that pops up when you highlight the "Queue service mode" field and press <Enter>.

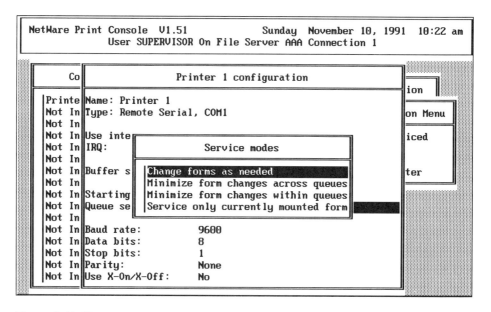

Figure 9-12: You can select one of these four possible queue service modes for each printer you configure.

The four queue service modes are:

- Change forms as needed. This is the default mode. It means that jobs in the queue will be serviced in sequence-number order. If a print job requires a form change, printing will stop until the new form is mounted.

- Minimize form changes across queues. If you select this mode, the print server will search all the queues assigned to the particular printer, looking for other jobs that require the currently mounted form. It will then service those jobs before servicing a job that requires a form change. In this mode, jobs in a low-priority queue might sometimes print before jobs in a high-priority queue.

- Minimize form changes within queues. This mode is much like the preceding one, except that entries in the highest priority queue will always be serviced first. However, within that queue, jobs might be serviced out of normal service sequence to minimize the number of form changes.

- Service only currently mounted form. As mentioned previously, some printers are dedicated to a particular form, such as labels or checks. This mode prevents a misdirected print job that calls for a form change from wasting the special form, as the print server will not service the stray job.

Highlight the queue service mode you want for the printer you are configuring and press <Enter>.

14g. *Set up the serial transmission parameters.*

The remaining fields define the transmission protocol for serial printers only. Check your printer manual for the protocols expected by your printer and set the fields to match.

Your serial printer might be capable of accepting data faster than 9600 baud; however, this is the fastest rate the print server software will allow. If your printer can use "X-on/X-off" flow control, selecting it here will improve overall printer performance.

14h. To save your changes, press <Esc>.

After you leave this screen, answer "Yes" to the confirmation prompt.

14i. Repeat Step 14 for another printer number, or press <Esc> to continue.

If you have other printers to configure, repeat Steps 14a through 14h for each one. When you are finished, press <Esc> to return to the "Print Server Configuration" menu.

The next two sections explain what to do differently when you are defining a remote parallel printer and a local parallel printer.

Configuring a Remote Parallel Printer

When you select a printer defined as "Remote Parallel, LPT1" in Step 14x, you see the same screen as for the serial printer, with the following two changes.

- The interrupt is set at IRQ 7, which is the default interrupt for LPT1. As with the serial port, it is highly unlikely that the default interrupt shown will be incorrect, but if it is, you can change it.

- The items below "Queue service mode" are blank, since they do not apply to parallel ports.

Configuring a Local Parallel Printer

When you select "Parallel, LPT1" for the printer type in Step 14x, you see the same selection options as for the remote parallel type, with one major exception: use of an interrupt is optional. The following section briefly describes printer interrupts versus polled printing and gives some suggestions on making the best selection.

Choosing Between Polling and Interrupts

An operating system, such as DOS or NetWare, has the ability to poll its parallel ports to determine if the attached printers are ready to receive more data. Under this scheme, the operating system chooses when to service the printers.

An alternative method is to enable interrupts for the parallel ports. When interrupts are enabled, the printer requests more data by sending a signal that interrupts the processor. Thus the choice of when to service the printer is made by the printer itself.

When you have more than one printer vying for the CPU, it is easily possible for one printer to interrupt the servicing of another. For this reason, polled printing is usually the better choice.

However, when the printer is attached to a machine other than the print server, the operating system running at the print server has no way of polling the remote printer. It must rely on a specific request for more data from that other machine. But at that other machine, the local operating system (DOS) isn't controlling the printer either. Rather, the printer is controlled by a small, memory-resident program called RPRINTER.

Since RPRINTER is not an operating system, it can't poll the printer; it must rely on the printer's ability to signal its readiness for more data. The printer does this by a process known as "raising an interrupt," while RPRINTER monitors the interrupt line. When the interrupt signal is received, RPRINTER sends a request to the print server for more data, which it then forwards to the printer.

In a typical installation, a newly-defined print server might be servicing a few remote printers and only one or two local ones. This print server should be set up so that the local parallel printers are polled, not interrupt driven. In this way, the print server will respond first to the requests of the remote printers (via RPRINTER and its own LAN card). The rest of the time, the print server will poll its own local printers to see if they need service.

As more and more remote (and possibly local) printers are added, the print server might not have much time to service its local parallel printers. When this happens, printing at the local printers will slow down. The supervisor should then experiment with enabling interrupts for the local printers. While using interrupts will definitely improve the print speed for the local printers, it will have a negative impact on the remote ones. Finding the best compromise is often a matter of trial-and-error experimentation.

Assigning Queues to Printers

We now resume our explanation of the print server configuration steps at Step 15.

15. Select "Queues Serviced by Printers."

Once you have defined at least one printer, press <Esc> to return to the "Print Server Configuration Menu." Then select "Queues Serviced by Printer" to bring up a list of all the configured printers, as shown in Figure 9-13.

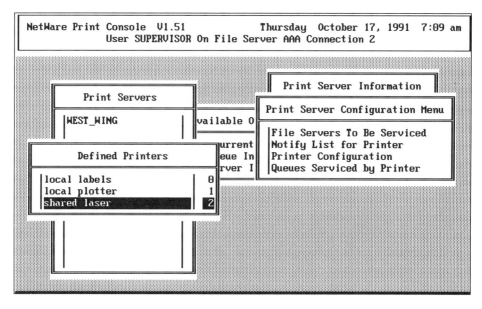

Figure 9-13: The "Queues Serviced by Printer" option lets you assign one or more queues to each printer you have defined.

Select the first printer to which you wish to assign queue(s). Note that the assignments you make here are "permanent"—every time you initialize the print server, these assignments will be in place. However, after the print server is up and running, it is possible to add or delete other queues on a temporary basis. (These temporary changes are discussed in Chapter 10.)

16. Assign one or more queues to each configured printer.

As explained in Chapter 8, you can set up a many-to-many relationship between queues and printers. To add queues, press <Ins>. This brings up the list of defined queues for that server, as shown in Figure 9-14. Highlight the queue you want to add and press <Enter>.

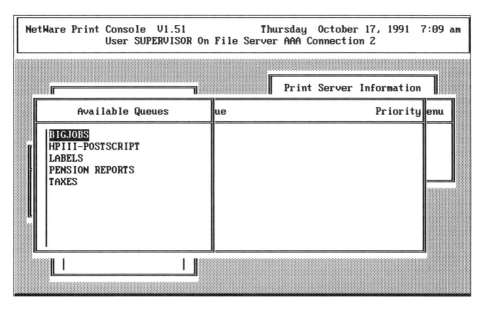

Figure 9-14: PCONSOLE displays a list of available queues you can assign to the selected printer.

You now have the opportunity to specify the priority of that queue for the selected printer. Priorities vary from one to ten; the lower the number, the higher the priority. Figure 9-15 shows the "Priority" entry box.

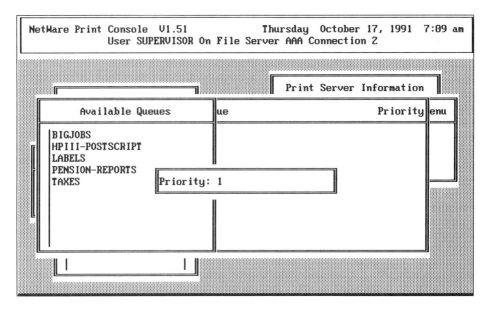

```
NetWare Print Console  V1.51          Thursday  October 17, 1991  7:09 am
                       User SUPERVISOR On File Server AAA Connection 2
```

Print Server Information

```
┌─────────────────────────────┐                    │ Print Server  Information │
│      Available Queues       │ ue                      Priority│enu│
│ BIGJOBS                     │
│ HPIII-POSTSCRIPT            │
│ LABELS                      │
│ PENSION-REPORTS    ┌─────────────────────────────┐
│ TAXES              │Priority: 1                  │
│                    └─────────────────────────────┘
```

Figure 9-15: When you assign a queue to a printer, you can also set the queue's priority.

You can assign another queue to the same printer by pressing <Ins> again and selecting the queue. If you want multiple queues assigned to a printer at the same priority, use the <F5> key to mark each one, then press <Enter> and assign them a priority all at once.

Repeat Step 16 for each defined printer. The same queue may be assigned to more than one printer, just as any printer may service more than one queue. When you are finished, press <Esc>.

17. Choose "Notify List for Printer" and set up the notification list.

Setting up a notify list is optional, but highly recommended. When the printer needs attention due to a paper jam, running out of paper, and so on, the print server will send a message to the users or groups you specify in the notify list. If you skip this step, the printer might remain idle due to paper outages or jams for a long time until somebody notices the problem.

17a. To establish a notification list, select "Notify List for Printer" from the "Printer Configuration" menu.

17b. You'll see the list of defined printers again. Highlight the one you want to set up and press <Enter>.

17c. Press <Ins> to bring up a list of all users and groups on your file server. You can select any existing user or group defined on that server for notification. (The entire list might not be visible all at once; if necessary, use the arrow keys or <PgUp> and <PgDn> to scroll through the list.) The choice at the top of the list is "(Job Owner)." It makes sense to select this entry first, since the job owner is the user with the most incentive to fix the problem.

17d. Once you have selected an entry, a "Notification Intervals" box appears on the screen, as shown in Figure 9-16. The "First:" number specifies the number of seconds before the first message is sent. "Next" is the number of seconds between subsequent messages. The text of the message alerts the recipient to the "printer off-line" condition. A reasonable pair of entries is 30/60, meaning a notice after the printer is off-line for thirty seconds and another notice every minute thereafter until the condition is resolved.

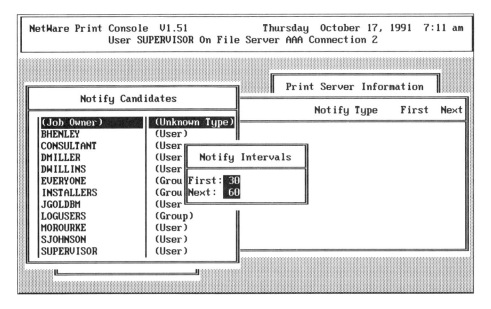

Figure 9-16: For each notify candidate you select, you can specify different intervals for the notification messages to be sent.

It is a good idea to always add at least one other entry besides "(Job Owner)" to the notification list. The job owner might not always be at his or her workstation, or may have issued the CASTOFF command so that NetWare disregards incoming messages. A good choice might be a group that shares the printer, or—in the case of a remote printer—the person who uses the workstation to which the printer is attached. For secondary choices, you can specify longer notify intervals such as 120/600 (first notice after two minutes, subsequent notices every five minutes).

18. Press <Esc> twice to return to the "Print Server Information" menu.

From here, there are just two details to complete.

19. Select "Change Password" (optional).

For the vast majority of installations, it makes little sense to assign a password for the print server. Before anyone can print anything from a queue, you have to start the print server. To be practical, every user of every queue serviced by the print server would need to know the password—but a password that everybody knows offers no additional security.

20. Enter a "Full Name" for the print server (optional).

As a final option, you can enter a full name for the print server. You can use this name to identify the print server's location or purpose. Many supervisors don't take the time to enter full names, but we encourage you to enter something. One purely cosmetic reason is that the SECURITY program (which supervisors should run from time to time to check for security holes in their network) displays the full name of the print server. If you leave the full name undefined, a series of garbage characters will appear where the full name should be.

21. If you are setting up more than one print server, repeat the entire process starting from Step 3. If you are finished, press <Esc> repeatedly to exit.

Setting Up a "Wildcard" Printer

Most of the time, you know precisely which printers are going to be shared on the network. They're either connected to the print server itself or attached to nearby workstations running RPRINTER. In some cases, you might have other printers that are never intended to be shared. Often these printers are located in private offices, or are otherwise reserved for one user's exclusive use.

Nevertheless, there might be times when even private printers need to be pressed into shared service. For Allied Accounting, this might be necessary at tax crunch time. Or it could be that the "owner" of the printer is away from the office for a week and someone else wants to have use of that printer. At Southern Confederacy Insurance, it is company policy to use "private" printers when their owners are away.

Here is one recommended way to set up your printing environment to handle "wildcard" printers that are shared only on occasion.

1. Create a separate print server just to handle wildcard printers. Southern Confederacy, for example, decides to use the print server that will be loaded as a VAP on their router. They name this print server "WILDCARD."

2. Configure all of the print server's possible printers as "Remote Other/Unknown." Follow Step 14 above, but choose the "Remote

171

Other/Unknown" option for all sixteen printer slots. Choosing a name such as "Wildcard Printer n" is a good idea, too.

With the "Remote Other/Unknown" option selected, you won't be able to specify interrupts, serial transmission parameters, and so on. You won't define any queues or set up any notifications here either.

3. Set up the print server to service queues on all file servers, as explained under "Servicing Queues on Multiple File Servers," which follows.

When someone needs to use a printer that is normally private, that user asks the supervisor or the print server operator to add the needed queue to that printer (and possibly set up proper notifications). When the user runs RPRINTER at the machine the private printer is cabled to and selects an available wildcard printer, RPRINTER will ask for the connection information (parallel or serial, and interrupt number) that it needs.

A specific example of using a wildcard printer is given in Chapter 10.

Servicing Queues on Multiple File Servers

A print server can service queues on up to eight different file servers, although it is unlikely that anyone will need to use all eight at once. However, it is easier to justify the cost of a standalone print server if it services two or three file servers (and thereby relieves these servers of the print management workload).

As mentioned in the previous section, Southern Confederacy Insurance plans to set up an entire print server to manage sixteen remote printers and service queues that might be on any of the four file servers at the company. They would use the following steps to accomplish this task.

Figure 9-17 summarizes the steps to follow in setting up a print server to services queues on multiple file servers.

1. Log in as SUPERVISOR or equivalent, go into PCONSOLE, and create a new print server on the first file server.
2. Select the new print server, choose "Print Server Configuration," then select "Printer Configuration."
3. Select any unconfigured printer. Specify the appropriate remote parallel or serial port, or choose "Remote Other/Unknown" if you want to define it later with RPRINTER.
4. Press <Esc> and save your changes. Now, unless this is a "wildcard" printer, select at least one queue for the printer to service from the list of queues defined on the first file server.
5. Press <Esc> until you are back at the "Printer Configuration Menu." Choose "File Servers to be Serviced." The first file server will already be on the list. Press <Ins> and add the second one.
6. Press <Esc> until you return to the main menu. Change to the file server you selected in Step 5.
7. Create a new print server on the second file server. Use the same name for the print server as the one you used on the first file server.
8. Select this new print server, then choose "Printer Configuration." Configure the same printer number as you chose for the first file server, but define its type as "Defined Elsewhere."
9. Press <Esc> until you are back at the "Printer Configuration Menu." Now (unless this is a "wildcard" printer), select at least one queue from the second file server's queues.
10. Repeat Step 5, but this time the second file server will be on the list and you'll add the first one.
11. Repeat Steps 6 through 10 for up to the maximum of eight file servers.
12. Exit PCONSOLE and save all changes.

Figure 9-17: Steps for setting up a print server to service queues on multiple file servers.

Most of these steps have been described already in this chapter. The following comments clarify some of the trickier steps.

Step 1. When you select a print server name, make sure the name is not already in use on any of the file servers that this print server will service. This print server name will be entered again in Step6.

Step 5. This is the only time you'll need to use the "File Servers to be Serviced" option. For print servers that service queues on only one file server, this information is filled in automatically.

Step 6. You don't have to leave PCONSOLE to change file servers. Just go back to the main menu and select "Change File Servers." You'll see a list of file servers you are currently attached to. If your target file server is not on this list, press <Ins> and select it from the resulting list of all available file servers. (Unless you are already logged in to a server, you'll be asked to supply a user name and password. Choose SUPERVISOR or an equivalent user.)

Step 8. Choosing the same printer number is essential. When you have finished defining the print server and start it up, you'll run RPRINTER from a workstation. For its start-up parameters, RPRINTER needs a print server name and printer number. That's why you have to choose the same name and number during this setup.

Step 11. You can repeat these steps for as many as eight file servers.

If you run this print server at a file server using the PSERVER NLM (the PSERVER VAP running on a NetWare 286 file server can't handle queues on another file server), you must run it on the file server where you first defined the printers. If you try to run it on a file server where the printers are "Defined Elsewhere," the print server will not load any of those printers.

Similarly, if you run this print server away from the file server (using PSERVER.EXE or the VAP at a router), make sure the file server where the printers are defined is up and running first. If you are running the VAP at a router, give that file server name when asked for the "Host Server." If you are running PSERVER.EXE at a workstation, your current drive should be mapped to that file server.

The other file servers should also be up and running. If they are not, you can add them to the already running print server through PCONSOLE's "Status/Control" and "File Servers Being Serviced" menu options.

CHAPTER 10

PSERVER, RPRINTER, and PSC

In the previous chapter, we discussed how to define a print server through the PCONSOLE program. In this chapter, we'll look at the various ways of running the print server software (PSERVER) and describe the use of the RPRINTER (Remote PRINTER) program. We'll also discuss how to manage your print server with the PSC (Print Server Control) program.

To minimize confusion in this chapter, we'll refer to the program that manages the printing as PSERVER, and to the definition of which printers and queues it manages as the "print server." PSERVER is the NLM, VAP, or EXE software that comes with the NetWare operating system; a print server is what you define or manage by using PCONSOLE. Admittedly, these definitions are somewhat arbitrary. Other literature, including Novell's documentation, uses these terms interchangeably, leaving the reader to determine their meaning from the context.

Conceptual Overview

Before Novell added the PSERVER software to its NetWare products, network printing services were an integral part of the NetWare operating system. All printers, therefore, had to be physically cabled to the file server. Of course, servicing network printers added to the workload of the file server, but this extra burden was seldom a problem for small LANs. As LANs grew, handling all printing at the file server was no longer a viable solution. The physical limit of five printers per file server, each within length of the printer's cable, also became unworkable for larger networks. Users wanted three things; less work for the file server, more printers, and the ability to place printers at remote locations.

At first, Novell did not provide a solution, which allowed many third-party software vendors to step in with their own products. But, with the release of NetWare

386, Novell added its own PSERVER software. Shortly after its release with Net-Ware 386, the PSERVER software was made available to users of NetWare 286 version 2.15 (the NetWare 286 product that was shipping at the time). Now, the PSERVER software is an integral part of both NetWare 286 version 2.2 and Net-Ware 386 version 3.11.

Once defined, a print server may be run at a file server (controlled by the VAP or NLM), at an external router (controlled by the VAP), or at a workstation (controlled by the EXE). The three implementations differ mostly in the control information placed in the file header. The header information allows them to load on top of their respective operating systems. In other words, the NLM contains the program code necessary to load into a NetWare 386 environment; the VAP has the ability to load at a router or on a NetWare 286 file server; and the EXE loads on top of DOS. Despite these differences, you can use any one of these three PSERVER versions to run any previously defined print server.

When you start up the print server, it will immediately begin to manage the printing on any local (physically attached) printers included in its definition. Servicing of remote printers will start when remote workstations run the RPRINTER program and establish a connection.

Users can run the PSC program to manage network printers. PSC allows you to make a shared printer private temporarily, indicate a form change, abort the current print job, and more. Both the RPRINTER program and the PSC program are examined in detail at the end of this chapter.

Starting the Print Server

The method for starting the print server varies slightly with the PSERVER version you intend to use. The following sections describe the method for each one.

Starting PSERVER.EXE

To start PSERVER.EXE, you must be logged in at a workstation and attached to the file server(s) on which the print server is defined. You need not log in as SUPERVISOR; merely logging in as GUEST (in other words, with minimum rights) will do.

In addition, the workstation must have the following line in its SHELL.CFG or NET.CFG file:

```
SPX CONNECTIONS = 60
```

A higher number of SPX connections is allowed; for fully configured print servers, it is recommended. A good rule of thumb for the "SPX Connections" setting is 50 plus 10 for each printer defined.

The command to start the print server is:

```
PSERVER printservername
```

As a security measure, PSERVER.EXE logs out any user who was previously logged in at that workstation when it loads. Therefore, when someone downs that print server (instructions are given later in this chapter), there is no potential security breach.

Starting PSERVER.VAP at a NetWare 286 File Server

To start the PSERVER VAP, copy the PSERVER.VAP file into the SYS:SYSTEM directory. When NetWare starts up, it checks that directory for any files with the .VAP extension. If it finds any, it issues a prompt that says:

```
"Value Added Processes have been found. Do you wish to
load them (Y/N) ?"
```

If you answer "Y," the VAP will be loaded. As the VAP starts, it will ask you for the name of the print server that you defined in PCONSOLE. If you are using version 1.2.2 of the PSERVER VAP (the latest as of this writing), it will save that name and, without prompting, re-use it each time.

If you want to change print server names, type the console command "PSERVER CLEAR." The VAP will then ask you for the name again the next time it starts.

To automate the VAP loading process (so that the file server can be started unattended), place the VAP WAIT command in the SERVER.CFG file. You can create the SERVER.CFG file in the SYSCON program, or with any text editor. The line "VAP WAIT 10," for example, causes the system to start a ten-second countdown timer. During this time, a prompt appears instructing you to press any key to abort loading of the VAPs. If you let the VAP WAIT time elapse, the VAPs will be loaded automatically.

Note: Loading VAPs is an all-or-nothing proposition. There is no way to load only some of them, short of moving the .VAP files into and out of SYS:SYSTEM. However, there is a way to force the sequence of VAP loading. If you modify the extensions of the VAPs to VP0, VP1, and so on, they will load in numerical order starting with VP0. Users of the PSERVER.VAP who use the password option might want to take advantage of this fact and make the PSERVER.VAP load last. That way, any other VAPs that write messages to the console screen as they load will not write over (or into) PSERVER's password request prompt.

Starting PSERVER.VAP at a Router

If you want to run the VAP at a router, first make sure that it is a protected mode router and that you have at least one megabyte of extended memory in the computer. Once you meet these requirements, you can use a single computer for two concurrent network tasks—as a router and as a print server.

To start PSERVER.VAP at the router, include the PSERVER.VAP file in the same directory as ROUTER.EXE. Since neither a router nor a print server needs a hard disk, these files may be on the router's boot diskette.

When loading VAPs at a router, you can't set it up for unattended startup. Even though the latest software will save the name of the print server definition to use, it will always have to ask you for the name of the "Host File Server." The reason is that a router is always located between two or more file servers; the print server definition you choose might be on any of them.

If you are using a print server definition that serves multiple file servers, choose as the host file server the one where the printers were defined by type, not the one where they were "Defined Elsewhere."

Starting PSERVER.NLM

Starting the PSERVER NetWare Loadable Module is the easiest of all. At the console of a NetWare 386 server, type:

```
LOAD PSERVER printservername
```

You can include this command in the server's AUTOEXEC.NCF file so that it will be issued automatically every time the file server is restarted.

Monitoring the Status of the Printers

Both PSERVER.EXE and PSERVER.NLM (but not PSERVER.VAP) have a built-in monitoring screen that looks like the one in Figure 10-1.

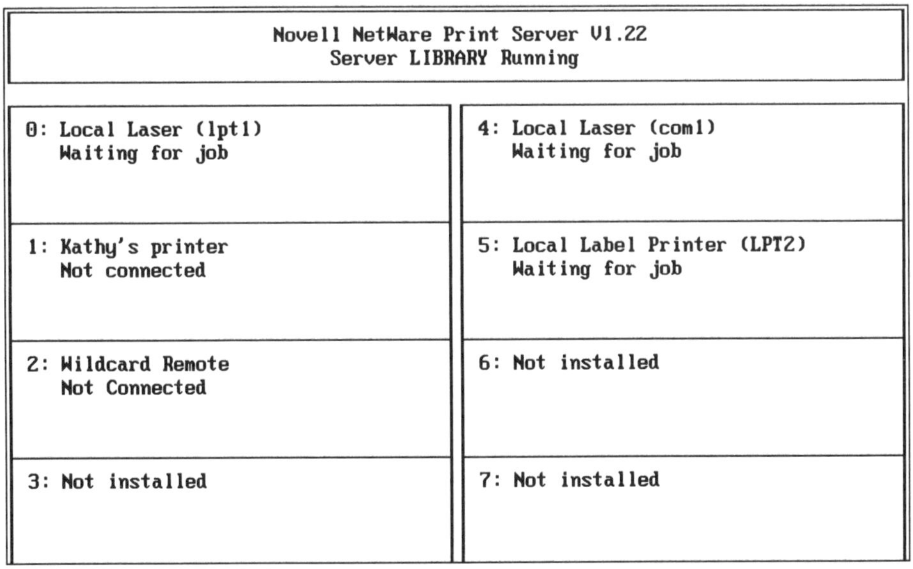

```
                    Novell NetWare Print Server V1.22
                          Server LIBRARY Running

  0: Local Laser (lpt1)          4: Local Laser (com1)
     Waiting for job                Waiting for job


  1: Kathy's printer             5: Local Label Printer (LPT2)
     Not connected                  Waiting for job


  2: Wildcard Remote             6: Not installed
     Not Connected


  3: Not installed               7: Not installed
```

Figure 10-1: The PSERVER monitoring screen (NLM and EXE only).

When creating a print server, you can define up to sixteen printers. There is no particular order for definitions that is better than any other. However, defining the printers numbered 0 to 7 first allows them all to fit on a single screen. In cases where printer numbers 8 to 15 are defined, you can use certain keys to switch to the other screen "page."

The particular key to be used varies, depending on two main factors; the kind of keyboard in use and the means by which the program is being accessed. Figure 10-2 lists some examples.

PROGRAM	KEYBOARD	KEY(S)
PSERVER.EXE	Enhanced	numeric keypad +/-
PSERVER.EXE	Standard	Page Up/Page Down
PSERVER.NLM	Enhanced	Page Up/Page Down
NLM via RCONSOLE	Enhanced	Any Function Key
NLM via RCONSOLE	Standard	Home/End

Figure 10-2: You can use these keys to switch the PSERVER page display.

Once PSERVER is started, each of the sixteen boxes will contain information about the status of a defined printer. Figure 10-3 shows a PSERVER to which several printers have been attached and to which a remote printer has connected. Notice the various status information—"Waiting for job," "Printing," "Out of Paper," and so on—that can be displayed.

```
              Novell NetWare Print Server V1.22
                    Server LIBRARY Running

  0: Local Laser (lpt1)          4: Local Laser (com1)
     Out of Paper                   Waiting for job
     Job # 21, README.DOC
     Queue: ADMIN/COMMON_Q

  1: Kathy's printer             5: Local Label Printer (LPT2)
     Mount Form 2                   Printing
     Job # 39, LPT1 Catch           Job # 39, MAIL.LST
     Queue: ADMIN/CHECKS            Queue: ADMIN/LABELS

  2: Wildcard Remote             6: Not installed
     Not Connected



  3: Not installed               7: Not installed
```

Figure 10-3: The monitoring screen for the PSERVER NLM and EXE displays printer status information.

Monitoring Printer Status in PCONSOLE

While the console display screens described above are useful, they are not absolutely necessary. You can find this same information, and much more, from within the PCONSOLE program.

Figure 10-4 lists the steps for monitoring printer status in PCONSOLE.

---

1. Start PCONSOLE.
2. Choose "Print Server Information."
3. Select the print server that owns the printer.
4. Choose "Print Server Status/Control."
5. After that, select "Printer Status."
6. Select the printer you want to manage and press <Enter>.

Figure 10-4: Steps for monitoring a printer in PCONSOLE.

To illustrate the printer monitoring process, here is an example from the Southern Confederacy Insurance scenario.

Southern Confederacy Insurance has eight print servers managing 100 permanently shared printers and another 20 normally private printers that can be added to the shared pool as needed. To help support the large amount of printing, Sara Abrams of the PC Support staff is permanently assigned to manage the printouts. Whenever anyone wants to modify a print job already in the queue, or even one that is already printing, they call Sara.

Her main tool is PCONSOLE. She uses the methods described on the following pages to handle users' printing control requests.

To get to the status screens, Sara follows these steps.

1. Start PCONSOLE.

From any network drive, she types "PCONSOLE" and presses <Enter>.

2. Choose "Print Server Information" from the main menu.

3. Select the print server that owns the printer.

In Sara's case, she highlights the print server named LIBRARY and presses <Enter>. Figure 10-5 shows the what the PCONSOLE screen looks like at this point:

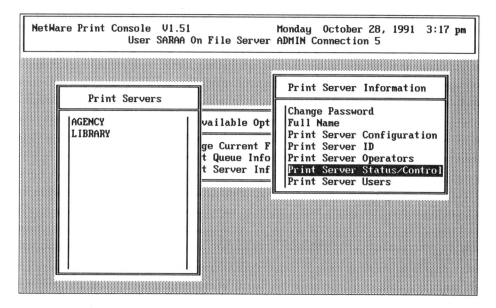

Figure 10-5: You can use the "Print Server Status/Control" option in PCONSOLE to control a printer.

4. Choose "Print Server Status/Control."

5. Select "Printer Status."

The resulting screen lists all the local printers and all the remote printers for which there is an active RPRINTER connection, as shown in Figure 10-6.

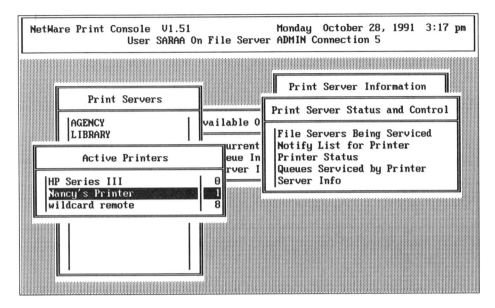

Figure 10-6: The "Printer Status" option leads to a list of currently active printers.

6. Select the printer you want to manage and press <Enter>.

Sara chooses the printer named "Nancy's Printer." PCONSOLE now displays the status screen shown in Figure 10-7.

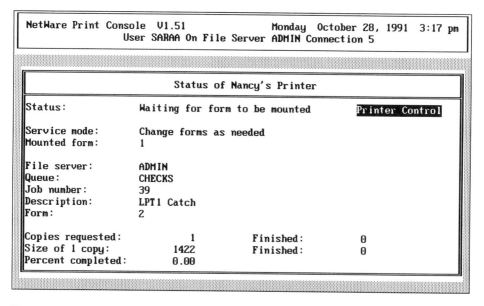

```
┌──────────────────────────────────────────────────────────────────────┐
│ NetWare Print Console  V1.51              Monday  October 28, 1991  3:17 pm │
│            User SARAA On File Server ADMIN Connection 5             │
└──────────────────────────────────────────────────────────────────────┘

        ┌─────────────────────────────────────────────────────┐
        │              Status of Nancy's Printer              │
        │ Status:        Waiting for form to be mounted  ▐Printer Control▌ │
        │                                                     │
        │ Service mode:  Change forms as needed               │
        │ Mounted form:  1                                    │
        │                                                     │
        │ File server:   ADMIN                                │
        │ Queue:         CHECKS                               │
        │ Job number:    39                                   │
        │ Description:   LPT1 Catch                           │
        │ Form:          2                                    │
        │                                                     │
        │ Copies requested:        1      Finished:      0    │
        │ Size of 1 copy:       1422      Finished:      0    │
        │ Percent completed:    0.00                          │
        └─────────────────────────────────────────────────────┘
```

Figure 10-7: From this "Status" screen, you can both monitor and control the selected printer.

The following sections describe each of the fields on this screen.

Status:

This is a two-line field. The first line shows the current (or last known) status of the job, while the second line shows the status of the printer. Possible values for the first line are:

```
Printing job
Online
Offline
Paused
Stopped
Waiting for job
Waiting for form to be mounted
```

For the second line, the options are:

```
[blank]
Out of Paper
Not Ready
```

Printer Control:

Pressing <Enter> on this field brings up the printer control pop-up list shown in Figure 10-8.

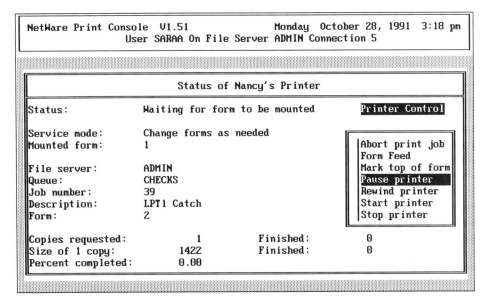

```
NetWare Print Console  V1.51              Monday  October 28, 1991  3:18 pm
                  User SARAA On File Server ADMIN Connection 5
```

```
                        Status of Nancy's Printer

Status:                Waiting for form to be mounted      Printer Control

Service mode:          Change forms as needed
Mounted form:          1                                 Abort print job
                                                         Form Feed
File server:           ADMIN                             Mark top of form
Queue:                 CHECKS                            Pause printer
Job number:            39                                Rewind printer
Description:           LPT1 Catch                        Start printer
Form:                  2                                 Stop printer

Copies requested:           1        Finished:         0
Size of 1 copy:          1422        Finished:         0
Percent completed:       0.00
```

Figure 10-8: Selecting "Printer Control" brings you to a list of printer control options.

Here is a description of each of these printer control options:

- Abort print job This option stops the current print job. (You can also use the PSC command to abort a print job, as described later in this chapter.)

187

- Form Feed This options sends a single form feed command to the printer. Form Feed is one of two commands that can be sent even when the printer is stopped.

- Mark top of form Use this option to generate a line of asterisks at the current print position. This mark is designed to assist you in aligning printing on preprinted forms. Like Form Feed, this command works even when the printer is stopped.

- Pause printer This option halts the printer until a "Start Printer" command is issued. The print job will resume where it left off.

- Rewind printer This command can be used to "back up" within the current print job. Use "Pause printer" first, then choose "Rewind printer." You will see a screen similar to the one shown in Figure 10-9. You can choose to back up a certain number of bytes in the copy currently being printed, or you can back up to any point in a previous copy as well.

- Start printer Use this option to resume sending data to the printer.

- Stop printer This command is like "Pause printer," except that when you start the printer again, the job resumes from the beginning.

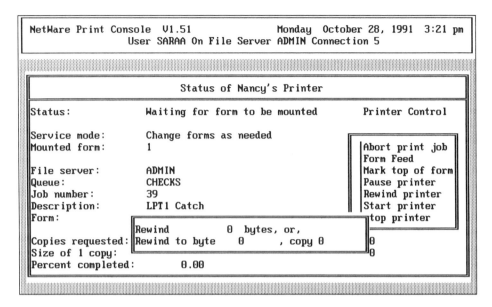

```
NetWare Print Console  V1.51              Monday  October 28, 1991  3:21 pm
                   User SARAA On File Server ADMIN Connection 5
```

```
                         Status of Nancy's Printer

Status:               Waiting for form to be mounted      Printer Control

Service mode:         Change forms as needed
Mounted form:         1                                   Abort print job
                                                          Form Feed
File server:          ADMIN                               Mark top of form
Queue:                CHECKS                              Pause printer
Job number:           39                                  Rewind printer
Description:          LPT1 Catch                           Start printer
Form:                                                      top printer
                      Rewind          0  bytes, or,
Copies requested:     Rewind to byte    0      , copy 0
Size of 1 copy:
Percent completed:         0.00
```

Figure 10-9: With the "Rewind printer" option, you can back up to any point in the current copy or in a previous copy.

Service mode:

These queue service modes are the same modes that were available for defining the printer. Figure 10-10 shows the list of queue service modes.

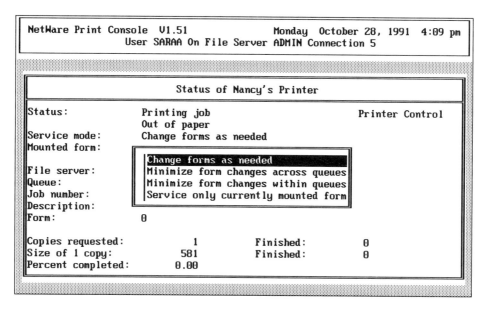

Figure 10-10: The "Service mode" option allows you to modify the rules for form changes.

Here is a brief description of each service mode.

- Change forms as needed This is the default mode. It means that jobs will be serviced without regard to form number. If a job that requires a form change arrives in the queue, printing will stop until the new form is mounted.

- Minimize form changes across queues This option causes the print server to examine all the queues assigned to a particular printer, searching for other jobs using the currently mounted form. It will select those jobs before selecting a job that requires a form change. Note that this might cause a job in a low-priority queue to print before a job in a high-priority queue.

- Minimize form changes within queues This option is much like the preceding one, except that entries in the highest priority queue will always get serviced first. However, to minimize form changes within that queue, jobs might be taken out of normal service sequence.

- Service only currently mounted form As was previously mentioned, some printers are dedicated to a particular form, such as labels or checks. This option prevents a misdirected print job from wasting the special form, as it will not call for a form change.

Mounted form:

This field displays the number of the currently mounted form. To see the defined forms and their numbers (or to create or modify them), use the PRINTDEF program as described in Chapter 7.

File server:

This field displays the file server from which the job is currently being printed.

Queue:

This field indicates which queue on that file server contains the job being printed.

Job number:

As entries are placed into the queue, they are assigned a unique job number. This field displays that job number.

Description:

For jobs submitted to the queue via NPRINT, this field shows the file name. For jobs that came in via CAPTURE, it will show "LPTn Catch." Either of these defaults can be overridden by a console operator using PCONSOLE, in which case the description entered by the operator is displayed.

Form:

This field indicates the form number that this job requires. This field must agree with "Mounted form" (above) before the job will print.

Copies Requested:

This field shows the number of copies called for in the CAPTURE or NPRINT command, or as modified via PCONSOLE.

Finished:

This field increments as each requested copy is completed.

Size of 1 copy:

This field displays the number of bytes of data that make up a single copy. (As a rule-of-thumb reference, a single-spaced printed page with standard margins and no graphics will take approximately 2,000 bytes.)

Finished:

This "Finished" field indicates the number of bytes sent to the printer, on a per-copy basis. In other words, for print files where the number of copies is greater than 1, this field will cycle from 0 to the size of one copy, then back to zero again, repeating this process until all of the copies are printed.

Percent Completed:

To save you some arithmetic, this field displays the results of the following calculation: the second "Finished" field divided by the "Size of one copy" field. For multiple-copy print jobs, the percentage displayed is not always accurate.

Making Temporary Changes to the Print Server

No matter how carefully you plan your print server definitions, there may be times when you need to change things temporarily. This section describes the means and methods for accomplishing this task.

We'll use an example from the Allied Accounting scenario. As a quick review of their printing setup, they have several printers defined for the "WEST_WING" print server. These include two remote laser printers in the Tax Department, three remote printers in the Pension Department, and two printers attached locally to the print server. (The other printers are managed by the "EAST_WING" print server.)

It's tax season at Allied Accounting, and the Tax Department is busy creating long, complicated returns. Their two laser printers are operating at full speed, yet the average wait time before a newly-submitted print job actually gets printed is almost an hour. Meanwhile, the three printers in the Pension Department are mostly idle.

The system administrator, Jennifer Pedraza, wants to reassign two of the Pension Department's printers to handle the Tax Department's overflow, but she doesn't want to make the changes permanent.

Figure 10-11 summarizes the basic steps for temporarily changing queue assignments.

---

1. Start PCONSOLE.
2. Choose "Print Server Information."
3. Choose the print server to modify.
4. Choose "Print Server Status/Control."
5. Choose "Queues Serviced by Printer."
6. Choose the printer to which you want to add a queue.
7. Press <Ins> to see a list of queues not already assigned to this printer.
8. Choose the queue you want to add.
9. Press <Enter> to accept the default priority of 1.
10. Choose the other queue. (If there are multiple other queues, you can mark them all with the <F5> key, then press <Enter>.)
11. Give the other queues a lower priority by assigning a higher number (2 or above).

Figure 10-11: Steps for temporarily reassigning print queues.

Here is how Jennifer uses these steps to reassign the Pension Department printers to the Tax Department.

1. Start PCONSOLE.

These steps assume that PSERVER is already running.

2. Choose "Print Server Information."

PCONSOLE displays a list of the defined print servers.

3. Choose the print server you want to modify.

This list contains all the print servers defined on the system, whether they are active or not. You can only modify or maintain an active print server. Figure 10-12 shows what the PCONSOLE screen looks like at this point.

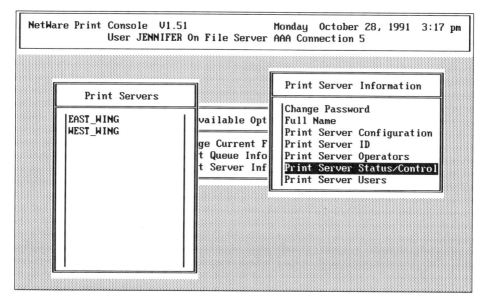

Figure 10-12: The "Print Server Status/Control" option also allows you to temporarily reassign queues to a printer.

4. Choose "Print Server Status/Control."

This option won't even be listed for print servers that aren't currently running.

5. Choose "Queues Serviced by Printer."

PCONSOLE displays the screen shown in Figure 10-13.

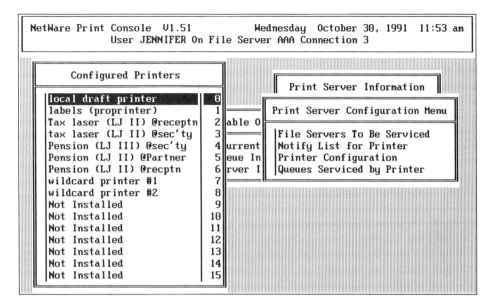

```
NetWare Print Console  V1.51          Wednesday  October 30, 1991  11:53 am
                 User JENNIFER On File Server AAA Connection 3
```

```
      Configured Printers              ┌──────────────────────────┐
  ┌─────────────────────────────┐      │   Print Server Information │
  │ local draft printer      0  │      ├──────────────────────────┤
  │ labels (proprinter)      1  │      │ Print Server Configuration Menu │
  │ Tax laser (LJ II) @receptn 2│able 0├──────────────────────────┤
  │ tax laser (LJ II) @sec'ty 3 │      │ File Servers To Be Serviced │
  │ Pension (LJ III) @sec'ty  4 │urrent│ Notify List for Printer    │
  │ Pension (LJ II) @Partner  5 │eue In│ Printer Configuration      │
  │ Pension (LJ II) @recptn   6 │rver I│ Queues Serviced by Printer │
  │ wildcard printer #1      7  │      └──────────────────────────┘
  │ wildcard printer #2      8  │
  │ Not Installed            9  │
  │ Not Installed           10  │
  │ Not Installed           11  │
  │ Not Installed           12  │
  │ Not Installed           13  │
  │ Not Installed           14  │
  │ Not Installed           15  │
  └─────────────────────────────┘
```

Figure 10-13: By choosing the "Queues Serviced by Printer" option, you prepare to make temporary queue assignments.

This screen shows the printers defined for the "WEST_WING" print server. Using the procedure described in Chapter 4, Jennifer defined the printers and assigned a queue to each of them. Notice that the mnemonic name for each printer indicates the kind of printer and its use or location.

To meet the temporary needs of the Tax Department, Jennifer will use two of the printers in the Pension Department. She will accomplish this by adding the queue named "Tax_Reports" to the list of queues serviced by two of the Pension printers. We'll illustrate the process of choosing the secretary's printer, and leave the assignment to the receptionist's printer as an exercise for the reader.

6. Choose the printer to which you want to add a queue.

Jennifer highlights Printer 4, named "Pension (LJ III) @sec'ty." Notice again how the mnemonic name allows you to easily identify the printer definition that you want. Press <Enter> to see the screen shown in Figure 10-14. This screen lists the queue(s) already assigned to the printer.

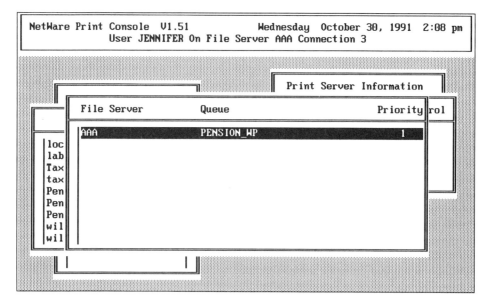

NetWare Print Console V1.51   Wednesday October 30, 1991 2:08 pm
                    User JENNIFER On File Server AAA Connection 3

Print Server Information

File Server   Queue   Priority rol

AAA   PENSION_WP   1

loc
lab
Tax
tax
Pen
Pen
Pen
wil
wil

Figure 10-14: When you select a printer, PCONSOLE displays the queues already being serviced by that printer.

7. Press <Ins> to see a list of queues not already assigned to that printer.

Figure 10-15 shows the list of queues for Allied Accounting's server AAA.

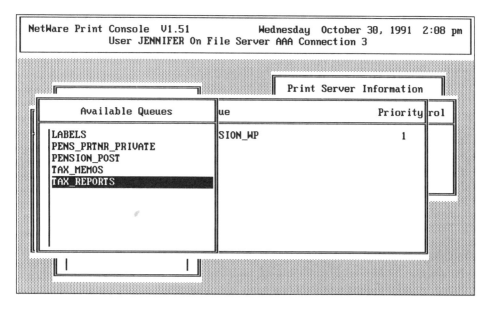

Figure 10-15: You can temporarily add a queue to the list of queues being serviced.

8. Choose the queue you want to add.

For our example, Jennifer highlights the "TAX_REPORTS" queue and presses <Enter>. If circumstances dictate, you can mark several queues (using the <F5> key) and press <Enter> to assign them all at once.

9. Press <Enter> to accept the default priority of 1.

When you press <Enter>, a small box like this one pops up:

```
Priority: 1
```

To accept the default priority, just press <Enter> again. You can change the priority to any number from 1 to 10. Lower numbers indicate higher priorities (1 is the highest priority).

10. Choose the other queue.

You should decide what to do about the other queue and its priority. Depending on your needs (and what you negotiate with the printer's owner), you might give the old queue a lower priority than yours, give it a higher priority, or delete it from the list.

If you choose to delete the old queue, make sure it is still being serviced elsewhere. To do that, go back and choose "Current Queue Status" from the "Print Queue Information" menu. The "Attached Servers" field should have a value greater than zero. To delete the queue, press the <Del> key and confirm your choice by answering "Yes" to the prompt.

11. Give the other queue(s) a lower priority by assigning a higher number (2 or above).

To change the priority of the old queue, highlight that queue and press <Enter>. You'll see the same "Priority" pop-up box. Just change the number and press <Enter> again.

There is one last, optional step. When you (or another network supervisor) defined the printers and queues, you might have placed some entries in the "Notify" list. This is the list of people who will be notified if the printer needs attention. Since this list is defined by printer, it's likely that the notify list includes the person who owns the printer, or a group of people who work near it.

As a courtesy, you should add the names (or group name) of the people who are now going to be printing on that printer. Start this process by choosing "Notify List for Printer" from the Status/Control menu. The remainder of the steps are the same as those for initially defining the notify list (see Chapter 9 for exact instructions).

The procedure for activating the Pension Department's remote printers is given under "Running RPRINTER as a Menu Utility" later in this chapter.

Stopping the Print Server

In the vast majority of cases, you'll start the print server and leave it running until you are ready to shut down the file server. At that time, you can bring the file server down by typing the following command at the file server console:

```
DOWN
```

The file server will respond by telling you that files are open and asking if you want to halt anyway. If you answer "Yes" to this prompt, any print servers that were up and running will be abandoned. If they were printing any jobs, those jobs will remain in the print queues. When you start the print server again, these jobs will start printing all over again from the beginning.

While this method of halting a print server works, it is not the preferred procedure. Besides, there will be other times when you want to stop the print server and reload a new copy. For example, after you have defined a new printer, you have to reload the PSERVER software to make it active.

There are three recommended methods for stopping a PSERVER. One is a universal method that works for all three types of PSERVERs. The second method works only for the VAP, while the third works only for the NLM. Figure 10-16 summarizes all three methods.

The Universal Method
1. Start PCONSOLE.
2. Select the file server.
3. Choose "Print Server Information."
4. Choose your print server by name.
5. Choose "Print Server Operators" and make sure your user ID is on that list. Then press <Esc>.
6. Choose "Print Server Status/Control."
7. Choose "Current Server Status."
8. Select "Down" or "Going down after current jobs."

The VAP Method
1. Go to the file server or router where the VAP is running.
2. At the colon prompt, type "PSERVER STOP."

The NLM Method
1. Go to the file server, or access the file server remotely via RCONSOLE.
2. At the colon prompt, type "UNLOAD PSERVER."

Figure 10-16: These are the steps for stopping the three versions of PSERVER.

The Universal Method

As an example of using the universal method for stopping PSERVERs, consider the following situation.

As the system administrator for Southern Confederacy Insurance, Sara has eight print servers running: one each on a NetWare 386 file server, a NetWare 2.2 file server, and a router, plus five standalone PSERVERS on dedicated workstations. Physically walking to the PSERVER location is both unnecessary and time consuming. She wants to be able to stop the print server from her own workstation. (Since anyone, not necessarily the network supervisor, can start a PSERVER, she can arrange to have someone located near the PSERVER on hand to restart it later.)

In situations like this, you almost always use the universal method to stop a PSERVER. The instructions that Sara would follow are detailed below.

1. Start PCONSOLE.

2. Select the file server.

From within PCONSOLE, you can use the "Change File Server" option to select the one on which the print server has been defined. In our example, case, Sara changes to the LEGAL file server.

3. Choose "Print Server Information."

4. Choose "Print Server Operators" and make sure your user ID is on that list. Then press <Esc>.

You must check the "Print Server Operators" list to make sure you are an operator and therefore have the rights to stop the print server. This is the only place in NetWare where being supervisor-equivalent is not exactly the same as being SUPERVISOR.

Sara has to make sure that her user name is on the list of print server operators. Since she is a supervisor-equivalent user on all the file servers, she can add her name to the list of operators if necessary. This will be a permanent assignment, so this step can be skipped in the future.

5. Choose your print server by name.

Sara chooses the print server LEGAL, which is running as a VAP on the LEGAL file server. When she defined the print server, Sara selected the name LEGAL because she knew it would always run as a VAP on the file server of the same name. (The other print servers in that area are LAW_LIBRARY, RESEARCH, and AD_HOC. This last one has been defined with all sixteen printers as "wildcard" printers.)

6. Choose "Print Server Status/Control."

7. Choose "Server Info."

PCONSOLE displays the screen shown in Figure 10-17.

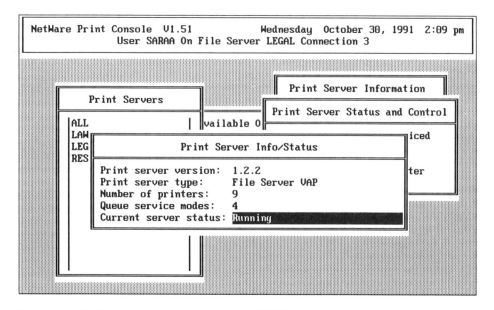

Figure 10-17: You can view the current PSERVER status in PCONSOLE.

Pressing <Enter> here brings up the following pop-up:

```
Print ser | Down
Print ser | Going down after current jobs
Number of | Running
Queue ser |_____
Current server status: Running
```

Figure 10-18: PCONSOLE gives you two options for downing a print server.

8. Select "Down" or "Going down after current jobs."

To bring the print server down, select either of the top two options. As their names imply, the top option downs the print server immediately, while the other allows current jobs to finish. If you choose "Down," the current job will restart from the beginning when you start the print server again.

The VAP Method

This method of stopping the PSERVER VAP is more likely to be used in small networks where the file server or router is more readily accessible. For example, in Hirsch and Cabot's small office the VAP runs on a NetWare 286 version 2.2 file server. It is easier for them to go to the file server and type "PSERVER STOP" when they want to bring down PSERVER.

To reload the same print server again, simply type "PSERVER START" at the file server console. To load a different print server, type "PSERVER CLEAR" at the console, then down the file server or router. When you bring it up again, you can enter the new print server name at the prompt.

The NLM Method

Jennifer, the printing administrator at Southern Confederacy Insurance, might use this method to bring down the PSERVER NLM running on their NetWare 386 file server. They have enabled the remote console feature through the RCONSOLE program. Therefore, the easiest way to stop PSERVER is to access the console

(either directly or remotely through RCONSOLE) and type "UNLOAD PSERVER."
To restart PSERVER, the command is:

```
LOAD PSERVER printservername
```

This command works for either the same print server or a different one, depending on the name you specify in the LOAD command.

Using the RPRINTER Program

The NetWare program that tells the print server where a remote printer is located is called RPRINTER. The RPRINTER program can be run as a menu utility or from the command line. In this section, we'll look at RPRINTER as a menu utility first. Then we'll explore the use of RPRINTER at the command line, especially as it applies to batch files.

Running RPRINTER as a Menu Utility

As an example of using the RPRINTER menus, we'll go through the procedure that Allied Accounting would use to reassign a remote printer in the Pension Department for use by the Tax Department during their rush period.

The first step is to start the RPRINTER program. After completing the installation process for either NetWare 286 version 2.2 or for any version of NetWare 386, the RPRINTER.EXE file will be located in the SYS:PUBLIC directory. Therefore, after logging in, any user can type "RPRINTER" to start the menu program. Figure 10-19 is a sample of RPRINTER's opening menu.

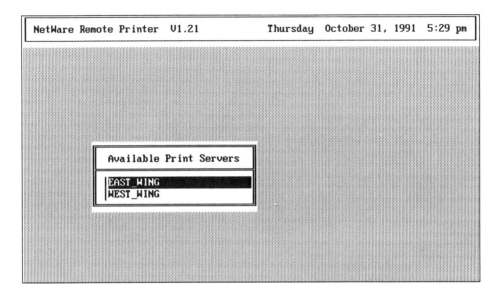

Figure 10-19: RPRINTER's initial screen lists the available print servers.

This list includes all print servers that are up and running and that have remote printer definitions not currently in use. In other words, if a print server is defined with ten remote printers, and all ten have been assigned to other users, that print server will not appear in the list.

Once you select the print server, RPRINTER lists all the remote printer names and numbers defined for that print server.

In our example, the Pension Department secretary would start the RPRINTER program and select the "WEST_WING" print server. Figure 10-20 is an example of the screen that the secretary would now see:

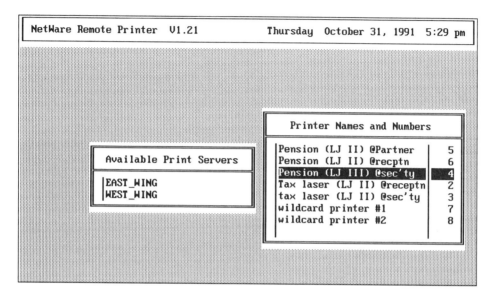

Figure 10-20: RPRINTER lists all the remote printers defined for the selected print server.

The user then simply highlights the printer he or she wants to activate and presses <Enter>. For our example, that would be printer number 4: "Pension (LJIII) @sec'ty" (the LaserJet III printer at the secretary's desk).

The RPRINTER program returns to DOS and displays a message similar to the following:

```
*** Remote Printer "Pension (LJ III) @sec'ty" (printer 4)
installed ***
```

Figure 10-21: RPRINTER displays this acknowledgement message when a remote printer has been successfully activated.

Since the supervisor at Allied Accounting has already reassigned the print queues on a temporary basis, the tax reports will now begin to print at the secretary's printer.

Running RPRINTER at the Command Line

One important aspect of the system administrator's job is to shield the users from as many network complexities as possible. The more we can make happen "behind the scenes" from our users' point of view, the more we can minimize user errors, omissions, and frustrations.

For remote printers, NetWare helps us accomplish that goal by allowing the RPRINTER program to run as a single command. The official syntax is:

```
RPRINTER printservername printernumber
```

So, for example, the command to activate the same remote printer as in the menu example above would be:

```
RPRINTER WEST_WING 4
```

In addition, you can unload the remote printer (as long as it was the last memory-resident program loaded) by using the command:

```
RPRINTER printservername printernumber  -R
```

And, finally, there is this form:

```
RPRINTER -S
```

which generates a status screen like the one in Figure 10-22:

```
Print server:    WEST_WING
Printer:         4
Printer name:    Pension (LJ III) @sec'ty
Printer type:    LPT1
Using IRQ:       7
Status:          Waiting for job
```

Figure 10-22: The RPRINTER -S *command* **displays status information about the remote printer.**

Running RPRINTER in a Batch File

When you run RPRINTER, you are making a connection between your workstation and the print server. In many ways, this is like the connection you make to the file server when you log in. The print server is started, then the RPRINTER connection is made, and printing continues from there. To automate this procedure, you can place the appropriate RPRINTER command in the workstation's AUTOEXEC.BAT file.

However, a user might reboot the workstation after having already connected with the print server. If RPRINTER is in the AUTOEXEC.BAT file, it will once again contact the print server and ask for a connection with its particular printer number. But since the print server was never made aware that the connection had been broken, it rejects the new request as invalid.

The first step in avoiding this problem is to put the RPRINTER command in the AUTOEXEC.BAT file twice: the first time with the -R (remove) option, and the second time in its basic form so it can make the attachment. In this way, when the workstation is started up for the first time that day, the print server *will* reject the remove request, but accept the attach. For subsequent reboots, the remove option will clear the connection so that the attach will work.

Unfortunately, that's not the end of the problem. The remove request is a low priority request for PSERVER; it is designed to take higher priority requests first. Therefore, it is possible that the RPRINTER -R command will be ignored, causing the subsequent attach to fail.

The final solution is to place the following lines in the AUTOEXEC.BAT file:

```
:LOOP
RPRINTER print-server-name printer-number  -R
RPRINTER print-server-name printer-number
IF ERRORLEVEL 1 GO TO :FAIL
GO TO :OK
:FAIL ECHO Rprinter failed to attach.....
ECHO Press CONTROL-C to stop trying, or ....
PAUSE
GO TO :LOOP
:OK
```

If the RPRINTER attach fails, the batch file informs the user and gives him or her the option to stop trying or to press any key to try again. (The PAUSE statement generates the line "Press any key to continue.")

Using the PSC Command

We have already discussed the methods for managing a printer by using the PCONSOLE program. To supplement that process, NetWare provides a simple command line program called PSC that has many of the same functions. The syntax for the PSC command is:

```
Usage: PSC PS[=]printserver P[=]printernumber FlagList
```

The user who works at the computer to which the remote printer is attached will likely use the PSC command the most. Occasionally, that user will need to make the printer private (take it away from the print server temporarily) and then make it public again later, or terminate a printout already sent to the queue, or perform any of the other functions with relation to his or her "own" printer. The various PSC "FlagList" options allow users to perform these functions.

PSC FlagList Options

In place of FlagList, you can include any of the following options (the minimum abbreviations are shown in caps):

```
CancelDown
FormFeed
PRIvate
SHared
STARt
ABort
STOp [Keep]
MArk [character]
MOunt Form=n
STATus
```

Most of these options perform the same function as the similarly-named commands in PCONSOLE's printer management screen. Here is a quick summary of each option.

CancelDown

Use this option to cancel a previously issued "Down after current jobs" selection in the print server management function. (See page ### for a description of that selection.)

FormFeed

Use this option to send a page eject command to the printer. This will work even if the printer is stopped.

PRIvate

When you declare a remote printer PRIVATE, you temporarily take use of the printer away from the print server. Only the user at the local workstation can use the printer.

SHared

This option gives the a printer previously declared as PRIVATE back to the print server for everyone to use.

STARt

This option restarts a previously stopped printer.

ABort

This option immediately cancels the current print job and deletes it from the queue. Printing will stop as soon as the printer's buffer empties.

STOp [Keep]

The STOP option alone also aborts the current print job. With the KEEP option, the print job remains in the queue. When the printer is restarted, the job will print again from the beginning.

MArk [character]

The MARK option alone causes a line of asterisks to print. This function helps you align printing on preprinted forms. If you want a character other than asterisks, you can specify it after the word MARK. This command works even on a stopped printer.

MOunt Form=n

When a print job requires a form other than the one currently mounted in the printer, printing stops until you tell the print server the requested form is mounted. To mount a particular form, change the paper, align it if necessary, and then issue the PSC command with the MOUNT FORM=n option. Be sure to specify the correct form number for n.

STATus

This option displays the current status of the printer: Waiting for Job, Printing Job, Offline, and so on.

Setting the DOS Environment Variable for PSC

To simplify the use of the PSC command, NetWare allows the user to place the print server name and the printer number into the DOS environment with a SET command. Once this is done, it is no longer necessary to include the print server name and printer number in the PSC command.

The syntax for the SET command is:

```
SET PSC=PSprintservername Pnumber
```

For example, to indicate remote printer number 4 for the WEST_WING print server, the command is:

```
SET PSC=PSwest_wing P4
```

With the print server name and printer number set in the DOS environment, the user can get the status of the printer by typing "PSC STAT." To get the status of a different printer, you would have to use the full form, as in "PSC PS=east_wing P=6 STAT."

You do need to be a print server user *to see the status*. If you're not, you'll be told that the print server isn't running. It is our recommendation that the group EVERYONE be kept as the print server user to avoid this problem. Access to queues, and therefore printers, can be controlled by managing print queue users.

> **Tip:** Whenever Hirsch and Cabot set up a new client, they always include the following line in the user login script for those users who have a shared printer attached to their workstation:
>
> ```
> DOS SET PSC="PSprintservername Pnumber"
> ```
>
> Of course, they substitute the proper print server name and printer number. That way, the users don't have to modify their AUTOEXEC.BAT or other batch files.

CHAPTER 11

Console Commands for Core Printing

In all versions of NetWare 286 (but not in any version of NetWare 386), it is possible to have built-in printer management as part of the operating system itself. This is known as "core printing." As we have explained previously, separate print servers are a relatively new concept to NetWare software. Prior to their introduction, all network printing was done on printers physically attached to the file server. Even with the latest NetWare 286 release (version 2.2), the installer has the option of either including core print services or relying on the print server VAP.

This chapter discusses the commands used to configure and control the core printing environment: the console commands PRINTER, QUEUE, and SPOOL. Since the majority of these commands and their parameters are the same in versions 2.1x and 2.2, these descriptions apply to all NetWare 286 versions. Commands new to the NetWare 2.2 environment are indicated by the † symbol.

Conceptual Overview

The console commands can be used to create or delete a queue, to assign a queue to a printer (and give it a priority), to redirect output destined for one printer and send it to a queue, and more.

To get a job from the user's workstation to a printer, the system administrator must perform several tasks. He or she has to create the queue, make sure the printer is defined, and assign the queue to the printer. Once this printing environment is established, the administrator has additional duties, such as deleting or resequencing print jobs, reassigning queues to other printers, and otherwise managing the print process.

In NetWare 2.1x, some of these setup duties were performed automatically at installation, resulting in a rudimentary default printing environment. But to go beyond that default setup, the system administrator had to get involved. (For a review of the default printing environment and the techniques for modifying it, see Section II.)

While some print administration tasks can be administered through the PCON-SOLE program, others cannot; in a few cases, there is some overlap. In this chapter, we'll look at each printing console command in turn and describe its use in the printing environment.

As mentioned, the three commands involved in the core printing environment are PRINTER, QUEUE, and SPOOL. They will be described in that order.

Command Abbreviations

Each command can be abbreviated to its first letter (P for PRINTER, Q for QUEUE, and S for SPOOL). All of the commands have subparameters which you can also abbreviate (and occasionally omit altogether).

However, the allowed abbreviations are different in various versions of NetWare 286. Since these console commands are often placed in the AUTOEXEC.SYS file for execution every time the file server is restarted, it is a good idea to spell them out in full. This serves both as documentation and as protection against changes in allowable abbreviations as the software is upgraded.

When you enter the commands at the console, however, abbreviations are often more convenient. The best advice is to abbreviate the key word to its first letter (for example, use P rather than PRINTER) and spell out the remainder of the command. The following discussion shows some of the allowable short forms.

Also, in the remainder of this chapter, we'll use the variables n and x. N always refers to the printer number; x represents any other value.

The PRINTER Command

Figure 11-1 lists all the variations of the PRINTER console command.

```
PRINTER
PRINTER n ADD QUEUE name AT PRIORITY x
PRINTER n CONFIG
PRINTER n CONFIG BAUD=x
           WORDSIZE=x STOPBITS=x
           PARITY=x XONXOFF=x POLL=x
PRINTER n CREATE DEVICE
PRINTER n DELETE QUEUE name
PRINTER n FORM FEED
PRINTER n FORM MARK
PRINTER n MOUNT FORM x
PRINTER n POLL x
PRINTER n QUEUE
PRINTER n REMOVE
PRINTER n REWIND x PAGES
PRINTER n START
PRINTER n STOP
           PRINTER ?  (or PRINTER HELP)
```

*Figure 11-1: The **PRINTER** console command is used to control a network printer.*

Following are some usage notes for each of the PRINTER command variations.

PRINTER

This command displays the current status of all configured network printers. The possible status indicators are:

```
"Running" or "Halted"
plus
"On-line" or "Off-line"
plus
"Form n mounted" or "Form n NEEDED"
plus
```

215

"Servicing *n* queues"

Here's an example of the response to this command:

```
:PRINTER
ADMIN is configured for 2 printers:
Printer 0: Running On-line Form 0 mounted Servicing 0 Queues
Printer 1: Running Off-line Form 0 mounted Servicing 1 Queues
```

Figure 11-2: The PRINTER command displays the status of each printer.

PRINTER *n* ADD QUEUE *name* AT PRIORITY *x*

Use this command to add a queue to a printer. The queue must already exist. If you omit the "AT PRIORITY *x*" phrase, the queue will be added at the default priority of 1 (the highest priority). If used, the priority must be a value between 1 and 10. You may omit (but not abbreviate) the key words QUEUE and AT.

Short form: P *n* ADD *name* PRI *x*

†PRINTER *n* CONFIG BAUD=*x* WORDSIZE=*x* STOPBITS=*x*
PARITY=*x* XONXOFF=*x* POLL=*x*

If you create a serial printer with the PRINTER CREATE command (described below), you can change its configuration with this command. Omit any parameters you wish to leave unchanged from the default values shown in Figure 11-3. In the figure, uppercase letters indicate allowable abbreviations.

Parameter:	Default:	Valid values:
Baud:	9600	300,600,1200,2400,4800,9600
Word**S**ize:	8	7,8
Stop**B**its:	1	1,2
Parity:	NONE	None, Even, Odd
Xon**X**off:	NO	Yes, No
Poll:	15	1-60

Figure 11-3: Configuration parameters for serial printers.

†PRINTER *n* CONFIG (no parameters)

With no additional parameters, this command displays the current configuration for the printer number you select. In addition to the parameters shown in Figure 11-3, the display also shows the printer number and the port name.

Figure 11-4 is an example of the display for both a parallel printer (printer 0) and a serial printer (printer1).

```
:P 0 CONFIG
Printer  Port  Poll  XonXoff  Baud  StopBits  WordSize  Parity


0        LPT1  15

:P 1 CONFIG
Printer  Port  Poll  XonXoff  Baud  StopBits  WordSize  Parity


1        COM1  15    No       9600  1         0         NONE
```

Figure 11-4: The PRINTER CONFIG command with no parameters displays the current printer configuration.

†PRINTER *n* CREATE *device*

In NetWare version 2.2, the printing environment you set up is not saved when the file server goes down. You must redefine it every time you restart the server. To use a printer attached to a file server, you must first tell the operating system that the print device exists and which port it is attached to. This is the command used for that task.

For example, to define a parallel printer attached to LPT1, the command is:

```
:P 0 CREATE LPT1
```

For a serial printer attached to COM1, the command is:

```
:P 1 CREATE COM1
```

PRINTER *n* DELETE QUEUE *name*

This command is the opposite of the ADD QUEUE statement. It removes a queue from the list of queues that a particular printer services. (Note that the queue itself is not deleted.) If a job is currently printing, this command will abort it and remove it from the queue.

Short form: P *n* DEL *name*

PRINTER *n* FORM FEED

Mainly used for printers with continuous forms mounted, this command causes a form feed (page eject) to be sent to the printer. You can send a form feed command even if the printer has been stopped with the PRINTER STOP command (explained below). However, if the printer is off-line, this command will generate an error message.

Short form: P *n* FF

PRINTER *n* FORM MARK

When changing paper, it is often necessary to check the form alignment before beginning the next printout. This command causes a single row of asterisks to be printed at the current line.

218

After adjusting the alignment, you can use the preceding command (P *n* FORM FEED) to skip to the top of the next page in preparation for printing.

PRINTER *n* MOUNT FORM *x*

Use this command to tell the core printing service that you have mounted the required form on the specified printer. The following three short forms are all valid:

```
P  n  MOUNT FORM  x
P  n  MOUNT  x
P  n  FORM  x
```

†PRINTER *n* POLL *x*

By default, NetWare polls a queue to see if there is a print job ready. This polling occurs at the completion of either of two events: immediately after a prior job completes, and after the poll time elapses. Poll time is the maximum amount of time the print management software will wait before checking to see if there is any data in the queue ready for printing. The default poll time is 15 seconds.

When using core printing with NetWare 2.2, you can change the poll time to any value ranging from 2 to 60 seconds. A shorter poll time increases network traffic, so you should decrease it only when there is a specific benefit to be gained. For example, a point-of-sale printer might justify a short poll time, so as to avoid keeping customers waiting while their receipts are printed.

> **Note:** The POLL option is only available with NetWare 2.2 core printing; there is no corresponding print server parameter. (You can include poll time as a parameter in the "P *n* CONFIG" command described above).

PRINTER *n* QUEUE

This command is an inquiry function. It tells you the current status for the printer (the same information as just "P" alone), and it reports on the queues that printer *n* is servicing, along with their priorities. (Queues are listed in descending priority order.) Here is an example of the response to this command.

```
:PRINTER 0 QUEUE
Printer 0:   Running On-line   Form 0 Mounted   Servicing 1 Queues


Servicing QNAME   at priority 1
```

Figure 11-5: The PRINTER QUEUE command displays both printer and queue status.

†PRINTER *n* REMOVE

This command is the opposite of the PRINTER CREATE function. Before you can remove a print device, you must first delete all of its queues, then check the status with the "P n" command. The status must be "Running, On-Line, Form n mounted, servicing 0 queues" before you can remove the printer. It often takes several seconds for the command to take effect.

PRINTER *n* REWIND *x* PAGES

When problems occur during a print job (the paper jams, the ribbon breaks, and so on), it is often desirable to back up a few pages before you resume printing. This command causes NetWare to scan backwards through the print job, looking for form feed characters. After passing x such form feeds, NetWare starts printing the job again. If no form feeds are found (or the number found is less than x), printing will restart at the beginning of the job. The maximum value for x is 10.

Here are some special cases:

Command:	Action:
P *n* REWIND	Rewind to the top of the current page
P *n* REWIND 0	Rewind to the beginning of the job
P *n* REWIND *n*	Rewind *n* pages

PRINTER *n* START

Use this command to restart a printer that you previously commanded to stop. In NetWare 2.2, a printer is automatically started when it is created; in prior versions, all defined printers are started when the file server is brought up.

PRINTER *n* STOP

You might want to stop a printer to perform maintenance tasks such as changing paper or rewinding the job some number of pages. A stopped printer will not accept data from the queues. However, some other PRINTER commands will work (for example, marking, mounting a form, or sending a form feed).

PRINTER ? or PRINTER HELP

This command displays the information shown in Figure 11-1 for those using NetWare version 2.2 with core printing enabled.

The QUEUE Command

Figure 11-6 lists all the variations for the QUEUE console command.

```
QUEUE
QUEUE name CHANGE JOB n TO PRIORITY x
QUEUE name CREATE
QUEUE name DELETE JOB n/*
QUEUE name DESTROY
QUEUE name JOBS
QUEUE ? (or QUEUE HELP)
```

Figure 11-6: The QUEUE console command is used to control print queues.

Following are some usage notes for these QUEUE command variations.

QUEUE

Without any parameters, the QUEUE command displays all the queues defined on the file server, along with a count of jobs in each queue and the number of printers currently servicing the queue. Only printers managed by core printing will be listed; QUEUE does not report on printers servicing the queue through a print server.

The sample display in Figure 11-7 is from the PAYROLL server at Southern Confederacy Insurance. Although this is a version 2.15 server, the results would be the same if it were upgraded to version 2.20.

```
:QUEUE


PAYROLL Print Queues

CHECKS     0 queue jobs   serviced by 0 printers.
REPORTS    2 queue jobs   serviced by 1 printers.
MEMOS      2 queue jobs   serviced by 1 printers.
```

Figure 11-7: The QUEUE command displays information about each queue serviced by the network printers.

QUEUE *name* CHANGE JOB *n* TO PRIORITY *x*

This command can be used to change the sequence in which jobs will print. To get the job number, use the "QUEUE *name* JOBS" command described below. (You can also change a job's sequence in the PCONSOLE program. See Chapter 9.)

Short form: Q *name* CHANGE *n* TO *x*

QUEUE *name* CREATE

While this command creates a new print queue, that queue cannot be serviced by a print server. It can only be serviced by the core printing service. The best advice is to create and delete (destroy) all queues through the PCONSOLE program.

QUEUE *name* DELETE JOB *n* | *

This is the command to "kill" a job in the queue. Using this command, you can delete a single job or all jobs in the queue. If you choose the job actively printing, there is no warning; printing will stop as soon as the printer's buffer empties. To kill a specific job, use its job number. To kill all jobs, use an asterisk in place of the *n*.

Short form: Q name DEL *n*

QUEUE *name* DESTROY

This command is the opposite of the QUEUE CREATE command. Like CREATE, the DESTROY command should be avoided if you have any print servers that service the queue.

QUEUE *name* JOBS

Use this command to see a list of jobs in a particular queue, along with their job numbers and priorities. The resulting display includes the following fields: Priority, User, File, Job, and Copies. When using the CHANGE or DELETE variations, you will need the job number (not the priority number) of the job you wish to manage. This command provides that information. Figure 11-8 shows an example of the output.

```
:QUEUE memos JOBS
Jobs currently in Print Queue MEMOS:


Priority          User          File        Job      Copies


1                 GUEST                      12        1
2                 SJONES        BUDGET.OUT   13        4
```

Figure 11-8: The QUEUE JOBS command displays the print jobs in the specified queue.

QUEUE ? or HELP

In NetWare version 2.2, this command displays the list of QUEUE commands shown in Figure 11-2.

The SPOOL Command

The SPOOL command is provided for backwards compatibility with previous versions of NetWare. It is the only print-related console command that is available in all versions of NetWare (including NetWare 386).

In earlier releases of NetWare, it was possible to capture to a printer number. In other words, "Printer=*n*" was an option for the CAPTURE and NPRINT commands. Users who chose this option were specifying that their output be printed on a specific printer, bypassing the queue altogether. The implication was that they were willing to wait for the printer to become available, rather than allow the system administrator to redirect the print job elsewhere using the PRINTER and QUEUE commands described above.

Figure 11-9 shows the data flow under this printing scheme:

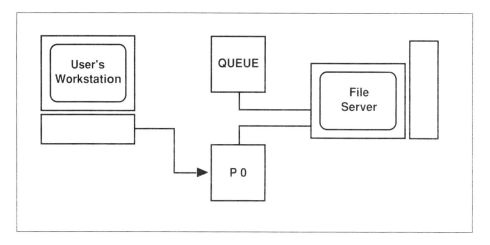

Figure 11-9: In old versions of NetWare, users could send print jobs to a printer by specifying its number.

This capability of sending print jobs directly to a printer no longer exists in NetWare. Now users must name a queue in their NPRINT and CAPTURE commands.

Nevertheless, there are still many copies of the old CAPTURE and NPRINT programs in use, as well as other programs that use the old NetWare function call libraries that included subroutines or functions for directing printouts to printers. To maintain compatibility with these types of programs, you can use the SPOOL command.

The SPOOL command tells NetWare to intercept output directed to a specific printer and redirect it instead to a particular queue.

The full format of the SPOOL command is:

```
SPOOL n TO QUEUE name
```

Its short form is: S *n* TO *name*

You can issue only one SPOOL command per printer number, and the printer numbers may range from 0 to 4.

Figure 11-10 shows the new print data path after the SPOOL command has been entered. The dotted line shows the intended path, while the solid line shows the redirected path.

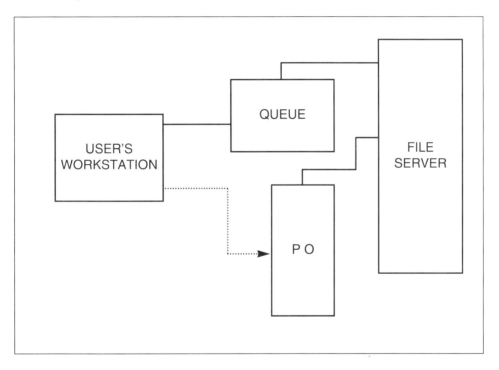

Figure 11-10: The SPOOL command redirects print jobs destined to a printer number to a specific queue.

Once the print data has been redirected to a named queue, the system administrator can complete the process by assigning printer 0 (or any other printer) to service that queue.

225

Section IV:

Third-Party Printing Products

NetWare has always provided the ability to share printers, but prior to the release of NetWare 386, those printers had to be physically attached to the file server. While this was not a problem for very small offices, it was unacceptable for large networks with workstations in more than one room. The absence of remote printing capabilities in NetWare created a market niche that several third-party companies attempted to fill. Over the years, numerous products have been introduced to provide the ability to print on printers attached to workstations distributed around the network.

With the first release of NetWare 386 in 1990, Novell began including its own print server (PSERVER) software to manage remote printing. Many people thought the advent of Novell's PSERVER would eliminate the market for third-party print server packages, but they were wrong. For one thing, the NetWare print server is an evolving product. Like any new software, it has some limitations and bottlenecks which will take time to be fully addressed. Furthermore, it's impossible to develop a single network print program that is best for everyone, because everyone defines "best" differently. For some people, it means the program that prints fastest; for others, it might mean the one that generates the least amount of LAN traffic, or the one that places the lowest demand on the file server's resources.

In addition, users will always want to be able to perform tasks within their print environment that NetWare programs do not address. Some of these tasks, such as accounting for print resources used or handling a shared PostScript and ASCII printer, are handled nicely by available third-party programs. As a result, the market for third-party network printing products is still alive and growing steadily.

This section examines printing-related software from several third-party companies. The products examined fall into three general classes: (1) programs that run at users' workstations and add to user functionality—these generally enhance the features of NetWare's CAPTURE, NPRINT, and PRINTCON programs; (2) programs that replace or supplement the PSERVER or RPRINTER programs; and (3) devices that allow printers to be attached directly to the LAN cabling system, without the need for an intervening PC.

This section is composed of four chapters. The first three correspond to the three classes of products described above:

- Chapter 12 looks at four programs designed to enhance network users' control of their printed output: LANPrint, LANQview, Q-Assist, and IQ.

- Chapter 13 examines three programs designed to take the place of (and improve upon) Novell's PSERVER and RPRINTER combination: LANSpool, Printer Assist, and Mosaic.

- Chapter 14 discusses various third-party hardware products for attaching printers directly to the LAN cable.

- Chapter 15 treats one of the most complex LAN printing problems: how to share PostScript printers, especially those that can be switched in to and out of PostScript mode.

The products examined in this section are a representative subset of the available products in each category. We'll briefly look at each program's installation method and features so you can get a feel for the general approach taken by each particular vendor. However, the intent is not to do a comparative review, but rather to give you an idea of the options that are available to enhance your printing environment. Of course, in this rapidly changing marketplace, it is likely that newer versions of these products will be released after this book is written. If you decide to acquire any of these products, be sure to carefully read and follow the installation instructions that come with the package.

All of the products described in this section work with NetWare 286, versions 2.1x and 2.20, and with all versions of NetWare 386. However, some of the products have separate versions for the NetWare 286 and 386 product lines.

CHAPTER 12

Programs to Help Users Manage Printing

Printing in a shared environment is a difficult concept for some users to understand. The idea that they can issue a print command without having a printer attached to their computer, or that someone else can print on "their" printer, seems like science fiction to them. Rather than being helpful, the slew of NetWare printing programs (PRINTCON, PCONSOLE, CAPTURE, NPRINT, and so on) are intimidating and often baffling.

System administrators might try to help by creating menus with easily understood options such as "Print on the laser printer" or "Print on wide computer paper." But users must remember to select the appropriate option before entering their application programs. Many times, users forget to make (or change) a selection before plunging into their work in the application. Only when they are ready to print do they discover that they must exit the application and redefine the printing environment.

When the jobs finally make it to the queue, changes sometimes need to be made. For example, you might want to increase the number of copies, put the job on hold, or move it to a different queue.

This chapter describes several third-party packages that can help in situations like these. Three of the programs—LANPrint, Queue Assist, and I-Queue—are designed to help users change the network printing environment without having to exit their applications. These easy-to-use programs "pop up" over any application when the user presses a certain key combination that allows the user to change virtually any CAPTURE parameter. Two other programs—LANQView and Qmanager (as well as Queue Assist and I-Queue)—provide system administrators the ability to manipulate jobs in the queues.

LANSpool Utilities: LANPrint, LANQView, and LANSel

LANPrint, LANQView, and LANSel are part of a suite of programs distributed with the LANSpool software package (LANSpool itself is discussed in detail in the next chapter). These are products of Intel's LAN Systems Group, 3311 North University Ave., Provo, Utah 84604. Suggested list price for LANSpool is $395.00.

LANPrint accesses the current CAPTURE settings, along with the user's PRINT-CON.DAT file, and allows the user to load a PRINTCON definition or modify the existing CAPTURE environment.

LANQView gives supervisors and print queue managers the ability to view any three queues simultaneously, and to move print jobs from any one to either of the others.

LANSel is a very small pop-up menu program available from Intel. It works by swapping the currently running program out to expanded memory (if available) or to disk, then executing any program listed in its menu options. Upon exiting that program, LANSel restores the previous program. The version of LANSel that is included with LANPrint and LANQView is permanently configured to provide this functionality for only these two programs. This runtime copy will not allow other programs to be added to the list of menu items.

Windows versions of LANSel (WLANSel) and LANPrint (LANPrntW) are also included with the LANSpool software.

Installing the LANSpool Software

The LANSpool installation program creates a subdirectory under SYS:LOGIN called SYS:LOGIN\LANSPOOL and copies all of the programs from the distribution disk there. As explained in the next chapter, this directory location allows any station to become an RPRINTER replacement without requiring the station's user to be logged in.

To continue the installation and load the LANSpool utilities, you need to set up a common directory and run the LQA (LAN Queue Administrator) program. Here is a quick overview of these steps.

1. Set up a common directory for the LANSpool utilities.

Having the utility programs in the SYS:LOGIN\LANSPOOL subdirectory is not much good for users because they typically don't have rights to SYS:LOGIN or its subdirectories once they have logged in. To set up a common subdirectory under SYS:PUBLIC for these utilities, follow these steps:

1a. Log in as SUPERVISOR or equivalent.

1b. Type "MAP N:=SYS:PUBLIC" (choose a different drive letter if N is in use).

1c. Type "MD N:LANSPOOL.USR."

1d. Type:

```
NCOPY SYS:LOGIN\LANSPOOL\*.* SYS:PUBLIC\LANSPOOL.USR
```

1e. In the SYSCON utility, modify the system login script (under "Supervisor Options") to include this line at a place where it will be executed by every user:

```
MAP INS S16:=SYS:PUBLIC\LANSPOOL.USR
```

2. Run the LQA (LAN Queue Administrator) program.

Once you have copied the files to the common directory and included the drive mapping in the system login script, you will be ready to give other users permission to run the LANQView program. The LQA program's main screen is shown in Figure 12-1:

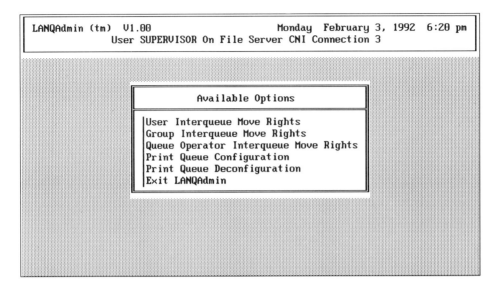

```
LANQAdmin (tm)   V1.00                      Monday  February 3, 1992  6:20 pm
                   User SUPERVISOR On File Server CNI Connection 3
```

```
                      ┌──────────────────────────────────────┐
                      │            Available Options           │
                      ├──────────────────────────────────────┤
                      │User Interqueue Move Rights             │
                      │Group Interqueue Move Rights            │
                      │Queue Operator Interqueue Move Rights   │
                      │Print Queue Configuration               │
                      │Print Queue Deconfiguration             │
                      │Exit LANQAdmin                          │
                      └──────────────────────────────────────┘
```

Figure 12-1: The LAN Queue Administrator's main screen displays the program's options.

Select "Print Queue Configuration" first. The program will run for several seconds and respond with the message box confirming that job movement between queues has been enabled.

At this point, only the supervisor can move jobs between queues. To give other users/groups the same ability, select "User Interqueue Move Rights" or "Group Interqueue Move Rights."

3. Exit LQA and run the LPCONFIG utility to specify which options you want the users to be able to change.

With LPCONFIG, you can set up the parameters that users will see on the LAN-Print "simple" changes screen (accessed by pressing <F3> from the LANPrint's initial menu). An example of this simple changes screen is shown in Figure 12-4, which follows.

4. You might want to modify each user's AUTOEXEC.BAT file to automatically load LANSel. For Windows users, add WLANSel and LANPrntW to the desktop.

Running LANSel

To give your print queue operators easy access to the LANSpool add-on programs, have them run the LANSel program. LANSel loads as a terminate-and-stay-resident (TSR) program. Pressing its "hot keys" (by default, CTRL-ALT-L) will bring up the screen shown in Figure 12-2.

```
┌─────────────────────────────────────┐
│              LANSelect               │
├─────────────────────────────────────┤
│ LANPrint          LANPRINT EXE       │
│ LANQView          LQV       EXE      │
│ LANSpool RStatus  RSTATUS   EXE      │
│ PConsole          PCONSOLE  EXE      │
└─────────────────────────────────────┘
```

Figure 12-2: When you press LANSel's hot keys, this pop-up screen appears.

This screen can pop up over any program, but be patient. It takes two or three seconds to load while it swaps the current program to extended memory or disk. The user can then select any of the four programs shown.

The bottom program is the NetWare PCONSOLE program, discussed in detail in Section III. Just above it is RSTATUS, a program for checking the status of a remote printer. It is described in the next chapter, along with its parent program, LANSpool.

Running LANPrint

LANPrint is a program that any user can run to check (or change) the current CAPTURE settings and display the target queues for all captured ports. It also looks at the user's PRINTCON.DAT file and gives the user several options for initiating any of his or her PRINTCON job definitions, or even creating a new, temporary definition on the fly. Figure 12-3 shows the initial LANPrint screen.

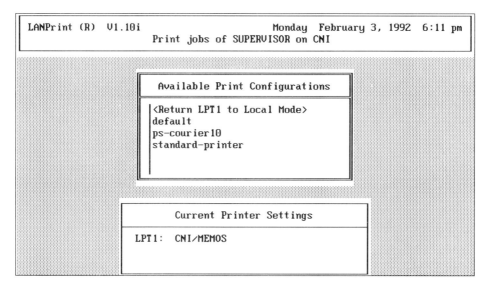

Figure 12-3: LANPrint's initial screen shows the available print job configurations and the current CAPTURE settings.

Highlighting one of the configurations listed and pressing <Enter> "executes" that configuration. Pressing <F3> brings up the small pop-up menu shown ir. Figure 12-4 that allows the user to make minor changes, such as choosing a different queue or form.

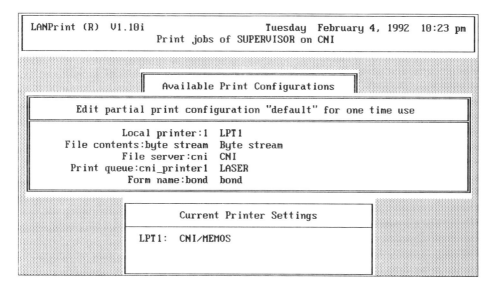

Figure 12-4: LANPrint's "simple" changes screen lets users make one-time changes to the selected configuration.

Pressing <F9> or <Ins> brings up a similar screen, shown in Figure 12-5. With <F9> access, the user can modify the selected configuration; <Ins> lets the user create an entire new, temporary print job configuration. This configuration is not saved in the user's PRINTCON.DAT file.

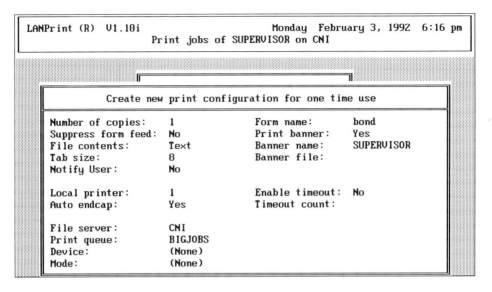

```
LANPrint (R)  V1.10i                  Monday  February 3, 1992  6:16 pm
                        Print jobs of SUPERVISOR on CNI


            ┌─────────────────────────────────────────────────────┐
            │       Create new print configuration for one time use │
            │                                                        │
            │  Number of copies:   1          Form name:      bond   │
            │  Suppress form feed: No         Print banner:   Yes    │
            │  File contents:      Text       Banner name:    SUPERVISOR │
            │  Tab size:           8          Banner file:           │
            │  Notify User:        No                                │
            │                                                        │
            │  Local printer:      1          Enable timeout: No     │
            │  Auto endcap:        Yes        Timeout count:         │
            │                                                        │
            │  File server:        CNI                               │
            │  Print queue:        BIGJOBS                           │
            │  Device:             (None)                            │
            │  Mode:               (None)                            │
            └─────────────────────────────────────────────────────┘
```

Figure 12-5: LANPrint users can also create a new, temporary print job configuration at any time.

Running LANQView

The final program in the LANSpool suite is LQV, an abbreviation for LANQView. LQV displays the contents of up to three print queues (by default, those currently being captured to LPT1, LPT2, and LPT3). A sample LQV screen is shown in Figure 12-6.

```
┌─────────────────────────────────────────────────────────────────────┐
│ LANQView (tm)  V1.10                    Monday  February 3, 1992  6:26 pm │
│                 User SUPERVISOR On File Server CNI Connection 3        │
└─────────────────────────────────────────────────────────────────────┘

╔═════════════════════════════════════════════════════════════════════╗
║ CNI/MEMOS  (LPT1)                            Size Form Status   Job   ║
╠═════════════════════════════════════════════════════════════════════╣
║  │ 7 SUPERVISOR    LPT1 Catch                2052  0 Ready     24    ║
║  │ 8 SUPERVISOR    LPT1 Catch                2052  0 Ready     25    ║
║  │ 9 SUPERVISOR    LPT1 Catch                2052  0 Ready     28    ║
╚═════════════════════════════════════════════════════════════════════╝

╔═════════════════════════════════════════════════════════════════════╗
║ CNI/LASER                                    Size Form Status   Job   ║
╠═════════════════════════════════════════════════════════════════════╣
║  │ 1 SUPERVISOR    LPT1 Catch                2052  0 Active    50    ║
║  │                                                                   ║
╚═════════════════════════════════════════════════════════════════════╝

╔═════════════════════════════════════════════════════════════════════╗
║ CNI/HP3SI                                    Size Form Status   Job   ║
╠═════════════════════════════════════════════════════════════════════╣
║  │ 1 SUPERVISOR    LPT1 Catch               67480  0 Adding    38    ║
║  │                                                                   ║
╚═════════════════════════════════════════════════════════════════════╝
```

Figure 12-6: This sample LQV screen shows three queues being monitored.

LANQView offers several function key-activated options:

F1	Display context-sensitive help
ALT+F1	Turn help line on/off
F3	Move a print job within a queue
ALT+F3	Move print job(s) to another queue
F4	Toggle user hold on a print job
ALT+F4	Toggle operator hold on a print job
F5	Mark the highlighted list element
ALT+F5	Mark all list elements
F7	Clear all marks
F9	Zoom/unzoom a print queue window
F10	Select a print queue
ALT+F10	Exit LANQView

Note that by marking one or more jobs in one queue, a print queue operator can move the jobs to any other queue, assuming permission to do so has already been granted via the LQA program.

239

Using LANSel and LANPrint within Windows

LANSpool also provides versions of LANSel and LANPrint for use with Windows. The Windows version of LANSel is called WLANSel. To use it, you must run LANSel before entering Windows. Then, while in Windows, run the WLANSel program. From that point on, you can access LANSel by pressing all four "control" keys (Left-Shift, Right-Shift, Ctrl, and Alt). Windows will be swapped out and LANSel will take control. When you leave LANSel, Windows will be swapped back in.

The Windows version of LANPrint is called LANPrntW. Starting it from within the Windows environment brings up a graphical version of the LANPrint program. This version also provides some of the interqueue job moving capabilities of LANQView.

Queue Assist

Queue Assist is a single program with several optional modules. At its most basic configuration, it merely allows users to change CAPTURE parameters. An additional module gives users the ability to read PRINTCON definitions (including a global definition, if desired) and initiate one as though a "CAPTURE J=name" command had been issued from the command line. A final option, intended for supervisors and print queue operators, provides queue management functions.

Queue Assist is a product of Fresh Technology Group, located at 1478 North Tech Blvd., Gilbert, Arizona. It is licensed on a per-file-server basis. Any number of users connected to a single file server may share a single copy of this product. Suggested retail price is $179.00. The following overview is based on version 5.4 of Queue Assist, dated 08/28/91.

Installing Queue Assist

Queue Assist is remarkably easy to install. The QAINSTAL program simply copies the distribution files to the directory of your choice. This should be a directory that all users have access to, such as a subdirectory of SYS:PUBLIC.

After that, you must run QACONFIG once to define the hot keys for each of Queue Assist's options. Figure 12-7 shows the main screen, and Figure 12-8 shows one of the options selected. Users can select the hot keys they want for each option, or just accept the defaults.

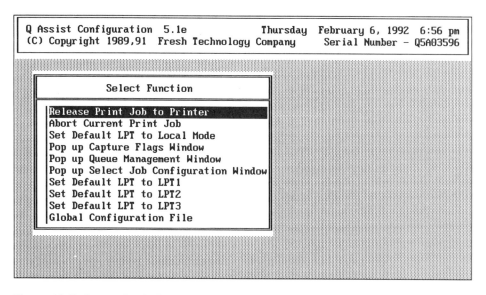

Figure 12-7: Queue Assist's configuration utility lets users specify hot key combinations for each option.

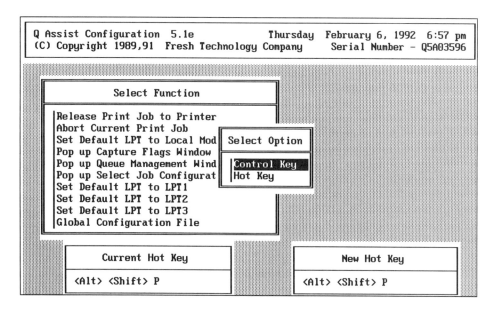

Figure 12-8: This screen shows a sample hot key configuration change.

The "Global Configuration File" option lets you specify a default global PRINT-CON.DAT, as shown in Figure 12-9. Users can substitute a different file on an ad hoc basis via Queue Assist's /P command line option (see Figure 12-10).

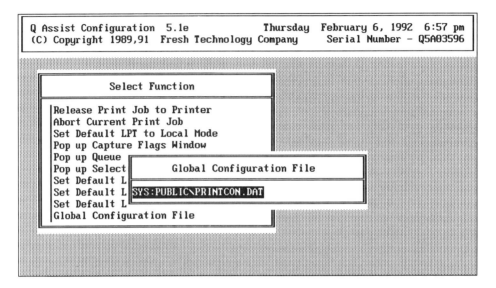

Figure 12-9: With Queue Assist, you can specify a global PRINTCON.DAT file.

Running Queue Assist

To run Queue Assist, you type "QA +" to load the program into memory. You can include additional parameters in the command line to customize the load module. For example, "QA ?" displays the help screen shown in Figure 12-10, which also lists the possible command-line parameters.

```
Z:\PUBLIC>QA ?
Q Assist will allow users to execute printing and queuing functions from
within other applications with the touch of a user configurable hot key.
The use of V, Q, or J flags will exclude the capability to pop-up over
Windows 3.0 and reduce the resident size of Q Assist.
  USAGE :  QA [+] [-] [?] [flags]
      +          Loads Q Assist into memory.
      -          Unloads Q Assist from memory.
      I          Displays copyright information.
      ?          Displays this help screen.
      /V         Loads the capture flags window.
      /Q         Loads the queue management window.
      /J         Loads the job configuration selection window.
      /UPPER     Loads Q Assist into high memory.
      /S         Disables beeps when a hot key is pressed.
      /B         Disables buzzing when printing.
      /N=name    Uses the job configuration file of user 'name'.
      /P=file    Uses 'server/vol:\path\file' as the job configuration file.
      /MONO      For users unable to see the cursor on mono screens.
      /MOUSE=X   Disables COM port X during pop-up.
      /IRQ=X     Disables specified IRQ (2 - 7) during pop-up.
```

Figure 12-10: Queue Assist's help screen lists the command line options.

When QA is first loaded, it lists its current hot key settings. An example is shown in Figure 12-11.

```
Z:\PUBLIC>qa +

 Q Assist loaded

    Manually change flags -loaded              <Alt> <Shift> V
    QUEUE functions -loaded                    <Alt> <Shift> Q
    Select Job Configurations -loaded          <Alt> <Shift> J

    Endcap/capture                             <Alt> <Shift> P
    Endcap - set to local mode                 <Alt> <Shift> S
    Abort - delete the current job             <Alt> <Shift> A
    Set default LPT port to LPT1               <Alt> <Ctrl> 1
    Set default LPT port to LPT2               <Alt> <Ctrl> 2
    Set default LPT port to LPT3               <Alt> <Ctrl> 3

Beeping when a hot key is pressed is enabled.
Buzzing when printing is enabled.

        ----------------------------------------------
                  Q Assist  - Version 5.1
           Copyright 1985,91   Fresh Technology Company
```

Figure 12-11: Upon loading, Queue Assist displays the current hot key settings.

To select from different print job configurations, Queue Assist can read a user's PRINTCON.DAT file, or use the global one set up in QACONFIG. Pressing <Alt>-<Shift>-J brings up a screen similar to the one shown in Figure 12-12.

```
┌──────────────────────────────┬──────────────────────────────────┐
│        Port Status           │          Configuration           │
├──────────────────────────────┼──────────────────────────────────┤
│ LPT1: CNI/MEMOS              │ pcl                      LPT1:   │
│ LPT2: CNI/BIGJOBS            │         (MORE ↑↓)        (*)     │
│ LPT3: Not Capturing         │                                  │
└════════════ Q Assist 5.1  Copyright 1985,91  Fresh Technology Company ═══╛
```

Figure 12-12: Queue Assist allows you to select a PRINTCON configuration.

You can use the cursor keys to cycle through the defined configurations. Pressing <Enter> selects the one currently shown. You can also enable a defined print job configuration for a different port, as though you had used the "L=2" or "L=3" command line parameters.

In Queue Assist, all users have the ability to manually change CAPTURE flags. Pressing the default hot key combination of <Alt>-<Shift>-V pops up a screen similar to the one shown in Figure 12-13.

```
┌────────────────────────────────────────────────────────────────────┐
│  SERVER/QUEUE        CPY FRM BANNER TEXT    TAB SIZE TIME AUTO  FF BUF│
├────────────────────────────────────────────────────────────────────┤
│ CNI/MEMOS            1   0   ON            OFF 8    0    ON    ON ( )  │
│ CNI/BIGJOBS          1   0   OFF           OFF 8    0    ON    ON ( )  │
│ CNI/ (none)          1   0   ON LST:       OFF 8    0    ON    ON (−)  │
└══════════ Q Assist 5.1  Copyright 1985,91  Fresh Technology Company ═══╛
```

Figure 12-13: Queue Assist provides a pop-up menu for changing CAPTURE flags.

You can use the cursor keys to move around from one field to another within this window. The <+> and <-> keys on the numeric keypad increment and decrement numeric values, flip-flop between toggle on/off values, and cycle through lists such as server or queue names. When you press <Esc>, your changes will be implemented.

If the AUTO (Autoendcap) flag is turned OFF, the <Alt>-<Shift>-P key combination will release the current print job to be printed. It will then reinitialize the CAPTURE parameters as if the command had been reentered. (If you were using

CAPTURE command line options, you'd have to either issue an ENDCAP command to close the print job and release it, or issue another CAPTURE command to both close the first print job and prepare for the next one. Queue Assist does this work for you.)

For supervisors and print queue managers, Queue Assist provides another pop-up window that allows jobs to be deleted, held, moved within a queue (sequence change), or moved between queues. An example of this window is shown in Figure 12-14.

```
┌────────────────────────────────────────────────────────────────────────────┐
║  Server = CNI                        Queue = MEMOS                            ║
║                                                                              ║
║ Seq# │ Job# │ User Name  │ Banner Name │Cpy│Fm#│ Status │ Size │ Date    Time ║
║  1   │ 34   │SUPERVISOR  │             │ 1 │ 0 │Ready   │  2K  │02/06/92 18:56 ║
║  2   │ 35   │SUPERVISOR  │             │ 1 │ 0 │Ready   │  2K  │02/06/92 18:57 ║
║  3   │ 36   │SUPERVISOR  │             │ 1 │ 0 │Held    │  2K  │02/06/92 18:57 ║
║  4   │ 37   │SUPERVISOR  │             │ 1 │ 0 │Ready   │  2K  │02/06/92 18:59 ║
║  5   │ 38   │SUPERVISOR  │             │ 1 │ 0 │Ready   │  2K  │02/06/92 19:00 ║
└═════════════ Q Assist 5.1  Copyright 1985,91  Fresh Technology Company ═══════┘
```

Figure 12-14: Queue Assist also provides a print queue management screen.

Again, you can use the cursor keys to move around within this window. Various key-activated commands include:

H	Place a job on hold
F	Increment the form number
C	Increment the number of copies
Shift-H	Release a held job
Shift-F	Decrement the form number
Shift-C	Decrement the number of copies

You can also change a job's sequence by moving the cursor to that job and pressing <S> to make it print sooner or <Shift>-S to make it print later.

Queue Assist and Windows

While Queue Assist is not a Windows application, it does have the ability to pop up over Windows. To enable this option, you must load Queue Assist (without using the /V, /Q, or /J command line options) before entering Windows.

I-Queue

The I-Queue program (also known as IQ) combines all of the functions described in the introduction to this chapter. It gives novice users the ability to make minor changes in their current print environment. It gives advanced users more complete control, including the ability to activate and modify print job configurations. It gives supervisors and print queue operators all the capabilities of Novell's PCONSOLE, PRINTCON, and CAPTURE.

I-Queue is a product of Infinite Technologies, 11403 Cronhill Drive, Suite D, Owings Mills, Maryland. The product is available for a 30-day free trial by downloading it from NetWire. Its purchase price is $199.00 for a file server license. IQ is available to all users logged in to a single file server. It is not a VAP or an NLM, and it takes no file server connections. IQ runs at the user's workstation in less than 2.5KB of RAM.

Installing I-Queue

IQ is easy to install. If you download it from NetWire, it will be in the form of a "ZIP" file called "IQUEUE.ZIP". A ZIP file is a single file comprised of several smaller files that have been compressed. You'll need a program such as PKUNZIP, which is also available on NetWire (download the self-extracting file PKZ110.EXE), to expand the ZIP file into its component parts. Choose or create a directory for the I-QUEUE files, make it your current directory, and unzip the distribution file into it.

You should first run the IQSETUP program. Its main screen is shown in Figure 12-15.

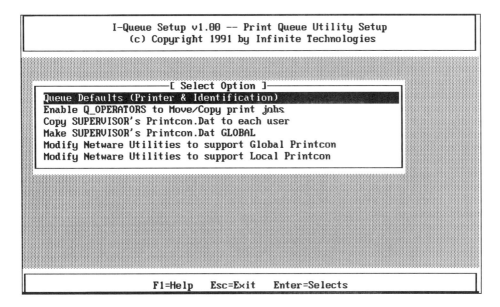

Figure 12-15: IQSETUP's main screen shows the various setup options.

The "Queue Defaults" option lets you assign an identification string (descriptive name) to each of your existing print queues. For each queue, you also define the type of printer that will normally be servicing it. This allows IQ to default to the proper printer definition (.PDF) file. (IQ reads the PRINTDEF database in SYS:PUB-LIC.) Figure 12-16 shows an example printer definition and queue identification.

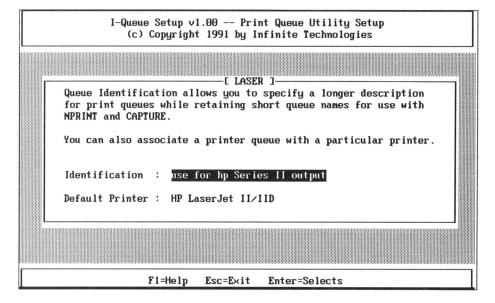

Figure 12-16: For each queue, you establish an identification string and printer type.

As you add additional queues, you should run this program again for the new queues. Figure 12-17 shows what the list of queues might look like after you have assigned them all descriptive names.

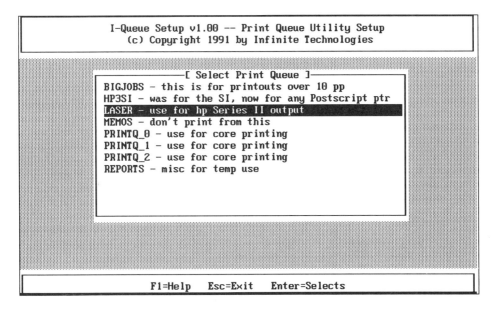

```
     I-Queue Setup v1.00 -- Print Queue Utility Setup
            (c) Copyright 1991 by Infinite Technologies

               ────────[ Select Print Queue ]────────
           BIGJOBS - this is for printouts over 10 pp
           HP3SI - was for the SI, now for any Postscript ptr
           LASER - use for hp Series II output
           MEMOS - don't print from this
           PRINTQ_0 - use for core printing
           PRINTQ_1 - use for core printing
           PRINTQ_2 - use for core printing
           REPORTS - misc for temp use




           F1=Help    Esc=Exit    Enter=Selects
```

Figure 12-17: You can assign descriptive names to each print queue.

The second option on the main screen, "Enable Q_OPERATORS to Move/Copy print jobs," should be chosen if you want any print queue operator or supervisor to be able to move or copy print jobs from queue to queue.

The rest of the options deal with global and local PRINTCON database files. For most users, the most obvious choice is to create a global PRINTCON database. However, there are some cases where individuals users need to use their own local database. One such case, albeit a rare one, is when PRINTCON's limit of 31 entries is too restrictive.

Running I-Queue

You load I-QUEUE by typing IQ at the DOS prompt. The program will use expanded or extended memory if available, and will swap to disk if not. You can tell it which choice to make by using command line switches. In addition, you can change the default hot key for popping up IQ (<Alt>-Q) to any <Alt>, <Ctrl>, <Shift>, or function key combination.

After loading IQ, pressing the hot key brings up the first screen. The exact appearance of the screen will vary depending on whether or not you already have LPT1 captured to a queue. If so, the screen will be a full-size screen showing your current CAPTURE parameters. If not, it will be a half-size screen that gives you the ability to start capturing immediately. Figure 12-18 shows a sample full-size screen.

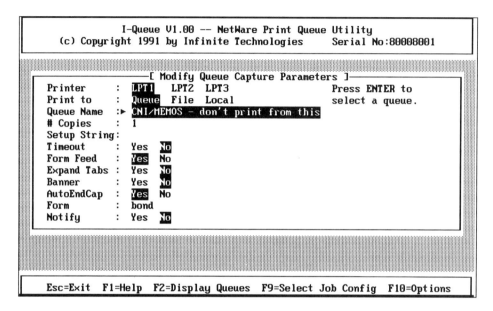

Figure 12-18: IQUEUE's first screen displays the current printing environment.

This screen shows the current CAPTURE settings, with those that are in effect highlighted. Moving the cursor to any option and pressing the right or left arrow key changes the option.

To capture LPT2 or LPT3, you would move the cursor to the top line and over to the desired port. The "Print to" option allows you to capture to a file, or end capturing and use a printer attached to the local parallel port. (If you capture to a file, the "Queue Name" line changes to "File Name" and you can type in the name of the file there.)

To change queues, you press <Enter> when the cursor is in the "Queue Name" field, as shown in the example. This will bring up a list of all defined queues to which you have access. Moving to the "Form" option and pressing <Enter> brings up a list of all defined forms from which you can select using the up and down arrow keys.

250

If you prefer to select a predefined print job configuration, you can press <F10> to pop up a list of all the available ones from which to choose.

The line labelled "Setup String" provides entry into a very sophisticated set of subscreens. While the details are beyond the scope of this book, they basically allow sophisticated users to select printer functions and modes from the PRINTDEF database (printer functions and modes are discussed in detail in Chapter 7).

When you want to manage jobs already in a queue, you can press <F2> to bring up a list of queues you have access to. A sample list is shown in Figure 12-19.

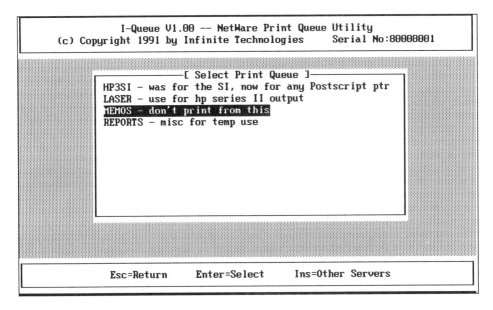

```
                I-Queue V1.00 -- NetWare Print Queue Utility
        (c) Copyright 1991 by Infinite Technologies    Serial No:80008001

                      ┌───────────[ Select Print Queue ]────────────┐
                      │ HP3SI - was for the SI, now for any Postscript ptr │
                      │ LASER - use for hp series II output          │
                      │ MEMOS - don't print from this                │
                      │ REPORTS - misc for temp use                  │
                      │                                              │
                      │                                              │
                      │                                              │
                      │                                              │
                      │                                              │
                      └──────────────────────────────────────────────┘

            Esc=Return     Enter=Select     Ins=Other Servers
```

Figure 12-19: Pressing <F2> from the main screen brings up a list of queues to manage.

You select the queue you wish to manage by highlighting it and pressing <Enter>. Figure 12-20 shows an example of the resulting screen display.

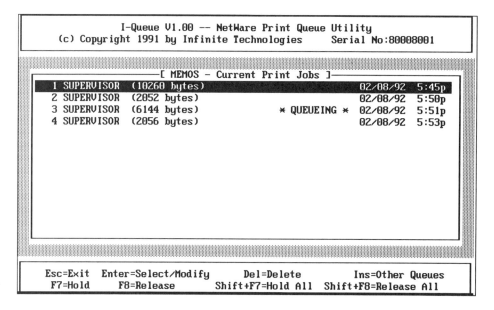

```
        I-Queue V1.00 -- NetWare Print Queue Utility
    (c) Copyright 1991 by Infinite Technologies    Serial No:80008001


                     ─[ MEMOS - Current Print Jobs ]─
   1 SUPERVISOR  (10260 bytes)                        02/08/92  5:45p
   2 SUPERVISOR  (2052 bytes)                         02/08/92  5:50p
   3 SUPERVISOR  (6144 bytes)          * QUEUEING *   02/08/92  5:51p
   4 SUPERVISOR  (2056 bytes)                         02/08/92  5:53p








   Esc=Exit   Enter=Select/Modify     Del=Delete          Ins=Other Queues
   F7=Hold    F8=Release        Shift+F7=Hold All  Shift+F8=Release All
```

Figure 12-20: I-Queue lists the jobs in a queue and lets you manage them in a variety of ways.

As you can see by the options shown at the bottom of the screen shown in Figure 12-19, you can put jobs on hold or release them, delete jobs from the queue, modify a particular job, and so on.

Running I-Queue within Windows

The IQ documentation file suggests loading IQ as a non-resident program (using the /NR command line switch) from any open DOS window whenever you need access to the program.

Another possibility is to load IQ before loading Windows, then open a DOS window exclusively for IQ's use. In this DOS window, you can pop up IQ by using its hot key. Press <Alt><Esc> when you want to return to Windows. This hot key combination leaves a DOS icon on the screen that you can reselect for instant access to IQ.

Special Feature of I-Queue

IQ comes with a program called ONHOLD that provides a function not supplied by any of its competitors. By typing "ONHOLD" before sending output to any queue, a user hold will be placed on the job immediately upon its arrival in the queue. Since you can't stop and hold a currently printing job in PCONSOLE, this feature is handy for those times when you send jobs to empty but active queues, knowing that you'll want the job held for printing at a later time.

While this may not be an option that will be used often, it is highly appreciated when it is needed. This feature alone is worth the purchase price for some users.

CHAPTER 13

PSERVER/RPRINTER
Replacements

In most environments, the NetWare PSERVER and RPRINTER programs work fairly well. The remote printing capabilities they provide are clearly sufficient for the vast majority of networks. However, there are a few areas where these programs fail to supply all of the needed functionality, or where their operating requirements are in conflict with other needs. Here are just two examples. First, remote printer workstations (the PCs on which RPRINTER is run) must have hardware level interrupt support for parallel ports. Without it, they will either print slowly or not at all. Second, NetWare makes no provision for printing a banner page on PostScript printers. In fact, if you don't disable banners on jobs you send to PostScript printers, the jobs won't print!

Fortunately, there are several third-party print packages that provide alternatives to the NetWare programs. In this chapter, we'll look at three of them: Printer Assist from Fresh Technology, LANSpool from Intel, and Mosaic from Insight Development.

The installation procedures summarized in this chapter are meant to give you a feel for each product's ease of use. Naturally, the manuals that come with the products cover installation and configuration in much more detail.

Printer Assist

Printer Assist is a program that can transform any workstation into a nondedicated print server. Printer Assist uses NetWare's built-in queue server facilities, so there is no limit to the number of printers that may be shared on a single network.

Even though no part of the product runs at the server (it is strictly workstation-based), Printer Assist is licensed on a "per file server" basis. In practical terms, this means that if any user runs Printer Assist to manage a single queue on a file server, then a copy of the program is needed for that file server. However, once that copy has been purchased, there is no license-imposed limit to the number of users who may service queues on that file server.

Printer Assist is a product of Fresh Technology Group, located at 1478 North Tech Blvd., Gilbert, Arizona. Suggested retail price is $249.00. The following overview is based on version 4.2c, dated 03/15/91.

Special Features of Printer Assist

Printer Assist does not require parallel ports to support hardware interrupts. It can handle a maximum of 26 queues per printer, and can manage as many as five printers on a single workstation. A typical one-queue, one-printer installation uses approximately 3KB of RAM. The program can be loaded into high DOS or upper memory if it's available.

Printer Assist also has the ability to print a banner page on PostScript printers. However, it is not the normal NetWare banner page. Rather, it is a rectangular box printed at the top of the page, containing the contents of the NAME and BANNER parameters of the CAPTURE or NPRINT commands (printed in Times Roman 24pt bold type).

Printer Assist comes in two versions: one (PA.EXE) is for DOS users, and the other (PAW.EXE) is for Windows users. A separate section of the manual thoroughly describes installation in the Windows environment.

A separate program, PAREPORT, generates printer usage reports. You can set various parameters to configure the report to be by person, by date, by queue, or without restriction. The report shows the number of line feeds and form feeds encountered, and the size of the printed file. It also estimates the number of pages printed. (The estimates are useless for PostScript or graphics files, but for typical text-based printouts they are quite accurate.)

Each time the Printer Assist program (PA.EXE) is loaded, it establishes a new connection at the file server. However, it is not necessary to be logged in to either load or run the program. This use of connections is not usually a problem, except for those sites where the number of logged-in users is nearing the maximum for that particular version of NetWare.

Installing Printer Assist

Loading the Printer Assist software onto the server is a one-step process. You simply log in as SUPERVISOR (or equivalent), insert the distribution diskette into drive A of your computer, and type "A:PAINSTAL." (Drive B may be used if you prefer.) The installation procedure copies all of the Printer Assist programs to a directory of your choice (creating it if you so request) and flags the files appropriately. It also copies the main program (PA.EXE) to SYS:LOGIN, so users can start it without having to log in.

Your next step is to go into PCONSOLE to create a queue server. (The formal definition of "Queue Server" is: "any bindery object that is allowed to attach to a queue". A more practical, unofficial working definition is that "a queue server is any device that directly accesses the queue's directory and services the queue, independent of a print server ".) Figure 13-1 summarizes the steps necessary to create the queue server. (Detailed instructions for creating print servers and print queues in PCONSOLE are given in Chapters 8 and 9.)

---

1. Start the PCONSOLE program.
2. Select "Print Server Information."
3. Press <Ins> to create a new print server entry.
4. Name your new print server.
5. Press <Esc>, then select "Print Queue Information."
6. Create a new print queue, or select an existing one by highlighting the queue name and pressing <Enter>.
7. Select "Queue Servers."
8. Press <Ins>, then choose the name of your new print server (specified in Step 4).
9. Repeat Steps 6-8 for additional queues, or steps 2-8 for additional queue servers.

Figure 13-1: Steps for creating a queue server in PCONSOLE.

After completing this procedure, change to the directory in which you installed the Printer Assist programs and start the PACONFIG program. This program creates a text file that you can use to simplify the loading of Printer Assist at the shared printer's workstation. (It's possible to enter everything on the command line, but that would be too much of a burden for even the most devoted user.) Figure 13-2 shows the initial PACONFIG screen.

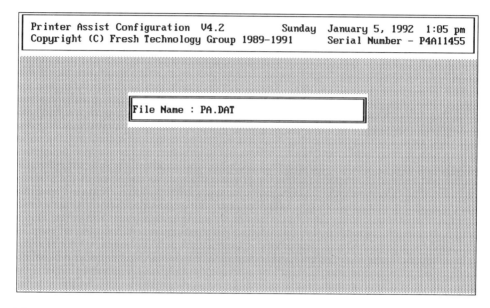

```
Printer Assist Configuration  V4.2        Sunday   January 5, 1992  1:05 pm
Copyright (C) Fresh Technology Group 1989-1991      Serial Number - P4A11455




                    File Name : PA.DAT
```

Figure 13-2: PACONFIG's initial screen asks you for a load file name.

You should change the default load file name (PA.DAT) to something that identifies the user or the printer. After creating the load file, you will move it to SYS:LOGIN so it can be used whether or not anyone logs in at that station. Unique (and mnemonic) load file names will help you distinguish between the files.

After specifying the load file name, the program prompts you for the copy number. If you have more than one shared printer at a particular workstation, you need to load more than one copy of Printer Assist. (The limit is fifteen copies; few users will ever have more than one or two.) This discussion assumes that you are loading only one copy; the Printer Assist documentation explains how to load more than one.

Other parameters are entered on the two configuration screens shown in Figures 13-3 and 13-4. Context-sensitive help is always available by pressing <F1>.

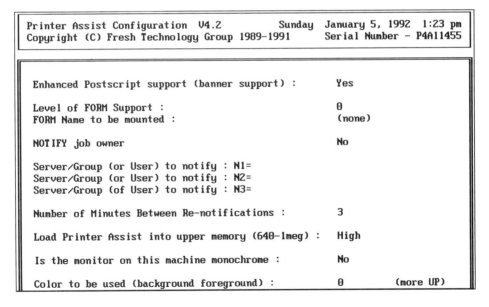

```
Printer Assist Configuration  V4.2        Sunday  January 5, 1992  1:22 pm
Copyright (C) Fresh Technology Group 1989-1991    Serial Number - P4A11455


Copy number of Printer Assist :                   1
Printer Type                                      LPT 1
Nonstandard Port Hex Address (S=xxxx or P=xxxx) :
Baud Rate :                                       (none)
Parity, Data Bits, Stop Bits :                    (none)
MAX characters to attempt to print per second :   990
Number of times to check for busy printer (LOOP): 680


        Server/Queue/PrintServer/Password
Q1=cni/laser_q/pa_server1
Q2=
Q3=
Q4=
Q5=
Total number of queues to reserve space for :     2


        Server/Volume:Path/Filename.ext              (more DN)
L= sys:public/passist/pasrv1.log-GRANT
```

Figure 13-3: This is the first of PACONFIG's configuration screens.

```
Printer Assist Configuration  V4.2        Sunday  January 5, 1992  1:23 pm
Copyright (C) Fresh Technology Group 1989-1991    Serial Number - P4A11455


Enhanced Postscript support (banner support) :    Yes

Level of FORM Support :                           0
FORM Name to be mounted :                         (none)

NOTIFY job owner                                  No

Server/Group (or User) to notify : N1=
Server/Group (or User) to notify : N2=
Server/Group (of User) to notify : N3=

Number of Minutes Between Re-notifications :       3

Load Printer Assist into upper memory (640-1meg) : High

Is the monitor on this machine monochrome :       No

Color to be used (background foreground) :        0        (more UP)
```

Figure 13-4: This is the second of PACONFIG's configuration screens.

It is possible to have as many as 26 queues serviced by each printer, but the configuration program only provides space for five. For the vast majority of users, five is more than enough. Those few users who need more can use any text editor to add the additional queue names. In either case, queue numbers also imply priority. That is, queue 1 will always be checked for new print jobs before queue 2. The only exception would be for form changes. As with the NetWare print server, it is possible to minimize form changes across queues.

Unlike NetWare's RPRINTER program, it is possible to load Printer Assist into high memory (the area between 640K and 1MB) or into upper memory (above 1MB) if you have the proper support on your PC. (Generally, you need to be running a memory manager like QEMM or 386MAX to use this feature.) The benefit for loading Printer Assist into high or upper memory is so it won't take up any of your PC's precious base memory. (Base memory is used for running applications; the more that is available, the better.) However, if you are running Windows, you'll need to load Printer Assist into base memory before you start Windows.

In addition, you can tell Printer Assist how much of your computer's processing power should be devoted to managing the shared printer. The MAX and LOOP parameters shown in Figure 13-3 control this. The values vary depending on the speed of the printer and the speed of the PC. The defaults are okay for a medium-speed computer and a slow printer, but need to be changed for faster PCs (especially ones with laser printers attached). Detailed instructions for optimizing them are given in the Printer Assist user's manual.

Once the configuration is complete, you'll need to copy the configuration file to SYS:LOGIN.

Running Printer Assist

To run Printer Assist at a workstation, modify the AUTOEXEC.BAT file to include a line similar to the one shown as line 4 below. (In this example, CONFIG.DAT represents a sample configuration file; you'd substitute the one you created.)

```
1:    IPX
2:    NETX
3:    F:
4:    PA @CONFIG.DAT
5:    LOGIN
```

From this point on, every time you restart that computer, the printer(s) you defined in the configuration file will be shared by anyone who has authority to place jobs into the queues that your printer(s) service.

Intervention on your part (to rewind a few pages, to mount a new form, or even to abort a print job) can be performed in two ways. One is to type "PA" at the DOS prompt. This brings up the first of four Printer Assist status and control screens. The bottom line of all screens is available for command input. The commands are clear and concise (START, STOP, MOUNT, KILL, and so on). However, you need at least 128KB of free memory to run this program. If you have "shelled out" to DOS from within an application, you probably won't have enough memory available.

The other way to manage the printer is to use the memory-resident program PAPC. This program takes almost 4KB of memory on a permanent basis, but once loaded it can be popped up over any application by pressing <Ctrl>-<Alt>-P.

Running Printer Assist within Windows

Printer Assist comes with a Windows application called PAW.EXE. To run in the Windows environment, type "PA" at the DOS prompt before starting Windows. Then run PAW from the Printer Assist directory.

PAW gives you the ability to modify the configuration files described above, to manipulate your current CAPTURE status, to move data between queues, and the equivalent of the PAPC hot key commands. You will probably want to set up Windows so this program starts up whenever you begin your Windows session, and keep it handy as an icon for instant access.

LANSpool

LANSpool runs as a VAP for NetWare 286 and as an NLM for NetWare 386. It can manage as many as 80 queues and 40 printers from a single VAP/NLM. Queues managed by LANSpool must be on a server running the VAP or NLM (called a "LANSpool" server), but a remote workstation may service queues concurrently on more than one LANSpool server.

There is no limit imposed by LANSpool on the number of shared printers on the LAN. LANSpool works across bridges and routers, but it will only service queues on those servers where a separate copy has been installed. However, in a multi-server environment where all servers have copies of LANSpool installed, the remote printer workstations may service queues on any (or multiple) file servers.

LANSpool is a product of Intel Corporation, 3311 North University Ave., Provo, Utah 84604. It is licensed on a per-server basis. Suggested list price is $395.00. LANSpool is bundled with LANPrint and LANQView (both of which are discussed in Chapter 12.) The version of LANSpool used for this overview is 3.0, dated 10/18/91.

Special Features of LANSpool

LANSpool does not require parallel ports to support hardware interrupts; it will support printing in a polled environment. If polled printing is chosen, the polling delay time may be varied as a means of balancing workstation performance with printer performance.

LANSpool has an excellent accounting interface. Accounting data may be reported by date, by user, by queue, by form type, by size, and by duration. Reports may be sent to the screen, or they can be saved in comma-delimited format for import into a database or spreadsheet program.

Installing LANSpool

The LANSpool installation process consists of several steps, but for the most part it is fully automated and trouble-free. The install program creates a print server named FSNAME_LS30. It also creates five print queues named FSNAME_PRINTER1 through FSNAME_PRINTER5 (substitute your file server name for FSNAME). For each of these queues, it assigns the print server it just created as a queue server. You are free to delete or rename these queue names or add new queues as desired.

After creating the print server and the queues, the install program creates a sub-directory under SYS:LOGIN called LANSPOOL and copies its installation files there. To define a shared printer, you must go to the workstation to which the printer is attached, change to the SYS:LOGIN\LANSPOOL directory, and type the "NODE NEW" command. Figure 13-6 shows the first LANSpool node configuration screen. The default print server password is LAN.

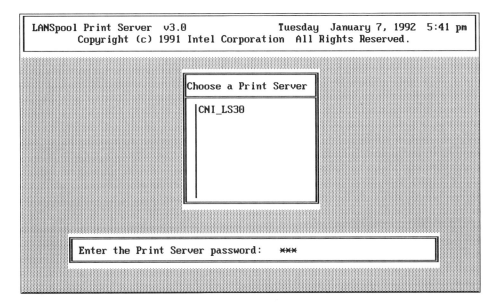

Figure 13-6: In the first LANSpool screen, you select a print server.

Once you choose the print server you want and enter the password, you see the screen shown in Figure 13-7.

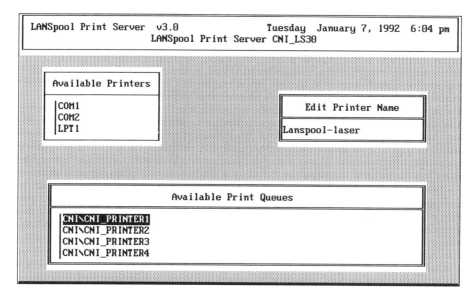

Figure 13-7: In this screen, you choose a LANSpool queue to assign to the node's parallel port.

From this screen, you can select one or more print queues, so long as they have been assigned to the LANSpool Print Server. The configuration files are stored in a subdirectory created by LANSpool: SYS:LOGIN/LANSPOOL/INI. LANSpool keeps track of which configuration file belongs to which workstation.

Running LANSpool

Once this configuration is complete, you can load the LANSpool VAP or NLM at the file server. After that, starting the remote printer requires only a few simple modifications to the AUTOEXEC.BAT file for the shared printer's workstation, as shown below:

```
IPX
NETX
F:
CD LANSPOOL
NODE
CD ..
LOGIN
```

To check on the status of the printer attached to your workstation, LANSpool provides the STATUS command. To check on the status of another printer, LANSpool provides the RSTATUS command.

LANSpool Add-On Programs

LANSpool also comes with a pair of programs called LQA (LAN Queue Administration) and LQV (LAN Queue View). LQA should be run once to set up users or groups with the rights to move print jobs between queues. Once that is done, you can use LQV to manage up to three queues concurrently.

LANSpool in the Windows Environment

LANSpool comes with a Windows application called LANPrntW. With this program, you can manage your LANSpool remote printers. It combines the features of the DOS programs LQV and RSTATUS.

Mosaic

Mosaic Print Manager is a product of Insight Development Corp. It is a replacement for NetWare's PSERVER software, but it uses Novell's RPRINTER program. The product comes with a two-volume set of documentation: one for the System Administrator and one for the Users. The optional Accounting package comes with its own matching volume.

Pricing for the Mosaic print server is $1995.00 for twenty printers, with the Accounting package included. (Priced separately, they cost $1195 and $995, respectively). In addition, Insight Development offers Mosaic for the Macintosh at $595 for 10 users. This product allows Mac users to send data to Hewlett-Packard and compatible laser printers anywhere on a Novell network.

Special Features of the Mosaic Print Server

All of the other PSERVER/RPRINTER replacement programs on the market, including the ones described earlier in this chapter, were developed as ways to incrementally improve on Novell's print server product. For example, they make it faster, smaller, or less overhead-intensive; they add or combine features, but they do virtually the same job in apparently the same way.

The Mosaic Print Manager was developed from a new point of view. It looks at printing on a large network as a corporate resource, and defines a way to manage it as such. Figure 13-8 presents this idea in graphical form.

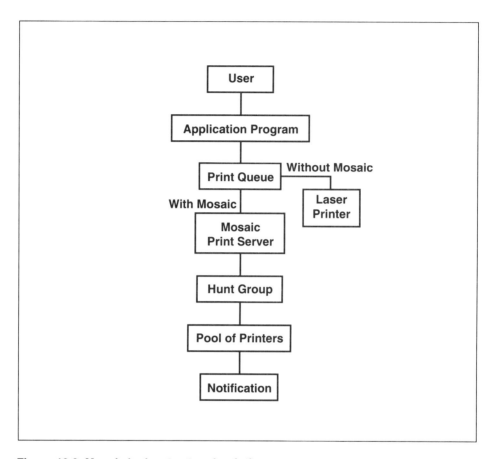

Figure 13-8: Mosaic looks at network printing as a corporate resource.

In this scheme, users send jobs to queues in the usual manner. Without Mosaic, some print server (or possibly a NetWare 286 file server with core printing services) takes the print job and sends it to a specific printer assigned to service that queue. The difference with Mosaic is that the Mosaic print server "owns" all of the printers and all of the queues assigned to it.

Queues are given descriptions that include the kind of printer that the user expects. Mosaic monitors the queues, and when a print job is ready, it looks for an available printer of the type that the queue description calls for—or better! In other words, if the user sends data to a queue that requires an HP LaserJet Series II, Mosaic might print it on a Series II, or on a IID, III, or IIID, because on the three latter printers the output will be the same. However, a job sent to a queue that specifies a Series III printer would not go to a Series II printer because that printer might not be able to handle it. Similarly, a request for a PostScript printer will only go to a printer that is equipped to handle PostScript jobs. Mosaic will generate a Post-Script banner page upon request.

Another great feature of the Mosaic server is that it manages font downloading. All too often, network users send the same fonts over and over to the same printers, resulting in a massive waste of network capacity and long delays in printing time. Mosaic keeps track of which fonts are already in each printer, how much font memory the printer has, and which fonts a given print job needs. It then downloads only the needed fonts, deleting unneeded ones if it needs the room.

Installing Mosaic

This discussion covers only the basic steps for installing a Mosaic print server. It does not go into detail about defining queues and printer pools.

1. Install the print server software on a dedicated workstation with a hard disk.

To install the software, insert the distribution disk labelled "Disk 1" into drive A (or drive B if you prefer) and type "A:INSTALL." Mosaic will ask permission to install on that machine. Then it will list all the non-removable drives it sees (which, if you are logged in, will include network drives) and will ask you to select a drive. After you specify a drive (the default is C:), the program will ask permission to create a \MOSAIC subdirectory. Once it receives that permission, it will load the contents of its distribution disks, creating several subdirectories as it proceeds.

To run, the Mosaic software requires a parameter of "files=120" in the CON-FIG.SYS file. Since very few machines have a setting this high, Mosaic asks permission to modify the CONFIG.SYS. (It will save the old one as CONFIG.BAK). In addition, two SHELL.CFG parameters are required: SPX CONNECTIONS=75 and FILE HANDLES=45. (The software seems more up to date than the manual; the FILE HANDLES parameter is mentioned by the install program but not by the installation guide.) However, Mosaic does not modify your SHELL.CFG. You have to remember to check this for yourself.

If you have purchased the Accounting feature, you should also install it at this point. This is a simple matter of placing the distribution disk in the A (or B) drive and typing "A:INSTALL." The installation takes only a few seconds.

2. Install the on-line portion of the software on each file server where Mosaic-managed queues will reside.

The instructions in the installation guide lead you through the procedure fairly well. However, the guide instructs you to insert the Mosaic Manager Disk-1 into the floppy drive, but that's the name of the print server workstation software disk. There is another disk labelled "Mosaic Manager"—it is the proper disk to use.

3. Assign the print server a name and password (optional).

This step provides a facility to change the name of the Mosaic print server, and to add or change a password. The default name is "MOSAIC" and there is no initial password. If you are installing more than one Mosaic print server, you will have to change the name of at least one of them.

4. Start the Mosaic print server.

The Mosaic print server screen is shown in Figure 13-9.

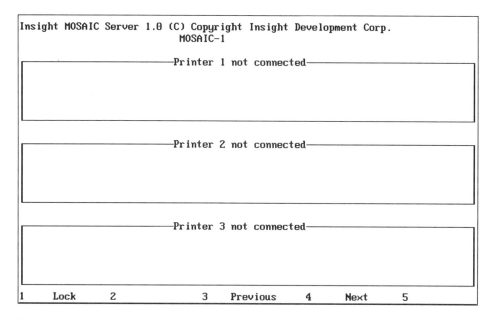

```
Insight MOSAIC Server 1.0 (C) Copyright Insight Development Corp.
                          MOSAIC-1
┌────────────────────────Printer 1 not connected───────────────────────┐
│                                                                        │
│                                                                        │
│                                                                        │
│                                                                        │
└────────────────────────────────────────────────────────────────────────┘
┌────────────────────────Printer 2 not connected───────────────────────┐
│                                                                        │
│                                                                        │
│                                                                        │
│                                                                        │
└────────────────────────────────────────────────────────────────────────┘
┌────────────────────────Printer 3 not connected───────────────────────┐
│                                                                        │
│                                                                        │
│                                                                        │
│                                                                        │
└────────────────────────────────────────────────────────────────────────┘
1    Lock      2            3    Previous    4    Next      5
```

Figure 13-9: This is the Mosaic Print Server's initial screen.

6. Run the MMANAGER program.

Go to a workstation and log in as SUPERVISOR to the server on which you installed the Mosaic Manager (MMANAGER) software. You must use the actual SUPERVISOR account the first time; after you've imported some users, you'll be able to use supervisor equivalents and print queue operators.

Change to the directory in which you installed the Mosaic Manager software and type "MMANAGER". The initial screen shows the Mosaic print servers that are up and running. Select the one you wish to work with. (For the first installation, there will only be one Mosaic print server on the list.)

When you do this, you should expect to get an error message. That's because even though the print server is up and running, it hasn't been defined to NetWare yet. An abbreviated Mosaic Manager menu will appear.

7. Define the Mosaic print server to NetWare.

Select the "NetWare PCONSOLE options" item. Then select "Print Servers" and choose a file server that contains queues to be managed by Mosaic. A list of known print servers will appear on the screen. Press <F5> (Create) to define a new print server. The default name for the new print server will be the same as the name of your Mosaic Print Server, currently running on its dedicated workstation. Although you can edit it here, you should just press <Enter>. (If you do edit the name here, you'll have to rename your print server).

If you gave your Mosaic print server a password in Step 3, select your new print server from this list and give it the same password.

In either case, press <Esc> to return to the "File Server" window. Here, if necessary, you can choose another file server and repeat Step 7.

When you've selected all the file servers that you want Mosaic to monitor, press <Esc> to get back to the screen that contains the "Login to Mosaic Server" command. Select this option to bring up the "Advertising Servers" list. Choose your Mosaic Print server from this list.

You'll only need to perform this procedure one time. After that, whenever you enter the Mosaic Manager program, you'll see the main menu shown in Figure 13-10.

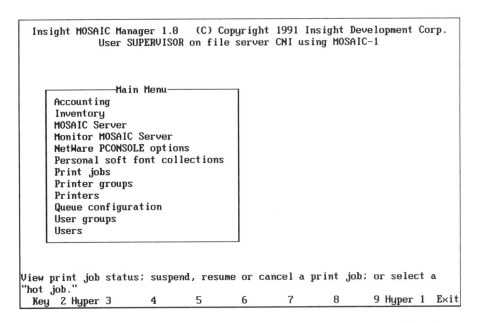

Figure 13-10: Once set up, the Mosaic Manager's main menu appears like this.

One of the nice features of this menu, especially for newly appointed Mosaic Print Manager Administrators, is the <F2> Hyper-Menu key. The Hyper-Menu key causes all of the submenu items to appear, making it much easier to find an option you're looking for. The Hyper Menu is shown in Figure 13-11.

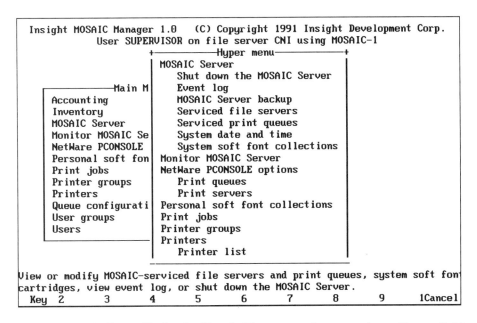

```
Insight MOSAIC Manager 1.0    (C) Copyright 1991 Insight Development Corp.
              User SUPERVISOR on file server CNI using MOSAIC-1
                        +────────────Hyper menu────────────+
                        | MOSAIC Server                     |
                        |    Shut down the MOSAIC Server     |
              ──Main M  |    Event log                       |
      ┌─────────────────┐  MOSAIC Server backup             |
      │ Accounting      |    Serviced file servers          |
      │ Inventory       |    Serviced print queues          |
      │ MOSAIC Server   |    System date and time           |
      │ Monitor MOSAIC Se|   System soft font collections   |
      │ NetWare PCONSOLE |  Monitor MOSAIC Server            |
      │ Personal soft fon|  NetWare PCONSOLE options         |
      │ Print jobs      |    Print queues                    |
      │ Printer groups  |    Print servers                   |
      │ Printers        |  Personal soft font collections   |
      │ Queue configurati|  Print jobs                       |
      │ User groups     |    Printer groups                  |
      │ Users           |    Printers                        |
      └─────────────────┘    Printer list                   |
                        +────────────────────────────────────+
 View or modify MOSAIC-serviced file servers and print queues, system soft fon
 cartridges, view event log, or shut down the MOSAIC Server.
   Key  2       3       4       5       6       7       8       9      1Cancel
```

Figure 13-11: In Hyper Mode, the Mosaic Manager main menu shows the available submenus to help you find the options you want.

At this point, the Mosaic Print server is up and idling. The system administrator still needs to define queues and their configurations, define hunt groups, import users, and more.

As you can see, the Mosaic Print Server is as complicated to set up as a file server. But once the setup work is finished, little additional attention is needed.

Running the Accounting Option

Accounting of print resources is sorely lacking from the NetWare suite of printing programs and facilities. Some of the third-party products have an accounting feature (see Chapter 12), but none approaches the depth and breadth of Mosaic's optional Accounting facility. This is because the other programs must rely on the information stored in the print queue and print server control files (the two hidden files in each print server and queue directory). It is simply not possible to report on data that is not collected.

Since Mosaic virtually takes control of printing and printing resources, it can collect and report on a much wider range of data. Reports can be produced that show:

- Which printers are used the most? The least?
- How much paper is used for print jobs
- What are the network printing costs? By department? By project?
- Which users submit the most jobs to the system?
- Which (cartridge/downloadable) fonts are used the most/least?
- Which forms are used the most/least?
- What is the print volume by department?

Mosaic also tracks the following data items, which may be reported in any manner:

- Printer-in-use time
- Count of jobs per printer
- Number of times any printer was idle (by printer)
- Total number of pages printed (by printer)
- Print server utilization, by any time period
- Forms usage, by name and number
- Font cartridge usage, by cartridge name
- Soft (downloadable) font usage
- Users/projects/departments that sent jobs

The Accounting package comes with a number of predefined reports that should satisfy almost any auditor. Nevertheless, Mosaic includes an ad hoc report generation feature as well.

Summary

Mosaic Print Manager is like no other NetWare add-on product. It doesn't merely attempt to do NetWare's job better; it does jobs that NetWare doesn't even try to do. This product is not aimed at the small-business or even at the departmental LAN. It is aimed at the kind of company that views networks and connectivity as a corporate resource and considers management of that resource to be a top priority.

CHAPTER 14

Third-Party Hardware

NetWare's open technology allows creative hardware and software developers to provide add-on services that Novell itself doesn't offer. Several companies that compete in the printing arena have capitalized on this open technology to provide innovative printing products for NetWare LANs. This chapter examines five hardware products that clearly manifest this creativity.

Two products—Intel's NetPort and Castelle's LANPress—are small, self-contained network print server devices. They attach directly to the LAN cabling system on one end, and then plug in via parallel or serial cables to the printers. A single device can manage two to four printers, with no PC involved. In fact, these devices are small enough to be affixed with velcro to the side of one of the printers they manage.

Two other products—Hewlett-Packard's optional LAN I/O board and Castelle's JetPress—are circuit boards that fit inside HP LaserJet Series II or Series III printers. With these adapters installed, the printers can be plugged directly into the LAN cable, bypassing parallel or serial port attachments altogether.

The last product we'll look at represents the state of the art in network printers: Hewlett-Packard's HP3si is a high-speed printer specially designed for heavy use on a LAN. While it can be ordered with a parallel or serial port, its key feature is its ability to plug directly into the LAN cabling. This LAN connection is an original design feature, not an add-on as it was for the Series II and Series III printers. As a result, the HP3si can accept and print data twice as fast as other HP laser printers.

Conceptual Overview

These new approaches to network printing offer three main advantages. The first advantage is space; the NetPort and LANPress devices take up little extra room, while the LAN I/O boards take up no extra room at all. The second advantage is convenience; you don't have to locate the printer near a workstation, nor is there any reason to keep a workstation up and running just to manage a printer. (Doing away with the workstation has some pleasant side-effects as well. Whenever an apparently idle workstation is left unattended, someone is bound to come along and either turn it off, or use it for a quick job and re-boot it when it's done. By removing the workstation altogether, you avoid these kinds of problems.)

The third and most important advantage is speed. Consider these facts:

- A standard parallel port can send data to the printer at a maximum rate of 50 Kbps (that is, 50,000 bytes per second).
- When printing is done in the background (as is the case with remote printer programs such as RPRINTER or Printer Assist), parallel port speed drops to about 10-15 Kbps.
- A serial port (as defined for RPRINTER) can transfer data at a maximum speed of 9.6 Kbps.
- A 16 page-per-minute laser printer prints one page in about four seconds.
- A typical printed page (single-spaced, one-inch margins) consists of about 2,000 characters.

Under normal conditions, then, the speed of a parallel port is more than sufficient to feed data to even a fast laser printer. However, "normal" conditions are changing as PostScript printers become the standard. A PostScript version of the same 2,000-character page of text translates into a print job stream 40,000 to 60,000 characters in size. Add some additional fonts or graphics, and you can easily inflate that number into hundreds of thousands of bytes per page. With today's increasing reliance on fancy fonts and three-dimensional graphics, the speed of the printer is no longer the bottleneck. Rather, it's the speed of the printer port that slows down the work.

In recognition of this trend, both the NetPort and the LANPress devices increase the speed at which the parallel port sends data. NetPort sends data at about 80 Kbps, while LANPress sends at about 200 Kbps (these figures came from the manufacturers). These higher transfer speeds are often sufficient to move the bottleneck back to the printer.

But what if you have a much faster printer, or larger print jobs (in the sense of more characters per page)? One solution is to attach the printer directly to an Ethernet or token ring cabling system so it can receive its data at LAN transfer speeds. For Ethernet, that's a theoretical maximum of ten million bits (1.2 million bytes) per second. Even allowing for a very generous 50% overhead, that's three times the speed of the LANPress parallel port, and ten times the speed of a standard PC parallel port.

Hewlett-Packard and Castelle both offer add-in cards for the HP LaserJet models II, IID, III, and IIID. The insertion of a LAN I/O card allows these printers to accept print jobs at the printer's best data throughput rate.

To take maximum advantage of this raw data speed, HP designed the HP3si printer especially for heavy LAN use. As mentioned earlier, the HP3si's direct connection to the LAN allows it to receive and print data at twice the speed of other HP laser printers.

Dedicated Print Server Devices

In this section, we examine the installation and use of two devices that act as dedicated print servers on the network: Intel's NetPort and Castelle's LANPress.

NetPort

The NetPort is a small, standalone print server device that attaches a printer directly to the network without the need for a workstation.

NetPort is a product of Intel, 15220 NW Greenbriar Parkway, Beaverton, Oregon 97006. Suggested retail price is $695 (Ethernet) or $1195 (token ring). The following overview is based on software dated 3/25/91, and a NetPort delivered for evaluation in November 1991.

You can set up a NetPort in one of two ways. The first way uses NetWare's Print Server (PSERVER) software to define the NetPort as though it were two printers attached to a remote workstation. The other method is to define the NetPort as a queue server, bypassing Novell's print server software. Figure 14-1 illustrates both options.

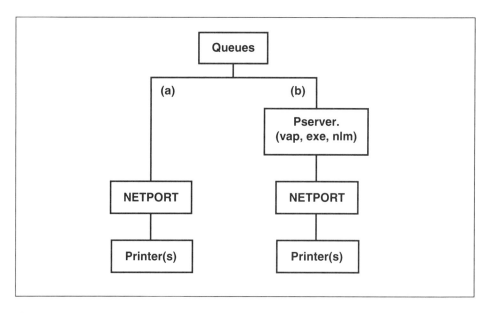

Figure 14-1: You can set up NetPort either with or without Novell's PSERVER program.

The advantages of option (a), the non-PSERVER method, are speed and ease of installation. The disadvantage is that it takes a network connection. This might be a problem if the current number of users on your LAN is close to the maximum number of users supported by your licensed copy of NetWare.

Option (b), with PSERVER, is a little slower, but it does not use a connection. Security-conscious users of NetWare 386 should choose this option as well, since option (a) requires you to allow unencrypted passwords on your system. However, this is not a serious security breach for the vast majority of users.

For those users who are already using Novell's print server software, adding a NetPort as another printer is a small maintenance task. For the rest, it is probably best to use NetPort in Queue Server mode.

Special Features of NetPort

The NetPort is designed to be used as a shared printer device. However, for those rare occasions when you need to use the NetPort's printer as if it were attached directly to a PC, there is an easy way to set this up temporarily. For those few applications that need two way communication with a printer or plotter, you can set up the NetPort in what Intel calls "virtual circuit" mode as well.

The official name of each NetPort is based on its serial number, which is a six-digit hexadecimal number. For ease of use, NetPort comes with a program called NPCON, which allows you to change the factory preset name to one that is easier to remember.

Installing NetPort

Figure 14-2 summarizes the steps to set up the NetPort as a queue server (option (a) in Figure 14-1). These example steps illustrate using the NetPort to place a printer in a very remote location, such as on a factory floor. Note the use of NPCON in Step 2 to rename the NetPort to "FACTORY_FLOOR."

---

1. Before installing the NetPort on a NetWare 386 network, enter the following command at the file server console:

   ```
   SET ALLOW UNENCRYPTED PASSWORDS=ON
   ```

2. Log in as SUPERVISOR (or equivalent) and create a NETPORT directory under SYS:PUBLIC. Insert the NetPort software diskette into drive A and type these commands:

   ```
   MD \public\netport
   COPY a:*.* \public\netport
   NPCON HP123456 NAME=FACTORY_FLOOR
   ```

3. Start PCONSOLE, choose "Print Server Information," then add these three print server names:

   ```
   FACTORY_FLOOR
   FACTORY_FLOOR-P
   FACTORY_FLOOR-S
   ```
   (continued)

(continued)

4. Press <Esc>, then choose "Print Queue Information." Highlight a queue name (or press <Ins> to add a new one), choose "Queue Servers," and insert these two print servers:

```
FACTORY_FLOOR
FACTORY_FLOOR-P
```

To set up the serial port instead of the parallel port, the second line would be:

```
FACTORY_FLOOR-S
```

5. Plug in the NetPort, then type:

```
NPCON FACTORY_FLOOR RESET
```

Figure 14-2: Steps for setting up the NetPort as a queue server.

The procedure for setting up the NetPort as a remote printer governed by PSERVER is given in Figure 14-3.

1. Log in as SUPERVISOR (or equivalent) and create a NETPORT directory under SYS:PUBLIC. Insert the NetPort software diskette into drive A: and type these commands:

```
MD \public\netport
COPY a:*.* \public\netport
NPCON HP123456 NAME=FACTORY_FLOOR
```

(continued)

(continued)

2. Start PCONSOLE. Choose "Print Queue Information" and create any additional queues you might want. If you are using only existing queues, skip this step.

3. Press <Esc> to go back to the main menu, then choose "Print Server Information." Choose an existing server to modify, or create a new one. Then press <Enter> and choose "Printer Configuration."

4. Select any "Not Installed" printer and press <Enter>. Change the printer name to "FACTORY_FLOOR." Then choose "Printer Type" and select "Remote Parallel, LPT1" for the NetPort's parallel port, or "Remote Serial, COM1" for the NetPort's serial port.

5. Press <Esc>, save the information when prompted, then choose "Queues Serviced by Printer" to bring up a list of all the printers defined for that print server. Select the printer you just defined (or, if you defined both, the parallel printer first, then the serial printer). Press <Ins> to bring up a list of queues. You may pick one or more queues, and assign them priorities if you wish.

6. Exit to the main menu, saving everything along the way when prompted. Then start (or restart) the print server. The method for starting the print server varies depending on whether you are using the VAP, NLM, or EXE. Details are in Section III, Chapter 5.

7. Plug in the NetPort, then type:

```
NPCON FACTORY_FLOOR RESET
```

Figure 14-3: Steps for setting up the NetPort with a Novell print server.

Note that the final step is the same in both setup procedures. You will need to repeat this NPCON RESET command whenever you modify the NetPort's environment, such as by adding or changing a queue.

The NPCON program also has several other uses. For example, it allows you to configure the NetPort's serial port. Like Novell's "PRINTER n CONFIG ..." console command, NPCON can be used to set baud, parity, word size, stop bits, and Xon/Xoff. An important point to note is that the NetPort's maximum baud is 19,200 cps, twice the Novell program's maximum. You also use NPCON to issue form changes, attach other queues, set up notification messages at job completion, and so on.

In addition to NPCON, the NetPort comes with several other programs to help you manage the NetPort and its attached printers. Most useful among these are NPQUERY and NPMON.

You can use NPQUERY in batch files to check the status of a NetPort's parallel or serial port. It returns an errorlevel that can be checked to determine if the printer is okay, off-line, out of paper, or in need of a form change. The NetPort manual gives an example of a batch job that displays the results of a status query.

NPMON is a small, memory-resident program that will tell "operators" that a printer needs attention. You use this program by issuing these two commands:

```
NPCON OPERATOR=username
NPMON ON
```

From that point on, any NetPort running in queue server mode will send its status reports to the specified user, on whatever workstation that user is logged in from.

Using the NetPort

To use the NetPort, you make three connections: (1) attach the printers to the device using parallel or serial cables; (2) plug the NetPort into the LAN cable; and (3) plug in the NetPort's power cord. When the NetPort is powered on, it runs through a startup diagnostic. If there is no LAN cable attached, or if no printer is attached to the port, the NetPort will report an error condition.

Whenever the NetPort is powered off and back on, you must issue the NetPort "NPCON *name* RESET" command.

After that, printing is merely a matter of sending data to a queue that a NetPort printer is servicing.

LANPress

LANPress is a small, self-contained print server that connects a printer to a LAN without the need for a workstation.

LANPress is a product of Castelle, 3255-3 Scott Blvd., Santa Clara, California, 95054. Several models are available, for use on Ethernet (thick, thin, or twisted pair) and token ring (4Mbps only or switchable 4/16 Mbps) networks. In addition, LANPress models are available with one parallel and three serial ports, or with two parallel and two serial ports. Prices range from $695 to $1395. The following overview is based on software dated 04-19-91 and a LANPress evaluation unit delivered in November 1991.

Special Feature of LANPress

The LANPress is remarkably fast. According to the manufacturer, its parallel port runs at almost 200Kbps. This is four times faster than a standard parallel port.

Installing LANPress

To install a LANPress, you first run the PSINSTAL program. This program creates a "master" file server and loads the LANPress software into a directory of your choosing. It also creates a new print server and assigns existing or new print queues to the printers it creates.

Next, you run LPCONSOL, Castelle's PCONSOLE look-alike program. You can use LPCONSOL to edit any print server on the network, but it is best to restrict your use of this program to Castelle LANPresses. Figure 14-4 shows LPCONSOL's main configuration screen.

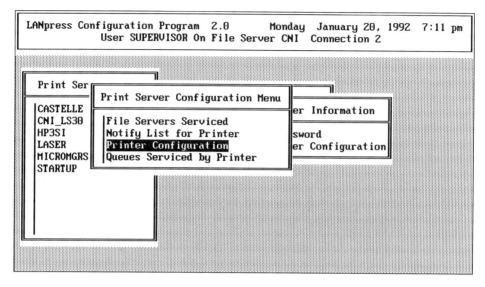

Figure 14-4: LPCONSOL looks a lot like Novell's PCONSOLE utility.

The LANPress sent for evaluation had two parallel and two serial ports. With this configuration, the configured printers list appears as in Figure 14-5.

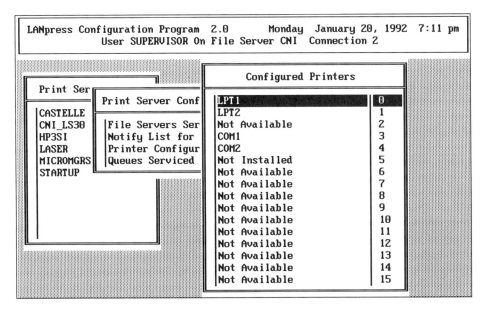

```
LANpress Configuration Program  2.0        Monday  January 20, 1992  7:11 pm
                 User SUPERVISOR On File Server CNI   Connection 2
```

```
                                        Configured Printers
    Print Ser
                  Print Server Conf    LPT1                            0
    CASTELLE                           LPT2                            1
    CNI_LS30     File Servers Ser      Not Available                   2
    HP3SI        Notify List for       COM1                            3
    LASER        Printer Configur      COM2                            4
    MICROMGRS    Queues Serviced       Not Installed                   5
    STARTUP                            Not Available                   6
                                       Not Available                   7
                                       Not Available                   8
                                       Not Available                   9
                                       Not Available                  10
                                       Not Available                  11
                                       Not Available                  12
                                       Not Available                  13
                                       Not Available                  14
                                       Not Available                  15
```

Figure 14-5: This sample printer configuration screen shows two parallel and two serial ports defined.

For the other LANPress configuration (one parallel and three serial ports), Figure 14-5 would show printer 1 as "Not Installed" and printer 5 as "COM3."

Configuring printers in LPCONSOL is similar to but easier than configuring printers in PCONSOLE. Figure 14-6 shows a serial port being set up. Note that the possible baud rates include speeds of 19,200 and 38,400 baud, as opposed to Net-Ware's 9,600 baud maximum. (The allowable limit is still defined as the smaller of the print server's maximum or the printer's maximum.)

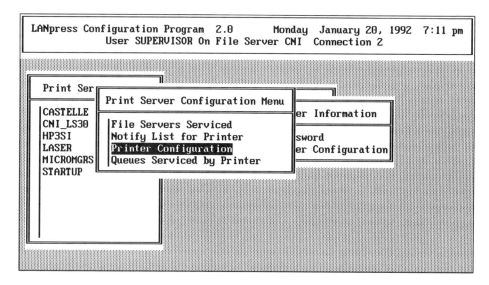

Figure 14-6: LANPress allows higher baud rates for serial ports.

From this point on, setting up a LANPress print server is exactly the same as setting up a NetWare print server. You use PCONSOLE to choose queue(s), priorities, and notification lists for each printer.

Once the LANPress is initialized, a "Status/Control" option will appear on the menu. Print server operators can use this option to select a printer and abort, pause, stop, or start a printer or print job. The only options that are not available are Mark Form, Eject Page, and Rewind.

Using the LANPress

Once the LANPress is properly configured, you simply plug it in and turn on the printers. If there is data in any of the LANPress printers' queues, it will begin printing.

LAN I/O Boards

There is more than one way to get data to a network printer. You can attach the printer to a parallel or serial port on a workstation or a file server; you can attach the printer to a standalone print server; or you can attach the printer directly to the LAN cable.

The two products discussed in this section fall into the last category. The Hewlett-Packard Network Printer Interface Card and the JetPress each plug in to the "optional I/O" slot on the LaserJet Series II and accept data directly from the LAN, without need for assistance from a workstation or print server.

Hewlett-Packard Network Printer Interface Card

The HP Network Printer Interface Card fits neatly into the optional I/O port on the LaserJet. It comes in three varieties: a token ring card and two Ethernet cards (BNC and twisted pair).

Once installed, the card can be configured in either of two ways: as a "queue server" or through Novell's PSERVER software. The queue server configuration is faster, while the PSERVER configuration adds a level of security for NetWare 286 users. Most users will want the additional speed and opt to configure the printer as a queue server. The following installation instructions assume this to be the case.

Installing the HP Interface Card

Here is a brief summary of the steps required to set up the HP Network Interface Card in the optional I/O slot.

1. Install the card inside the LaserJet printer.

The card fits into the "Optional I/O" slot found at the back of the printer. You need a small Phillips-head screwdriver to remove two screws holding the original cover plate in place. Once the cover plate is removed, you can see two rails; the new card fits into and slides down along these rails. The card has an edge connector in the back, so after sliding the card down about 90% of the way, you will meet with some resistance. A slight push will seat the card fully into the connector slot. Fasten the card using the two screws that you just removed. Be sure to refasten the screws securely to ensure that the card is properly seated.

Next, remove the parallel or serial cable that was previously attached to the printer and attach your LAN cable. If there is a PostScript cartridge in place, you will have to remove it. Now power on the printer. The printer will take longer to start up than you are used to, because the printer is internally set for parallel or serial I/O. However, the power-on self-test (POST) will find the I/O card.

2. Set the printer to recognize the new I/O card.

Here are the steps for telling the printer about the new card.

2a. Press the **OnLine** button to take the printer off-line (the "on-line" indicator light should go off).

2b. Hold down the **Menu** key for several seconds until AUTO-CONT= or SYM SET= appears in the display window.

2c .If the "I/O=PARALLEL, SERIAL, or OPTIONAL" message is not displayed, press the **Menu** key until that message appears in the display window.

2d. Press the "**+**" or "**–**" keys until I/O=OPTIONAL message is displayed.

2e. Press **Enter** to select optional I/O as the default. An asterisk should now appear in the display: I/O=OPTIONAL*

2f. Press **Continue** to exit the configuration menu.

2g. Wait for a message similar to 43 OPT INTERFACE or OPT I/O ERROR 43 to appear in the display window. Press **Continue** to clear this message.

2h. Reach behind the printer to the newly installed card and press the **Status** button, located underneath the card handle.

2i. A page will be printed after you press the **Status** button. Keep this page; you'll need it later in the process.

3. Initialize the I/O card using the HP software.

At this point, you have essentially added a new station to your LAN. Since this "station" has no diskette or any other way to initiate communications with the server, you must go to a workstation and run some software supplied by HP to initialize the I/O card.

4. "Log in" the printer to the NetWare file server.

After you initialize the I/O card, the act of powering on the printer will cause it to "log in" to the server. (In this example, it will log in as a queue server, not as a user; there is no user ID associated with the device.)

The printer will always have a password; it might be blank or null, but it's there. In NetWare 386, passwords are encrypted by default. When an unencrypted password is sent, the server will reject it. To allow the printer card to log in, you must enter the following command at the file server console:

```
SET ALLOW UNENCRYPTED PASSWORDS=ON
```

You should also add this command to the server's AUTOEXEC.NCF file so it will be issued whenever you reboot the server. You can do this in SYSCON, under "Supervisor Options.")

5. Set up the printer as a queue server in PCONSOLE.

To define a queue server in PCONSOLE, follow these steps:

5a. Start PCONSOLE.

5b. Choose "Print Server Information" and create a new print server. (Details are given in Chapter 9.)

5c. Choose "Print Queue Information" and either select a print queue or create a new one.

5d. From the menu that appears (shown in Figure 14-8), choose "Queue Servers," then press <Ins> and choose the print server name you defined in Step 5b.

5e. If you want the printer to service more than one queue, repeat Steps 5c and 5d.

287

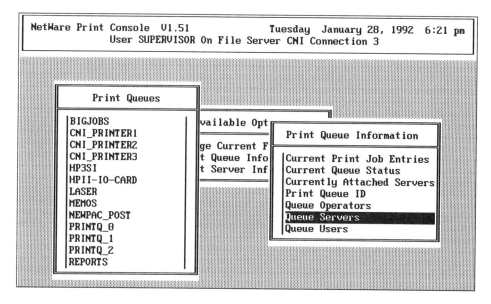

```
NetWare Print Console  V1.51              Tuesday  January 28, 1992  6:21 pm
                 User SUPERVISOR On File Server CNI Connection 3
```

Figure 14-8: Use PCONSOLE's "Queue Servers" option to assign the printer to service the selected queue.

6. Run the PCONFIG utility supplied by HP.

6a. In SYS:SYSTEM, create a subdirectory called HP-CARD (or something equally mnemonic). Copy the contents of the distribution diskette to that subdirectory. Then change to that subdirectory and start PCONFIG. Figure 14-9 shows the initial screen.

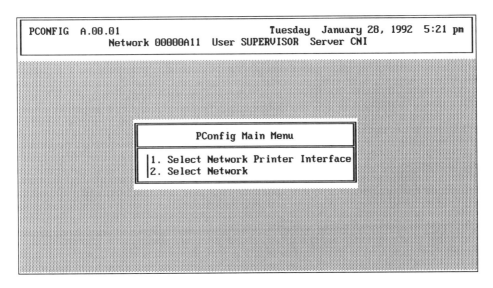

```
PCONFIG  A.00.01                    Tuesday  January 28, 1992  5:21 pm
              Network 00000A11  User SUPERVISOR  Server CNI


                        ┌──────────────────────────────────┐
                        │         PConfig Main Menu         │
                        │ 1. Select Network Printer Interface│
                        │ 2. Select Network                 │
                        └──────────────────────────────────┘
```

Figure 14-9: PCONFIG's initial screen lists two main menu options.

6b. Choose option 1, "Select Network Printer Interface." You'll see a list of node addresses. Select the node address that matches the node address on the status page you printed out at the end of Step 2. The node address will be in the form NPIxxxxx, with the x's replaced by hexadecimal numbers.

6c. Choose "Select/Configure Queue Server Mode."

6d. For the Node Name, type the name of the print server you defined in Step 5b.

6e. For the File Server Name, select the name of the file server on which you created the print server. (You can use the <Ins> key to bring up a list of file servers.)

This completes the installation and configuration of the HP printer with an optional I/O card. To test the printer, use CAPTURE or NPRINT to send a print job to the queue you named in Step 5c. Printing should start almost immediately. If not, turn the printer off and on again. Then send another test print job to the queue.

JetPress

The JetPress board by Castelle (3255-3 Scott Blvd., Santa Clara, California 95054) is designed to fit inside HP LaserJet model II, IID, III, and IIID printers. Suggested retail price is $595. As of this writing, the JetPress is designed only for Ethernet LANs (BNC and twisted pair). According to Castelle, a token ring board will be available "soon."

Special Features of JetPress

Castelle's JetPress board is a direct competitor of the HP Optional I/O board. Their lists of features and benefits match almost exactly. However, the JetPress offers two features not found in the HP board.

- JetPress can work with a PostScript cartridge. According to Castelle's technical support people, the timing on the board had to be altered to match the speed of the CPU on the PostScript cartridge.

- JetPress uses SPX at the Network layer to enable peer-to-peer communication. This gives standard NetWare utilities (such as PCONSOLE) the ability to monitor and manage print jobs on a JetPress-equipped laser printer. Users can go into PCONSOLE, choose "Status/Control," and actively manipulate the print jobs. (Details on how to do this are given in Chapter 9.)

Installing JetPress

Installing the JetPress board involves both hardware and software setup procedures. These are summarized below.

1. Install the JetPress board inside the printer.

If you are using the Ethernet board over twisted pair wiring (known as 10BaseT), you have to move two switches on the JetPress board before installing it into the laser printer. The switches are clearly marked on the board and are described in the manual.

The board's serial number is printed on its face. Also, the initial power-on sequence produces a status page that displays it. Write this number down or save the status report; you must have the number to complete the configuration.

The JetPress fits into the "Optional I/O" slot at the back of the LaserJet. Turn the printer off. To guard against the possibility of accidentally pressing the power-on rocker switch while installing the board, it's best to unplug the power cable as well. If you had a parallel or serial cable attached to the printer, remove it.

Next, use a small Phillips-head screwdriver to remove the cover plate, then slide the JetPress board in, component side down. The board is actually about an inch longer than the space provided; Castelle accommodates this with an extension to the cover plate.

If you are using a PostScript cartridge, remove it during the configuration process. You'll reinstall it after configuration is complete.

Plug the LAN cable into the board, then turn the printer back on. The JetPress will produce a configuration report.

2. *Configure the printer to recognize the JetPress board.*

2a. Press the **Online** key to take the printer off-line.

2b. Press and hold the **Menu** key for about 5-7 seconds. When the printer responds, it will display AUTO CONT=OFF (Series II machines will show SYM SET=Roman-8). If you've previously set the symbol set to something else, this response will show that setting instead.

2c. Press the **Menu** key repeatedly until the I/O SELECTION option is displayed.

2d. Use the "+" or "–" keys to change the selection to I/O=OPTIONAL.

2e. Press **Enter** to save this choice.

2f. Press **Online** to put the printer back on-line. The JetPress will print another configuration report.

This completes the hardware installation. Next, you must complete the software setup.

3. Run the JPINSTAL program to configure the JetPress.

3a. Insert the JetPress installation disk into drive A: and type JPINSTAL. Or, you can copy the contents of the disk to a directory on a file server or local hard disk and run the program from there.

3b. When the program starts, it asks for the serial number of the JetPress card. This is the number you wrote down during the hardware installation. It is also printed on the original configuration report. Enter that number.

3c. The installation program then asks you to name the "master" file server. Figure 14-10 shows this JPINSTAL screen. Choose the master file server as prompted.

```
          << JetPress Installation - Master Designation >>

JetPress can serve queues on up to eight servers. However, one (and only one)
must be the "master file server".

JetPress cannot operate without a master file server. The master file server
contains information pertinent to JetPress operation: the list of file
servers to serve, port configuration, etc.

A non-master file server contains queues to be served by JetPress, but does
not contain the data above.

Choose JetPress master file server according to the following recommendations:

    -The file server should be on the same network segment as JetPress.
    -JetPress should serve queues on the file server.
    -The file server should not be down often.

Is CNI the master file server for 06001106? [Y/N]:
```

Figure 14-10: This JPINSTAL screen asks you to designate a "master" file server.

3d. The JPINSTAL program also asks you to name any additional file servers that contain queues to be serviced by the JetPress. Name these additional file servers (if any), as shown in Figure 14-11.

```
          << JetPress Installation - Assigned File Servers >>

Print server 06001106 is configured to service the following file servers:

1. CNI (master)

If print server 06001106 is to serve additional file server(s)
(up to eight are allowed), please enter a file server name.
If no additional file servers are to be served, Press ENTER.

Enter File server name:
```

Figure 14-11: In this screen, you name additional JetPress file servers.

3e. You will then be asked to name the queues that the JetPress will monitor, as shown in Figure 14-12. All queues are serviced at the same priority. If you wish to make changes to these choices at a later date, you can do so in the normal way via the NetWare PCONSOLE program.

```
          << JetPress Installation - Queue Assignment >>

JetPress parallel port LPT1  can print jobs via Print Queues to
connected printer.

To configure Print Server 06001106 to serve existing or new
queues on File Server CNI, you will need to enter a Print
Queue Name.

REMEMBER
 - Press <Enter> if you do not want to assign queues at this time.

Enter Queue Name:
```

Figure 14-12: In this screen, you assign queues to the JetPress.

3f. The last question that JPINSTAL asks is whether or not you are going to use a PostScript cartridge. If so, all future configuration reports and banner pages will have PostScript-formatted headers.

3g. After asking for all the required and optional choices, JPINSTAL displays your choices and asks for confirmation. Figure 14-13 shows this summary and confirmation screen.

```
           << JetPress Installation - Configuration Summary >>

JetPress print server name: 06001106
File server name: CNI  (Master)

File server to be served:
1. CNI (master)

   Queue name                               Port(s):           Priority
1  LASER                                    LPT1                  1
2  HP3SI                                    LPT1                  1


Note: After installation, to change the priority of a queue,
please refer to the JetPress Installation and Operation Guide.

Client utilities will not be copied

If this configuration is satisfactory, press Y [Y/N]:
```

Figure 14-13: The JetPress summary screen lets you confirm your configuration choices.

Once you give your okay, the JPINSTAL program creates a print server whose name is the same as the serial number. It then assigns queues to that print server. If you chose to have the JetPress manage queues on multiple file servers, the program will create print servers on those file servers as well.

Using the JetPress

To reboot the JetPress, turn the printer off and then back on again. When the printer finishes its self-test, the JetPress board will attempt to log in to the master file server. A successful login causes the master server to recognize the JetPress as a print server, servicing one locally-attached printer. From that point on, any jobs sent to a queue serviced by the JetPress will print on the laser printer.

Users with proper rights can use NetWare's PCONSOLE program to manage the queues and jobs, just as if the printer were attached to a computer running the NetWare PSERVER.EXE software.

The HP3si Printer

As the industry leader in laser printer technology, Hewlett-Packard offers laser printers for every budget, from small personal lasers to the top-of-the-line printers designed for network use. The HP3si represents the high-end of their printer line.

The HP3si is based on the HP LaserJet Series III printer, a high quality printer capable of producing remarkably clear graphic images. In its default PCL mode, it has many of the features normally expected only in PostScript printers (multiple scalable fonts, the ability to rotate output to any angle, and more). In addition, the HP3si offers a much faster printing speed; it is rated at 17 pages per minute, compared to 8 for the HP III.

Looking at the figures presented in the conceptual overview to this chapter, some simple arithmetic tells us that a printer can print faster than a standard parallel port can supply data— assuming that the pages are relatively full. To avoid wasting this high speed capacity, the HP3si printer has a special version of the Hewlett-Packard LAN I/O card (see the discussion earlier in the chapter).

To install the printer on a network, you remove the parallel/serial board that comes with the printer and insert the LAN I/O card into that slot. Once the card is in place, the installation program is the same as for other HP LaserJet printers with optional I/O cards. However, one feature is different: you can order the HP3si with Postscript ability built in (it's an optional chip on the motherboard). Using the LAN I/O card does not preclude simultaneous PostScript use.

The HP3si has several other useful LAN features. For example, it has two large paper trays that each hold a full ream (500 sheets) of paper. As jobs are printed, the printer "jogs" them in the output tray; in other words, the feed mechanism moves 1/2" to the right or left so that the output stack can be easily sorted by job. The output tray is very deep, holding several hundred sheets of printed paper. A sensor halts printing when the output tray is full (the printer signals "Out of Paper" to the server as well).

The HP3si uses a different toner cartridge than the other HP laser printers. While these cartridges are about 20% more expensive than the original ones, they are rated for almost twice as many copies. The net result is a consumables cost of around 2 cents per page, compared with an industry average of 3 cents. In a high-volume printing environment, this can add up to a very significant savings.

All in all, the HP3si is a workhorse printer skillfully designed for the LAN marketplace.

CHAPTER 15

PostScript Printing on a LAN

With the growing popularity of PostScript printers, a serious network problem arose: how do you share a single printer with users who send PostScript output to a queue and those who send generic printer output? One of the problems with sharing PostScript printers is that they won't accept print streams that do not contain the proper PostScript control information at the head of the file. If a job stream without this control information is sent to the printer, the printer ignores it. (PostScript printers actually delete any non-PostScript job streams they receive.)

In addition, NetWare has the ability to add a banner page to the beginning of any print job on the network. The Novell banner page data does not contain PostScript control codes; therefore sending a banner to a PostScript printer will cause the intended output to be lost. Conversely, if a printer that is not set up for PostScript receives PostScript-formatted data, it will print the PostScript header information as though it is part of the output to be printed. (These lengthy PostScript commands often run for several pages).

This chapter looks at four solutions to these problems. One solution is the Pacific Page PostScript cartridge, which adds PostScript capability to the LaserJet series of printers. Bundled with the cartridge is a software package called PacificPrint, which can switch a cartridge-equipped LaserJet in and out of PostScript mode as necessary.

The second solution is a printer definition file (POSTTEST.PDF) that takes a generic printer file and prefixes it with proper PostScript commands.

The third solution is a VAP (or NLM) called PS Manager that runs at the file server and monitors the queues, performing much the same function as the PRINT-DEF definition file described above.

Finally, we'll briefly examine the SCRIPT program that comes with (and is dependent on) DR DOS. Like the .PDF and the .VAP, this program prepends PostScript code to standard output so that PostScript printers will accept it.

The Pacific Page PostScript Cartridge

The Pacific Page PostScript cartridge is a product of Pacific Data Products, 9125 Rehco Road, San Diego, California, 92121. At this writing, the suggested list price is $499.

The cartridge comes in various models for HP LaserJet Series II, IIP, IID, III, and IIIP printers. Cartridges for Series II printers include a 2MB memory board. The package also includes software called PacificPrint, which allows the printer to be shared by PostScript and non-PostScript users on a LAN.

The cartridge will work in only one printer at a time. The software may be installed on a server and used at the workstation connected to the printer. Any user on the LAN may submit jobs to the print queues that the printer is servicing.

Special Features of Pacific Page

To solve the problem of PostScript and non-PostScript jobs going to the same printer, Pacific Page includes a software package called "PacificPrint." This software sets up two queues: one for PostScript-formatted output and one for other output. Print jobs entering either queue will be printed on the designated printer. If the printer is already set to the proper mode, the job simply prints. If not, the PacificPrint software issues the command to change modes before releasing the print job to the printer.

For PostScript jobs that have banners enabled, the PacificPrint software also generates a PostScript banner page.

Installing the Pacific Page Cartridge

To install the Pacific Page PostScript cartridge, you simply turn the printer off, slide the cartridge into the slot (the left slot if your model has two), and turn the printer back on.

In addition, you must modify your word processor and other application programs to take advantage of your new PostScript capability. To help you accomplish this, the Pacific Page documentation includes directions for modifying the following popular programs: Microsoft Word, WordPerfect, Aldus PageMaker, Ventura Publisher, and Microsoft Windows.

After that, everything sent to the printer must be in PostScript format. You can switch back and forth between PostScript and PCL (Printer Control Language, the native mode on any Hewlett-Packard LaserJet) by sending a particular escape code. The code to go from PostScript to PCL is:

```
<ESC>&11057.32259J
```

If you are in PCL mode and want to go to PostScript, the code is:

```
<ESC>&15257.5257.1058J<CTRL-D>
```

The <ESC> character is ASCII value 27; <CTRL-D> is ASCII value 4.

You might find it worthwhile to create two batch files, one called TO-POST.BAT and one called TO-PCL.BAT. The contents of each are shown as Figure 15-1. If some of your users have exclusive use of a printer with a cartridge, all they have to do to switch modes is send the appropriate batch file to the printer before sending their print jobs.

```
                    TO-POST.BAT
                    _____

     ECHO <ESC>&15257.5257.1058J<CTRL-D> > lpt1


                    TO-PCL.BAT
                    _____

     ECHO <ESC>&11057.32259J > lpt1
```

Figure 15-1: These two batch files convert the printer to and from PostScript and PCL modes.

Installing the PacificPrint Software

The use of such batch files is not appropriate in a network environment, however. Since the batch file is separate from the print stream, there is no guarantee that they will arrive in the queue together in the proper order without another user's print job intervening. It wouldn't be long until users would complain about lost print jobs and unreliability.

To fix the problem, Pacific Page includes software called PacificPrint. The steps for installing this software are summarized below.

1. Log in as SUPERVISOR (or equivalent).

2. Create (or change to) a directory on the server that is available to anyone who will be operating a workstation to which the LaserJet/PostScript cartridge combination is attached.

3. Insert the PacificPrint diskette into drive A and type "A:INSTALL." Be prepared to provide the serial number on the PacificPrint diskette and the name of the organization or user that purchased the software. (The installation program serializes the software as it is installed.)

The default queues created by the install program are named PPA_POST and PPA_TEXT. However, it is easy to set up new PacificPrint queues for people who prefer more mnemonic queue names, or for those who have acquired cartridges for several printers.

The program used to create additional queues for PacificPrint to manage is called PAC-CFG. Figures 15-2 through 15-5 show samples of its screens. The program is simple to use, but there are two things to watch out for:

- The name of any queue that is to contain PostScript-formatted print streams must end in "_POST." Names for queues that will contain anything else must end in a different string.
- PacificPrint defines queue servers as "network members whose workstations host shared printers." Figure 15-3 demonstrates setting up a queue as a queue server.

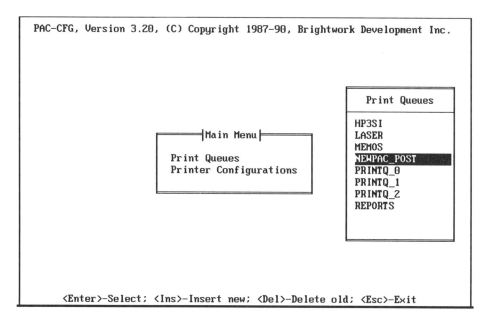

Figure 15-2: In the PAC-CFG program, names of queues that handle PostScript print streams end in "_POST."

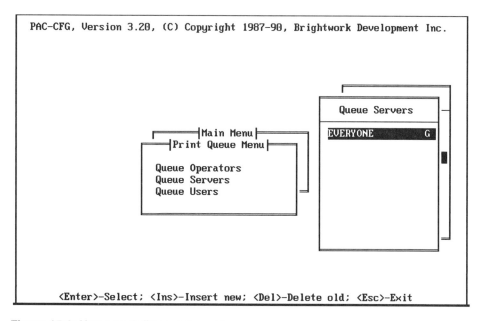

Figure 15-3: You can define a group of users as a queue server.

Once you define the queues, the next step is to define the printer configuration. This configuration will be saved in SYS:PUBLIC, and will be used by the user at the workstation serving as host for the shared printer.

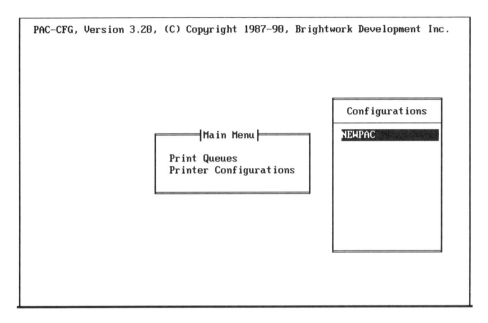

Figure 15-4: The "Printer Configurations" option lets you define a printer configuration.

When defining a printer configuration, you must make several decisions. The program is fairly intuitive, and the manual is easy to read and understand. Figure 15-5 shows a completed printer configuration screen.

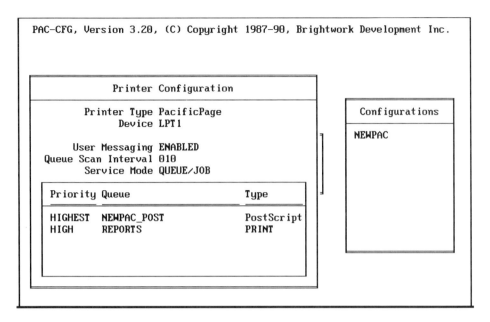

```
PAC-CFG, Version 3.20, (C) Copyright 1987-90, Brightwork Development Inc.


            Printer Configuration                      Configurations

        Printer Type PacificPage
             Device LPT1                                NEWPAC

        User Messaging ENABLED
   Queue Scan Interval 010
          Service Mode QUEUE/JOB

    Priority Queue                  Type

    HIGHEST  NEWPAC_POST            PostScript
    HIGH     REPORTS                PRINT
```

Figure 15-5: When you define a printer configuration, you specify its queues, priority, type, and other information.

Running the PacificPrint Software

To establish a printer attached to a workstation as a shared printer (using the configuration shown in Figure 15-5 as an example), you log in and issue the following command:

```
PACPRINT NEWPAC
```

The PACPRINT program will take approximately 12KB of the workstation's memory.

You must remain logged in for the printer to remain in its shared state. However, if you log out and another user logs back in, the printer will continue to work, so long as the second user to log in is also defined as a "queue server" for the queues that are named in the PACPRINT configuration. (The PACPRINT program polls its queues every 10 seconds. It is not possible to poll a queue when no user is logged in at the workstation.)

The Pacific Print software package also includes a program called PSP-CON.

This program allows the user to manage the PACPRINT configuration that is already loaded. Management options include such things as job sequencing within a queue and form changes. Figure 15-6 shows the PSP-CON configuration screen; Figure 15-7 shows its queue management screen.

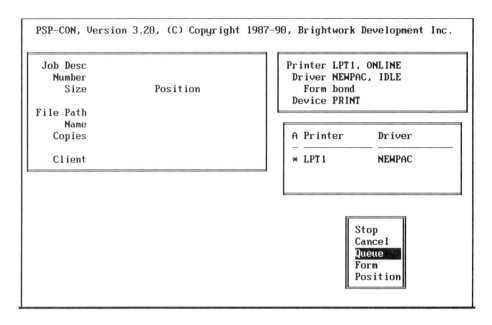

Figure 15-6: PSP-CON's initial screen is a control window.

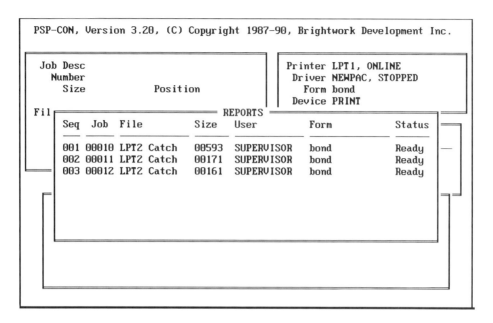

```
PSP-CON, Version 3.20, (C) Copyright 1987-90, Brightwork Development Inc.

  Job Desc                              Printer LPT1, ONLINE
    Number                               Driver NEWPAC, STOPPED
      Size          Position               Form bond
                                          Device PRINT
  Fil                         REPORTS
        Seq  Job  File        Size  User          Form       Status

        001 00010 LPT2 Catch   00593 SUPERVISOR    bond       Ready
        002 00011 LPT2 Catch   00171 SUPERVISOR    bond       Ready
        003 00012 LPT2 Catch   00161 SUPERVISOR    bond       Ready
```

Figure 15-7: This is a sample of PSP-CON's queue management window.

Using PacificPrint with Windows

PacificPrint works with Microsoft Windows if it is loaded into memory before Windows is started.

To use a laser printer from within Windows, you should select the Apple Laserwriter driver from the Windows Print Setup screen (found in the Accessories group). Details on printing from Windows can be found in Appendix II.

PRINTDEF Header Control with POSTTEXT.PDF

This section discusses several files contained in a file named POSTTE.ZIP. (A ZIP file is a single file that contains several other files within it. Each component file is compressed, resulting in a whole that's smaller than the sum of its parts.) POSTTE.ZIP can be downloaded from NetWire (a part of the CompuServe Information Service) in the NOVLIB forum, Lib 15. There is no charge, aside from the connect time charged by CompuServe (about a dollar's worth—it's a small file).

PostScript is a complex command language that can generate a wide range of special effects, such as outline, shadow, reverse print, rotation, and much more.

However, like many languages with an abundance of features, PostScript exacts a minimum overhead just to print a simple text file. The files contained within POSTTE.ZIP include a PRINTDEF definition file that places a carefully written PostScript control file ahead of any text file submitted to a queue. The result is that simple ASCII-only text files can be printed on a PostScript printer.

Installing POSTTEXT.PDF

First, you'll need to run a program such as PKUNZIP to break the ZIP file into its three component files: POSTTEXT.PDF, PSHEAD.PS, and README.DOC (PKUN-ZIP itself is in NOVLIB, Lib 15.) The .DOC file contains installation instructions, which we'll summarize here. It also explains that the .PDF is a derivative of work performed by Glen Reid of Adobe Systems. Glen's original work is in the PSHEAD.PS file, which is included for anyone who wants to work with the original.

POSTTEXT.PDF is a printer definition file suitable for importing into your NET$PRN.DAT database via the PRINTDEF program. After unzipping the original file, run PRINTDEF and import the POSTTEXT.PDF file. (For more information on running PRINTDEF, see Chapter 7.) A sample of the functions included in Posttext.pdf is shown in Figure 15-8.

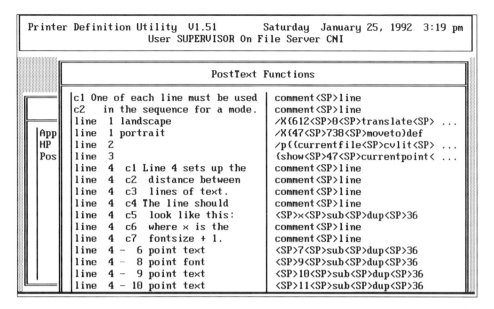

Figure 15-8: The functions in the POSTTEXT.PDF file are self-documenting.

You can easily make changes to these functions. As you can see from the figure, the author of the .PDF made the functions self-documenting. The liberal use of comments makes it easy to create additional lines that define other fonts and point sizes.

Once functions are defined, they must be gathered together into modes for use in PRINTCON. The modes that come with POSTTEXT.PDF are shown in Figure 15-9.

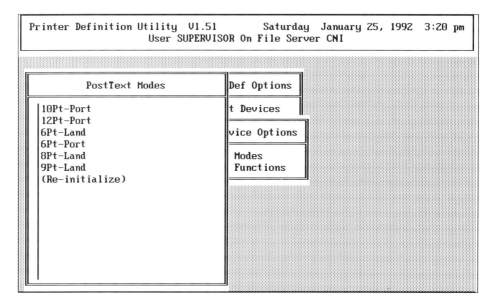

```
Printer Definition Utility  V1.51        Saturday  January 25, 1992  3:20 pm
                     User SUPERVISOR On File Server CNI


        ┌──────────────────────────┬──────────────┐
        │      PostText Modes       │Def Options   │
        │                           │              │
        │ 10Pt-Port                 │t Devices     │
        │ 12Pt-Port                 │              │
        │ 6Pt-Land                  │vice Options  │
        │ 6Pt-Port                  │              │
        │ 8Pt-Land                  │  Modes       │
        │ 9Pt-Land                  │  Functions   │
        │ (Re-initialize)           │              │
        │                           └──────────────┘
        │
        │
        │
        │
        │
        │
        │
        └───────────────────────────
```

Figure 15-9: The POSTTEXT.PDF functions are grouped together to form various modes.

The underlying functions comprising the 10Pt-Port mode are shown in Figure 15-10. From the figure, it is easy to see that creating a new mode is merely a matter of selecting the proper functions, one from each "line."

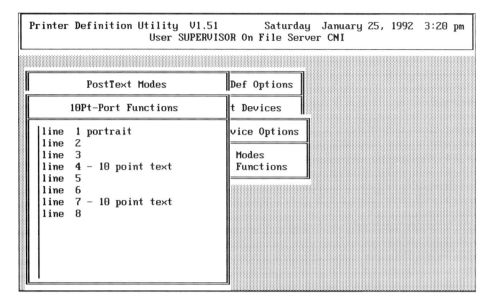

Figure 15-10: The 10Pt-Port mode consists of several POSTTEXT.PDF functions.

To make use of this new mode, you must run PRINTCON to create a new print job configuration. Figure 15-11 is a PRINTCON screen showing a new configuration called "ps-courier10."

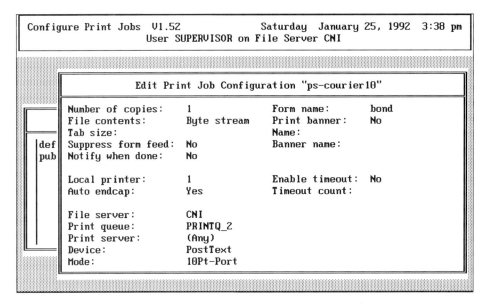

```
Configure Print Jobs  V1.52              Saturday  January 25, 1992  3:38 pm
                        User SUPERVISOR on File Server CNI
```

```
                Edit Print Job Configuration "ps-courier10"

     Number of copies:    1            Form name:        bond
     File contents:       Byte stream  Print banner:     No
     Tab size:                         Name:
def  Suppress form feed:  No           Banner name:
pub  Notify when done:    No

     Local printer:       1            Enable timeout:   No
     Auto endcap:         Yes          Timeout count:

     File server:         CNI
     Print queue:         PRINTQ_2
     Print server:        (Any)
     Device:              PostText
     Mode:                10Pt-Port
```

Figure 15-11: In PRINTCON, you can select one of POSTTEXT.PDF's modes for a print job configuration.

When you select a device and mode that you set up in PRINTDEF, NetWare will include the control characters that make up that mode in a part of the job stream known as the print head. The default size of the print head is 64 bytes. The modes that come with POSTTEXT.PDF take up almost 255 bytes (the maximum size). To have NetWare allocate a larger print head, add the following line to your workstation's SHELL.CFG file:

```
PRINT HEAD=255
```

You will have to reload the shell in order for this command to take effect.

Using the New Print Job Configuration

To use this new PostScript job configuration, include the "JOB=ps-courier10" parameter in your CAPTURE and NPRINT command lines. You can direct the output to any queue, so long as that queue is served by a PostScript printer. However, you must be sure that the data stream sent to the printer includes only regular text—

no PCL control codes, fonts, or graphics. If you are using a word processor, let it use its own PostScript driver.

Since NetWare sends its banner page before the print head, you must turn banners off (using the "/NB" parameter).

PS Manager

PS Manager is a program that runs as a VAP (on a NetWare 286 file server) or as an NLM (on a NetWare 386 file server). PS Manager is a product of the National Software Company, located at 3316 Kilkenny Street, Silver Springs, Maryland 20904. The VAP version has a retail price of $195; the NLM is priced at $295.

PS Manager works by splitting the normal function of a queue into two parts: input and output. Users send data to the input queue, and printers service the output queue (which is a different queue). PS Manager monitors the input queue for incoming data. If the data is already in PostScript format, it simply copies the data to the output queue. If the data is in PCL format, PS Manager converts the data to PostScript format and then copies it to the output queue.

PS Manager also has the ability to examine documents formatted for the IBM ProPrinter (a dot matrix printer) and retain the formatting codes. In other words, it will recognize and convert codes to create boldface or underlining, or to change fonts or point sizes.

Installing PS Manager

PS Manager installation is remarkably easy. Simply create a directory on your server (a subdirectory of SYS:SYSTEM called PSMGR would be a good choice, but you can use whatever directory you want.) Copy all the files from your distribution disk to that directory and start the installation program by typing "PSMGR." Figure 15-12 shows PSMGR's initial screen.

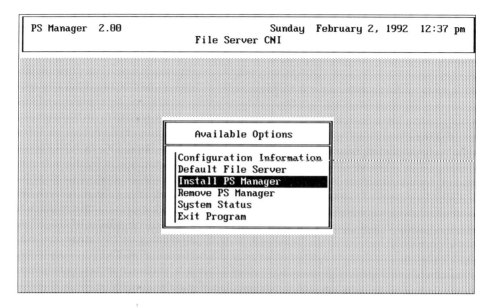

Figure 15-12: PSMGR's initial screen contains several options.

From the "Available Options" menu, choose "Install PS Manager." PS Manager is capable of detecting whether the file server it is being installed on is running Net-Ware 286 (thus requiring the VAP) or NetWare 386 (thus requiring the NLM). In the case of NetWare 286, you would choose "Install VAP on Server" from the menu shown in Figure 15-13. (On a NetWare 386 server, the screen shown in Figure 15-13 would indicate that it is installing the NLM.)

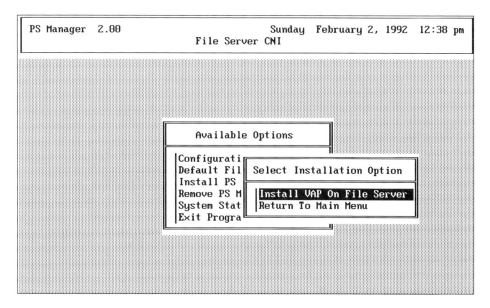

Figure 15-13: PSMGR automatically detects whether you need to install the VAP or the NLM on the file server.

Once the VAP or NLM has been installed, the next step is to configure the input and output queues. Figure 15-14 shows a sample configuration with one input queue and one output queue. PS Manager imposes no limit on the number of input and output queues it can manage.

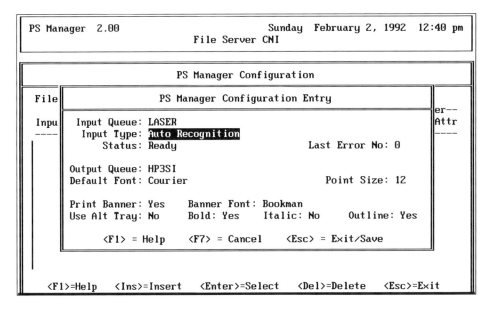

Figure 15-14: This sample PSMGR screen shows the program configured for one input queue and one output queue.

Notice the "Input Type" field highlighted in Figure 15-14. PS Manager has the ability to set three different input types. The first type is "PostScript Only." Data from input queues set to this type will simply be copied to the output queue for printing. The second type is "Text / Emulator." Data from these types of queues will always be converted to PostScript. The third and default option is "Auto Recognition." Data from this type of queue will be examined to see if it is already in PostScript mode. If so, the data will be copied to the output queue without modification; if not, the data will be converted along the way.

After you finish the configuration process, you must load the PS Manager VAP or NLM on the file server. If you are using the VAP version, you must bring down and restart the file server. For the NLM, you simply load it at the file server console prompt using the LOAD command.

You can modify PS Manager configurations while the VAP or NLM is running. Those changes will take effect immediately and will be saved for future use.

One of PS Manager's nicer features is the ability to pull the banner page from an alternate paper tray. If you are using a PostScript printer with a second tray, you can load colored paper into it and thereby create colored banner sheets that are exceptionally easy to locate.

Running PS Manager

PS Manager itself doesn't print anything! All it does is move data from one queue to another. The system supervisor must arrange for the data in the output queue to be printed.

In some informal tests of PS Manager running in conjunction with Printer Assist, LANSpool, PacificPrint, and NetWare 286's core printing, all of these packages worked as expected. Test data was sent to a HP LaserJet Series II with a Pacific Page PostScript cartridge installed.

SCRIPT.EXE

SCRIPT.EXE is a program that comes with DR DOS from Digital Research (now a wholly-owned subsidiary of Novell). Aside from the cost of the DR DOS operating system, there is no charge for this program. However, SCRIPT is written to detect whether the loaded operating system is, in fact, DR DOS.

The SCRIPT program has the ability to read a print stream destined for any PCL-based printer, such as an HP LaserJet, and convert the stream to PostScript. SCRIPT also handles downloaded fonts.

SCRIPT may be installed as a terminate-and-stay-resident (TSR) program, in which case it intercepts output destined for LPT1, LPT2, or LPT3 and converts it on the fly. Or, it can be run on an existing file and will either create another file or send the output directly to a parallel port. It also has the ability to make minor modifications to the text, such as switching to landscape from portrait orientation, or changing the default point size.

> **Note:** The Digital Research documentation says SCRIPT will work as a resident program with LPT1. But SCRIPT, as delivered with DR DOS v6.0, fails to load as a memory-resident program when directed to intercept LPT1 output. Digital Research provided a fix. It can be downloaded from their CompuServe forum.

Solutions to the Banner Page Problem

Another major headache that LAN administrators face when working with Post-Script printers is the NetWare banner page. As we've mentioned, NetWare print services (either core printing or the PSERVER software) can be set up to insert a banner page into the job stream before any of the user's data. This banner page data is in plain ASCII format; the only control codes it contains are line feeds and a form feed. All dot matrix and laser printers handle it properly, but PostScript printers don't. When a PostScript printer receives a print stream without the proper control information, it drops the entire stream.

The easy solution is to instruct users to disable banner pages by including the "No Banners" option in their printing commands. However, for some shared network printers, this solution is not completely satisfactory.

Three of the products we've discussed in this section provide better solutions for accommodating PostScript banner pages. They are PS Manager and PacificPrint (discussed in this chapter) and Printer Assist (a PSERVER/RPRINTER replacement described in Chapter13).

Summary

Each of the third-party solutions we've looked at in this chapter takes a different approach to sharing PostScript printers on a LAN. Some, like the PacificPrint software, assume that the best course is to leave the data alone and switch the printer between PostScript and PCL modes. Others, like the PS Manager VAP or NLM, convert the data from PCL to PostScript format before sending it to the printer.

None of these programs handles downloaded fonts in PCL format. All of them add additional overhead to the print processing load, and they all require the user to be careful in selecting the proper output queue, or in using the proper printer configuration file. But despite these limitations, they all manage to solve the problem of having two very different output streams coming from users' workstations aimed at a printer with very specific requirements.

Section V:

Troubleshooting Common Printing Problems

This section deals with identifying and resolving problems in the NetWare printing environment. The hardest part of resolving any problem is identifying the point of failure. As you'll see in some of the examples that follow, a single problem is often caused by several different factors. In situations like this, most people try to find a solution by examining each of the possible causes one-by-one, until they discover the true culprit. While this method often works, it isn't a very efficient use of time. It's like searching for a word in the dictionary by starting with aardvark and looking at each subsequent word until you find the one you want.

A better technique would be to attempt to isolate the problem, thereby limiting the number of possible causes. To do this, you must learn to ask "isolating questions." Here is an example of asking isolating questions:

Suppose you are the person who answers the telephone at a roadside automobile service center. Your job is to dispatch the proper assistance when motorists call in with a problem. The center employs an apprentice mechanic who can go to the customer, taking along any parts necessary to fix minor problems. A tow truck is also available for more serious problems. You have been instructed to try to determine the cause of the customers' problems first. That way, you can determine what form of assistance to dispatch: the apprentice mechanic (with appropriate parts) or the tow truck.

One day, a customer calls and says, "My car won't start." For the sake of the example, pretend that there are only three reasons why a car won't start: the battery is dead, it's out of gas, or the starter motor is broken. The apprentice mechanic can take booster cables or extra gas, but if the problem is with the starter motor, you'll need to send a tow truck.

To identify the cause of the problem, you have to ask some isolating questions. Your first questions might be "Do the headlights work?" and "If so, are they bright or dim?" The caller answers that the headlights do work and they're bright. You therefore rule out a dead battery as a possible cause. In other words, you are beginning to isolate the problem. Your next question might be, "What happens when you turn the ignition key?" The caller answers, "It just makes a clicking sound." Now you've isolated the problem—the starter motor is bad. Your course of action is clear: send the tow truck.

A word of caution: it's sometimes easy to draw the wrong conclusion, even after you've asked isolating questions. Consider the following story which is often told to graduate students in any area of scientific research:

An animal behavior researcher spent several months teaching a cockroach to climb onto his finger whenever he said, "Up!" Once the cockroach learned that, the researcher cut off two of the insect's six legs and said, "Up!" Although losing two legs slowed the cockroach down a little, it was still able to climb up onto his finger. The researcher made note of that, and then cut off two more legs and gave the "Up!" command once again. This time, the cockroach had to struggle quite a bit, but finally made it up onto the finger. After noting these results, the researcher cut off the two remaining legs and again said, "Up!" The cockroach failed to move. The researcher gave the command again, even more emphatically, but still the roach did not move. The researcher therefore concluded that cutting off all of a cockroach's legs causes it to go deaf.

Of course, the moral of this story is that sometimes, to find the right answer to a question, you need to re-examine the data and look for alternate meanings.

This section is organized around the concept of isolating questions. Chapter 16 has headings for the major NetWare printing programs. Chapter 17 is divided into conceptual areas such as upgrading and PostScript printing. Within these divisions are typical questions and answers relating to the particular programs or concepts. The first few questions cover simple problems; later questions tackle increasingly more complex issues.

To use this section as a guide to solving your own printing problems, first try to isolate the problem to at least one of the NetWare printing programs or concepts. Then turn to that section and look for a question that represents your problem. If you find one, follow the suggested solutions. If you can't find a question that covers your exact problem, keep looking: there should be something close enough to at least give you a hint.

CHAPTER 16

Questions and Answers by NetWare Utility

This chapter is devoted to the resolution of printing-related problems in a NetWare environment. The solutions presented come from a variety of sources, including questions and answers provided on NetWire (Novell's forum on CompuServe), and problems and solutions found in the NetWare Support Encyclopedia and in the NetWare documentation.

Unlike the rest of the book, this chapter and the next chapter are in question-and-answer format. This chapter contains headings that correspond to the print programs supplied by Novell (CAPTURE, PCONSOLE, and so on). The next chapter contains questions and answers organized by conceptual area (such as setup, upgrading, and PostScript printing).

CAPTURE and NPRINT

We just acquired our first laser printer and most of the jobs we send to it print out okay. But whenever we print a graph from our spreadsheet program, or use our word processor to print a graphic image, the output has missing spaces or stray lines at random places on the page. What should we do to correct this problem?

Both CAPTURE and NPRINT have a "Tabs" parameter. By default, NetWare monitors jobs as they leave the queue and replaces every occurrence of the Tab character (value 09 in the ASCII character set) with eight spaces. This isn't a big problem on dot matrix printers because most files sent to these printers don't contain Tab characters any more. However, the files sent to laser printers often have characters with the binary value "09" sent to them as part of a font or graphic image. With "Tabs" left to its default, NetWare will still convert it to eight spaces, thus distorting the graphic or ruining the font.

To keep this problem from happening, include the /NT (No Tabs) parameter in your CAPTURE and NPRINT statements. This parameter prevents NetWare from looking for Tab characters and converting them to spaces.

We're getting "Memory Overflow" errors on our HP LaserJet Series II when we print from NetWare via RPRINTER. The same file prints fine when sent to a local parallel port by the application. What's wrong?

This problem can also be solved using the /NT (No Tabs) parameter. When sending from the application to the local parallel port, NetWare doesn't have a chance to erroneously expand Tab characters. For an explanation, see the previous answer.

We recently added a new department to our network. Printing worked fine before, but now whenever I try to print a long report I get a banner page and a few report pages, followed by another banner page and a few more report pages, and so on until the job is done. Sometimes a report will even break off mid-page. How can I get my long reports to print all together?

You need to increase the timeout value by adding a few seconds to the /TImeout parameter in your CAPTURE and NPRINT commands. Whenever you start sending data to the print queue, NetWare keeps track of the time between characters. When that time interval equals or exceeds your timeout value, NetWare assumes the print job is complete and sends it off to be printed. When it receives another character, NetWare treats it as the start of a new job. The additional network traffic generated by the new department is apparently causing more delay in the transmission of your print jobs. If you increase the timeout value, the problem will go away.

We run a nightly inventory report that takes five or six hours to generate and about an hour to print. One of the managers starts the report just before leaving for the day, and the generation process ends around midnight. The first person to arrive at the office in the morning logs the manager out, which causes the report to begin printing. Our problem began when we instituted a nightly tape backup procedure. The consultant who installed the backup system set a time restriction on all user accounts so that no one can log in between 1:00 and 4:00 a.m. when the backup is run. He informed us that, since the backup program skips open files, setting the time restriction would ensure that all files would get backed up—even if people leave files open and go home without logging out. The backup seems to work all right, but now the inventory printout doesn't appear. When we try to log the manager out, the system says he wasn't even logged in. What can we do?

The success of the original report printing scheme hinged on the following fact: when a user who has print jobs pending in a queue logs out properly, NetWare automatically closes the print jobs and sends them off to the printer. But most people don't realize that when you set a time restriction in NetWare, anyone who is already logged in when the restricted time period begins will have their connection cleared. This automatic "Clear Connection" command results in roughly the same effect as if the user had shut off his or her machine without exiting any applications or logging out. NetWare simply closes any files that were left open. Any changes the user made since the last save are lost. This does not apply to print jobs in queues.

If a user's connection happens to be cleared while the user has a print job in the queue, NetWare treats it as an abandoned print job and deletes it from the queue.

Fortunately, the solution is simple: add the /KEEP parameter to the CAPTURE command for that user. This parameter causes NetWare to close, rather than abandon, the print job. Since the job will start printing as soon as it is closed, this solution offers the added advantage that the report will have already finished printing before the first person arrives the next morning.

We have an application that runs as part of a batch process. The batch program first issues up a CAPTURE command with No Autoendcap and Timeout=0. It then copies a file of control codes to LPT1 and enters a database program. When that program ends, the batch file logs the user out. According to the NetWare documentation, logging out should be equivalent to issuing an ENDCAP command and the job should print. Experience shows that the print job is lost. Do you have any solutions?

This problem is due to a bug in the CAPTURE program. However, there are two workarounds. One is to issue an ENDCAP command before logging the user out. The other is to add the /KEEP parameter to the CAPTURE command line.

My banner pages are coming out wrong. Usually the name is wrong or missing altogether, but sometimes there are other problems as well. What can I do to fix this?

Obtain a new version of CAPTURE. The easiest way is to download the latest version from NetWire. You can also call Novell and have them ship it to you (for a fee).

We have a problem with NPRINT. If the file to be printed is in the current directory it prints OK, but if we specify its path (either by using a drive letter or by giving a full path including the file server name, volume name, and subdirectories) it won't be able to find the job. What's wrong?

These problems occur with an older version of NPRINT (v3.03). To get a newer version that works correctly, download the latest NPRINT.EXE from NetWire.

Jobs don't appear in the queue. What should we do to fix this?

Check your CAPTURE settings by typing "CAPTURE SHOW" to see which queue and file server the jobs are being sent to. Then go to another workstation and start PCONSOLE, select that queue, and choose the "Current Print Job Entries" option. Watch the screen as you or an assistant sends a job to the queue from the workstation on which you issued the CAPTURE command. If the job does not appear on the screen, update your NetWare shell to the latest version. If it still fails, try to CAPTURE to another queue. If that works, delete the first queue and re-create it.

We recently upgraded to NetWare v3.11, and now whenever we try to print via NPRINT an error message that says "An unknown Queue error

0x0004 occurred" shows up at the workstation. This error appears on every one of our old workstations, but not on any of the ones we added as part of the upgrade. Is there a fix?

At one of the workstations that gets the error message, go into the directory in which IPX.COM is located and type "IPX I." The first line of the resulting output will tell you the version number, which is probably 2.15 or lower. You should have version 3.02 or higher. (IPX and shell version numbers do not necessarily correspond to NetWare version numbers; NetWare v2.20 users should also be using at least IPX version 3.02.)

To create a new IPX.COM file, you need the NetWare diskette labelled WSGEN. You'll also need to know the hardware settings of the LAN card in your machine. These settings are also displayed by typing "IPX I" (either write them down, or press <Shift><Print Screen> to print out a hard copy).

We just added a NetWare 386 file server to our network. But when we log in to it and try to NPRINT a file, we get the error message "An unknown queue error 0x0004 occurred." How can we fix this problem?

You're probably still using old versions of IPX.COM. Both NetWare 386 and NetWare v2.20 come with a diskette labelled WSGEN. Run this program to generate a new IPX.COM file for all of your workstations that have access to the new file server.

In general, it's a good idea to watch NetWire and acquire the latest IPX and shell versions. These programs form the interface between NetWare and your workstation's operating system and applications. Keeping them up to date will significantly reduce the number of problems you encounter with NetWare.

PRINTDEF and PRINTCON

We recently upgraded to NetWare v2.20 and we are making use of all the new modes and functions included in the new Printer Definition Files (file with the .PDF extension). We're finding that some of these work and some don't, but we cannot find a pattern. What's wrong?

You use PRINTCON to set up print job configurations that include modes defined in PRINTDEF. The control codes from PRINTDEF are sent to the queue in two areas of the print job file: the print head and the print tail. As a result, the print stream actually sent to the printer looks like this:

```
|Banner info (if any) | Print Head | Data | Print Tail
```

The default length for the print head is 64 characters; for the print tail, the default length is 16 characters. A few of the new mode definitions are a bit longer than these defaults, so they are truncated. The solution is to place the following lines in every SHELL.CFG or NET.CFG file:

```
PRINT HEAD 80
PRINT TAIL 24
```

You can use larger numbers if you need to.

We've been using PRINTCON job configurations for a while now, and suddenly we find that the printer doesn't reset between jobs the way it used to. What can we do?

Some of the shells that shipped with various versions of NetWare (and which were available for download from NetWire) contained a bug. Most frequently, this problem occurs with the EMSNETx shell, but the others had problems as well.

Upgrade to the latest shell versions. If that fails, check to see that the PRINT TAIL parameter in SHELL.CFG (or NET.CFG) is not too short. (The default length is 16 bytes.)

Is there an easy way for all network users to share the same PRINT-CON job configurations?

Yes, there is. Follow these steps:

1. Log in as SUPERVISOR.

2. Run PRINTCON and create all the configurations you need.

3. Copy the Supervisor's PRINTCON.DAT file from
   SYS:MAIL\1\PRINTCON.DAT to SYS:PUBLIC.

4. Change the Search mode of the following NetWare utility files to 5
   by typing:

```
SMODE CAPTURE.EXE 5
SMODE NPRINT.EXE 5
SMODE PCONSOLE.EXE 5
```

These steps are explained in detail in Chapter 7.

There seems to be a limit of 31 configurations per PRINTCON.DAT file. Our company needs many more than that. Is there a way to get around this limit?

If a single user needs more than 31 entries, the only solution is to assign that user multiple login IDs and have the user create different print job configurations for each ID. The user will have to keep track of which ID go with which configurations.

If you are using global print job configurations (see the answer to the previous question), there is a workaround. The global method hinges on changing the search mode (SMODE) for the programs that access the PRINTCON.DAT file. When set to search mode 5, these programs search the DOS path for the PRINTCON.DAT file as though it were an executable file, rather than just a data file. Since the .DAT file is placed in SYS:PUBLIC (normally the first directory in the path), everyone finds and uses the same file. If you are willing to maintain separate PRINTCON.DAT files in separate subdirectories, you can use the system login script to place the appropriate directory ahead of SYS:PUBLIC in the path and thereby create group or departmental PRINTCON.DAT files.

We use global PRINTCON configurations. The problem we're having with it is that every banner page displays the name "SUPERVISOR." How can we get the real user's name to show on the banner page?

Go into PRINTCON as Supervisor and edit the configurations so that the banner name is blank. Then copy the Supervisor's PRINTCON.DAT file back into SYS:PUBLIC. Thereafter, the banner name will contain the user ID of the first user to log in at each workstation. This is sufficient in cases where one user has exclusive use of a given workstation. If you need a more flexible method, use the "NAME=" parameter in your CAPTURE and NPRINT commands. You can also use the %LOGIN_NAME login script variable or a DOS environment variable, as in the examples below.

- In user login scripts:

```
#CAPTURE NAME=%LOGIN_NAME...
```

- In the system login script, include the command:

```
SET NAME="%LOGIN_NAME"
```

Then, in a batch file, use the CAPTURE statement:

```
CAPTURE NAME=%NAME% ...
```

We recently purchased several HP3si printers with the PostScript option. However, when we try to use the print definition with the software switch to change from PostScript to PCL mode, it always works on some of the printers but always fails on others. What's wrong?

On the original HP3si models, PostScript support was a dealer-added option. Enabling this support involved adding a chip to the motherboard and using the front panel switches to set SYS SWITCH to "on" (the default is "off"). On later models, the chip was installed at the factory.

Chances are your dealer installed the chip but forgot to change the switch settings. The printers that work are probably models in which the chip was factory-installed.

We have several HP laser printers in which we've recently installed PostScript cartridges. We created PRINTDEF code strings and PRINT-CON job configurations to switch between PCL and PostScript mode. It seems to work when going from PCL to Postscript, but not the other way around. Do you have any solutions?

The problem lies in the fact that when switching from PCL to PostScript, the printer sets the "printer busy" line on, which causes NetWare to wait before sending the next job. However the switch in the other direction doesn't do that. So the server just sends the data, which is discarded by the printer. Chapter 15 outlines several solutions for using PostScript printers on a LAN.

PCONSOLE - Queues

I've used CAPTURE to redirect print jobs to a NetWare print queue. But now, when I try to send print jobs, I get a "Not Ready writing Device LPT1:" message. The printer is on-line and the ready light is on; I can even use the <Print Screen> key to send text to the printer. How can this be?

Someone has changed the queue's status. Have the network supervisor or a print queue operator go into PCONSOLE and select "Print Queue Information." Then select the queue you are capturing to. Choose "Current Queue Status" and change the first operator flag, "Users can place entries in queue," to "Yes."

I'm very particular about the appearance and format of my print jobs. Consequently, I often want to delete a job after only a page or two has printed. Back when we had NetWare v2.15 and the printers were all attached to the server, I just went into PCONSOLE, selected the queue, chose "Current Print Job Entries," and deleted the job. We've now upgraded to NetWare v2.2, complete with a print server and a remote printer. It's a lot more convenient for me to have the printer here at my desk. But when I delete a print job, nothing else will print until I reboot my machine. Somehow, the connection between the print server and the remote printer gets lost. How can I fix this problem?

The easiest way is to use PSC to abort the job instead of deleting it. The command syntax is:

```
PSC PS=pservername P=printernumber ABORT
```

An alternate method is to use PCONSOLE. Choose "Print Server Information," then the "Status/Control" option, and then your printer number. From the resulting status screen, press <Enter> to pop up a window from which you can choose ABORT.

Since you want to abort jobs frequently, the first method is your best choice. You can make it even easier by placing this command in your AUTOEXEC.BAT file:

```
SET PSC=PSprintservername Pnumber
```

Then, when you want to abort a job, just type "PSC ABORT."

PCONSOLE - Print Servers

In PCONSOLE, when I select "Print Server Information" and choose a print server, the only options I see are "Change Password," "Print Server ID," and "Full Name." How can I define printers and so forth?

Get a newer version of PCONSOLE. You are probably using version 1.02a (which came with NetWare v2.12 and the early releases of NetWare v2.15). You need version 1.32 or later, which you can download from NetWire.

If you created print servers using that old version of PCONSOLE, you should delete them and then re-create them using the new PCONSOLE. If you don't, you might get this error message: "Read property value returned an error code of *xxx*."

When defining a local printer in PCONSOLE, I have the option of using interrupts or polled. My parallel port has interrupt capability, so I can go either way. Which option should I choose?

Generally, polled is better. If your print server is managing a lot of printers (near its maximum) and printing on the local printers becomes very slow, you can experiment with enabling interrupt-driven printing on the local printers. Enable this on one printer at a time, and watch the performance on both the local printer whose configuration you are adjusting and on all the remote printers. Finding the right balance is often a matter of trial and error.

On some of our printouts we're finding dropped characters or words at intermittent intervals. We checked the data while it was still in the queue, and it's all there. What's wrong?

You probably need to increase the buffer size you defined for the printer in PCONSOLE. Increase it in 2KB increments until the problem goes away. (You might have to go as high as 20KB, especially if you print graphics.) Remember, every time you increase the buffer size you give up some of your computer's base memory. Since base memory is limited to 640KB, it pays to be very stingy when it comes to allocating it to programs (such as RPRINTER) that remain memory-resident permanently.

We're running NetWare v3.11 with the PSERVER.NLM. Whenever we modify the print server, we unload the NLM, then reload it. However, this sometimes hangs the server. Shouldn't we be able to do this?

If the print server is actively servicing a print job at the moment you type the UNLOAD command, it might hang the server. The proper way to bring down a print server is to go into PCONSOLE, choose "Print Server Information," then the "Status/Control" option, and down the print server from there. Once the print server is down, you can safely unload the NLM from the file server console.

PSERVER (NLM/VAP/EXE)

> *I used to be able to just hit the power switch on my NetWare 286 server and it would start up without any further intervention from me. Now that I've added the PSERVER.VAP, I have to answer the "Do you want to load VAPs?" question, plus tell it the print server name. How can I make my server start up unattended again?*

The first step is to go into SYSCON under "Supervisor Options" and choose "Edit System SERVER.CFG File." Add the following line to that file:

```
VAP WAIT 10
```

This command changes the "Do you want to load VAPs?" message to "Press any key to abort loading VAPs." The bootup procedure will start a 10-second count-down timer. If no key is pressed in 10 seconds, the server will begin loading the VAPS. (You can have a longer wait time, but 10 seconds is the minimum.)

The next step is to download the latest copy of PSERVER.VAP (version 1.2.2)— the NetWire file name is PSERV1.ZIP. Copy the VAP file to SYS:SYSTEM and restart your file server. You'll be asked to name the print server as usual, but this time the name will be saved. After that, you won't have to retype the print server name when you restart the file server.

> *When we defined our print server, we set up job owner notification. But when the printer goes off-line, no notification messages are ever sent. Doesn't this feature work?*

Upgrade to the current version of PSERVER. Both the NLM and the EXE had this bug, which has now been fixed.

> *We recently added PSERVER.VAP to our file server and we're noticing unusually high server utilization. We've only defined four printers—two local and two remote. Is the VAP a resource hog?*

Don't worry about the high utilization figure. It only occurs when polled printing is in effect.

At the end of the day, we turn off all the workstations and then bring down the file server. Since we've added the PSERVER.VAP, the file server takes a very long time to go down. How can we fix this?

There are actually three answers to this question. Try all three and see which works best for you.

1. At the file server console, type PSERVER STOP and wait for the acknowledgement that it has stopped. Then bring down the file server.

2. Run PCONSOLE from a workstation to "Down" the print server. Then bring down the file server.

3. If you are running over Arcnet, leave one station turned on when you bring down server. (You can turn it off afterwards.)

We're just getting used to having a print server, so we're still making a lot of minor changes and adjustments. Every time we make a change, we have to down the file server and bring it back up. These interruptions are making our users very unhappy. Is there any way to avoid this?

Yes. At the console, type PSERVER STOP. After you receive an acknowledgement that it has stopped, type PSERVER START. This stopping and restarting causes the print server program to look into the bindery and read the updated information. Your remote workstations will have to unload and reload RPRINTER, but the others should be unaffected.

We're running PSERVER.EXE on an old AT with a monochrome display. We've defined this one print server to handle 14 printers and 20 queues (both numbers are less than the maximum). Printing is very slow. Do you have any suggestions?

You've overloaded the print server. Allowable maximums should not be interpreted as guarantees. The limit of 16 printers and 32 queues are merely the maximums that the software will let you define. Perhaps if you dedicated a fast 386 machine with 32-bit LAN cards, you might see decent performance on a maximally-loaded print server. However, the cost of a fast machine typically exceeds the cost of two or three older, slower machines that could share the load.

> *We're running PSERVER.VAP on a dedicated router. We've even upgraded to version 1.2.2 (the version that "remembers" the name of the print server). All was well until we renamed the print server through PCONSOLE (all we did was append a suffix to indicate the revision number). Now, when we start the router and VAP, it still looks for the old print server. Is there any way to tell it to forget the old name and pick up the new one?*

Yes—in fact, there are two ways. The VAP information is stored in a hidden file named VAPINFO.DAT, located in the same directory as ROUTER.EXE and PSERVER.VAP. Use the DOS ATTRIB command to remove the Hidden attribute, and then delete the file. The next time you bring up the router and VAP, it will ask you for the print server name.

In the future, you'll probably find it easier to use the second method. Before you bring down an old print server for the last time, go to the router console and type "PSERVER CLEAR." This command causes the VAP to erase the file for you.

> *When I tried to load the PSERVER NLM at my file server, I got a message about not having enough free buffers. Just how big is this NLM, anyway?*

PSERVER.NLM is not very big at all. Your message is indicative of a much more serious problem—a shortage of file server RAM. The formula for calculating minimum memory requirements for a standard NetWare 386 file server is:

$$((.023 * \text{total disk capacity}) / \text{block size}) + 4$$

In addition, the percentage of free cache buffers (compared to total server memory) should be at least 65%. The MONITOR program will show you how many free cache buffers your server has. Type "LOAD MONITOR" at the file server console; then choose "Resource Utilization." The number of buffers in each of the various memory pools, along with their respective percentages, is displayed on the screen. However, since you've already seen the "not enough buffers" message, you should install more server memory as soon as possible. Then you can worry about getting the print server up and running.

We're loading PSERVER.VAP on our file server. When it loads, it asks for the name of the print server and the password. Meanwhile, another VAP (PS-Manager) loads and overwrites much of the screen, leaving it a mess. Is there any way to control the order in which VAPs load so that the screen stays clear?

Rename the VAPs so that the extensions are VP0, VP1, and so on, up to VP9. (It's unlikely that you'll ever have more than two or three VAPs.) NetWare will then load them in that order. If you load the print server last, it will leave you with a screen free of interference.

We're running PSERVER.EXE in several remote locations. For the most part, the dedicated print servers run continuously. (We've even turned the monitors off.) Occasionally, we get errors that end in "Abort, Retry" on one LAN segment or another. The only solution is to reboot all the workstations on that segment. The users handle that okay, but someone has to remember to reboot the print server. Is there any way to do that automatically?

Get the file NETERR.ZIP from NOVLIB, section 16. This file contains a collection of free utilities written by Infinite Technologies (the same people who created the I-Queue program discussed in Section IV). With these utilities, you can have a print server reboot when the "Abort, Retry" message appears. These utilities also work with other types of servers such as MHS mail servers, gateways, and the like.

We use NetWare's resource accounting feature, but not to track print server usage. We're getting a message telling us that the print server is out of accounting funds. How can we turn this off?

A bug in some older versions of SYSCON caused print servers to have account balance problems. Get the latest version of SYSCON from NetWire. Then either delete all of the print servers and re-create them, or remove Accounting and reinstall it (whichever is easier).

RPRINTER

We want to run RPRINTER from within a login script. But when we use the # command, we find that there isn't enough memory left to load our application programs. When we run RPRINTER after the login script finishes, it only takes 7-10KB. Is there any way to load it from the login script without wasting almost 100KB of base memory?

RPRINTER stays memory-resident after it is loaded. It does this by passing DOS a marker that indicates where the end of RPRINTER code is in memory. DOS then knows where it can begin loading subsequent programs.

When you shell out to DOS by using the # command from within the login script, the LOGIN.EXE program remains loaded in memory. The first available byte after the end of the LOGIN.EXE code is given to the program following the # command so it will know where to start loading. If you specify a program that terminates normally and releases all of its memory space (such as CAPTURE), you can return to the login script and continue executing it with no problem.

However, if you specify a terminate-and-stay-resident program (such as RPRINTER) after the # command and then return to LOGIN.EXE, that marker RPRINTER passed to DOS is still in effect. Thus, any program you execute after LOGIN ends must begin loading after RPRINTER in memory. The part of memory that is used to contain the LOGIN code is an unusable "hole" in the workstation's RAM.

The solution is to use the EXIT login script command to exit to a batch program that loads RPRINTER. For example, you could include this line at the end of the login script:

```
EXIT "RPLOAD.BAT"
```

Once an EXIT command is encountered, no further commands in the login script will be executed. So be sure this is the last line in the login script. The RPLOAD.BAT file would contain the full RPRINTER command. (See the next answer for a sample batch file that loads RPRINTER.)

> *I have an RPRINTER command in my AUTOEXEC.BAT file ("RPRINTER COMMON_PRINT 3" is the exact command). When I boot my system for the first time every morning, any print jobs that happen to be waiting in the queue begin printing out almost immediately. However, if I reboot later in the day, printing almost never seems to work. (If I leave my machine off for 10-15 minutes, it works again when I start it back up.) How can I fix this so that it works right away when I reboot?*

When you first issue the RPRINTER command in the morning, you establish a connection between your workstation and the print server. The print server then "knows" that your workstation is host to printer number 3. If you reboot your machine, the AUTOEXEC.BAT file will reissue that same command. But the print server rejects it because it still thinks you are connected as printer 3.

If you wait a while (30 seconds to several minutes, depending on how busy the print server is), the print server realizes that your workstation isn't there any more and it will drop your connection. After that, it will accept your request to reconnect as printer 3. That's why RPRINTER works again if you take a 10-15 minute break.

To fix the problem, change your AUTOEXEC.BAT file to look like this:

```
:LOOP
ECHO OFF
RPRINTER COMMON_PRINT 3 -R
RPRINTER COMMON_PRINT 3
IF ERRORLEVEL 1 GO TO :FAIL
GO TO :OK
:FAIL ECHO Rprinter failed to attach.....
ECHO Press CONTROL-C to stop trying, or ....
PAUSE
GO TO :LOOP
:OK
```

The PAUSE statement generates the line "Press any key to continue."
The "-R" parameter in the first RPRINTER command line asks the print server
to drop the connection. (If there currently isn't a connection, this request will be
ignored.) The command in the next line attempts to establish the connection again.
It should succeed, but if the print server is busy it might fail, because the request
to drop the connection is a low priority task for the print server. If it's busy managing printers, the print server might defer or ignore the request. The retry loop
compensates for that possibility.

> *I have a printer attached to my workstation's LPT1 port. When I print
> directly from DOS, the printer works at full speed. Printouts sent to the
> printer via RPRINTER are very slow (sometimes one character every
> three seconds). What's wrong?*

There are several possible answers, listed here in order of how easy they are to
check and fix.

• Go into PCONSOLE and make sure that hardware interrupt support is enabled
  for the printer. Remote printers must use interrupts, even though earlier versions
  of PCONSOLE made this optional. (This problem has since been fixed.) When
  you check the interrupt setting, re-enter the interrupt number, even if it displays
  the one you want. For example, even if the screen displays IRQ 7 for LPT1, go

ahead and type the "7" again. (Another bug in an old version of PCONSOLE caused it to display the default interrupt, even if another one had been chosen.)

- Make sure your workstation actually supports hardware interrupts. Since DOS polls the parallel ports, many workstation manufacturers didn't provide that support. You can check it by moving the printer to a workstation where remote printing works, or by using a hardware interrogation program such as Check-It (by Touchstone Software Corporation) or Sleuth (by Dariana Technology).

- Get an add-on I/O board. These usually contain one parallel and one serial port, and both support hardware interrupts. They sell for under a hundred dollars.

- Obtain a new parallel cable from the printer manufacturer. Some printers require a non-standard cable to go from the Centronics port on the printer to the computer's parallel port. The printer manufacturer probably included this cable with the printer, but as printers get moved from one location to another, they often become separated from their cables. While generic parallel cables often work with DOS (polled) printing, the non-standard, original cable is needed for interrupt driven printing to work. Here is a pinout diagram of a well-made parallel cable compared to a generic one:

Parallel port		GOOD CABLE		GENERIC CABLE
1 - 14	_____	1 - 14	_____	1 - 14
15	_____	32	_____	32
16	_____	31	_____	31
17	_____	36	_____	36
18	_____	33		nc
19	_____	19		nc
20	_____	21		nc
21	_____	23		nc
22	_____	25		nc
23	_____	27		nc
24	_____	29		nc
25	_____	30	_____	16

(nc = not connected)

We have several remote printers defined. Mostly they work okay, but on some of them printing just stops. If we turn off the host workstation for a while and then reboot it, things work again for a while. What causes this problem?

The answer to the previous question will help you understand the symptom you are describing. But to solve the problem you'll need to increase some of your shell parameters. Add the following lines to your SHELL.CFG file (located in the same directory as IPX and NETX; create it if you don't have one already):

```
SPX ABORT TIMEOUT=800
IPX RETRY COUNT=50
```

You might need to experiment with higher values, up to about 2000 for SPX ABORT TIMEOUT and 100 for IPX RETRY COUNT.

We've set up a lot of remote printers, using a wide variety of comput-ers as workstations. From time to time, someone hits the <Print Screen> key on their keyboard while someone else's job is printing, thus ruining the printout. Is there any way to prevent this from happening?

There are two different ways to prevent this problem. One is to make sure that the user at that workstation issues a CAPTURE command. That will redirect the output of any <Print Screen> pressing to a print queue. However, this remedy is no longer in effect if the user logs out. (Remember, a user doesn't have to be logged in to run RPRINTER at the workstation.)

The other option is to add a line to the user's SHELL.CFG file (found in the same directory as IPX and NETX; create it if one doesn't exist):

```
LOCAL PRINTERS=0
```

With this parameter in effect (and the shell loaded), it is no longer possible to print directly to the workstation's parallel ports. The only drawback is that there is no way to print directly from the user's workstation. The "PSC ... PRIVATE" com-mand will no longer work.

CHAPTER 17

Questions and Answers by Concept

This chapter is devoted to the resolution of printing-related problems in a Net-Ware environment. The solutions presented come from a variety of sources, including questions and answers provided on NetWire (Novell's forum on CompuServe), problems and solutions found in the NetWare Support Encyclopedia, and the Net-Ware documentation.

Unlike the rest of the book, this chapter and the preceding one are in question-and-answer format. This chapter is organized by conceptual area such as setup, upgrading, and PostScript printing. The previous chapter contains subsections that correspond to the print programs supplied by Novell (CAPTURE, PCONSOLE, and so on).

Core Printing

We're trying to decide whether to use core printing or the print server VAP with NetWare 286. Which is the better choice?

I'd opt for the PSERVER VAP, even though it uses a lot more server memory than core printing does. (The VAP uses 512KB, compared to 3340 bytes for core printing.) The reason I advise against core printing is that it is one of the processes that uses "DGroup" memory. When NetWare 286 is loaded, it allocates DGroup memory to the processes that need it; the remainder is allocated to File Service Processes (FSPs). VAPs, on the other hand, do not use DGroup memory. It's easy to add more memory to a file server, but that won't buy you any more FSPs if you're experiencing an FSP shortage. The following analogy will help explain why it's always best to maximize FSPs.

When looking in a reference book, have you ever used your finger to mark your place while you looked somewhere else in that book for more information, then marked that place with a different finger while you looked in a third place? Did you ever run out of fingers? It happens to me all the time when I look up recipes. Take glazed, stuffed chicken as an example. First I look up the chicken, then put a finger on that page while I look up glazes, then hold that page with another finger while I look up stuffing, only to find that the stuffing requires a clear chicken stock, which I have to look up too. Pretty soon, I have more places to hold than fingers to hold them with.

FSPs are NetWare's fingers. A process gets an FSP and proceeds until it gets interrupted or has to wait for something to complete, so another process using a different FSP can begin. When that one gets halted before finishing, a third FSP takes on a third process, and so on until the server runs out of FSPs. If your server doesn't have enough FSPs, performance really suffers.

By contrast, adding a VAP to a server is like slowing down your reading speed from 500 words a minute to 475. Surely that's better than having fewer fingers.

Can we use core printing and the PSERVER VAP at the same time?

If your print server does not define any local printers (in other words, if all defined printers are remote printers), it should work. However, if you tell the print server to manage a printer attached to a port and core printing is also told to manage a printer attached to the same port, the file server will eventually lock up.

When we had SFT NetWare v2.12, printing worked fine with three printers attached to the server. We just upgraded to version 2.2, using the upgrade option in the INSTALL program. The manual says everything should be the same when you upgrade using this option. But all three printers have stopped working. Why?

You need to check two things. First, check to see if you included Core Printing when you ran INSTALL. The easiest way to check is to go to the file server console and type

```
:PRINTER ?
```

If this command generates a screen full of PRINTER command syntax help, you have enabled Core Printing. If you get an error message, go back into INSTALL, choose the Maintenance option this time, and specify that you want Core Printing enabled.

In either case, you must also check (and possibly modify) your server's AUTOEXEC.SYS file. This file, analogous to DOS's AUTOEXEC.BAT, contains user-selected commands that NetWare reads when it starts up. You can easily view and update it through SYSCON's "Supervisor Options." Make sure that it contains a line like this for each printer attached to your server:

```
PRINTER n CREATE port
```

where n is a number from 0 to 4 and port is a parallel or serial port. NetWare 2.2 with core printing requires that the ports be defined every time the server is restarted.

> *We can't seem to bring down our file server. Whenever we type the DOWN command (or try it through FCONSOLE,) the server hangs. So we have to just turn the server off, but in subsequent restarts we get a message that there are transactions to be backed out. What can we do?*

You actually have two solutions available. One is to type "DISABLE TRANS-ACTIONS" at the console before you type the "DOWN" command. The other is to modify the poll time for your file server's printers so that the minimum time is at least six seconds. Setting a poll time shorter than that prevents the "DOWN" process from closing the print queues.

Setup

> *What are the SHELL.CFG and NET.CFG files? Where can we find them? How are they used for printing?*

These files are located in the same subdirectory as IPX and NETX. They are used when loading those programs to control the interface between the workstation and the LAN. Most workstations can use either NET.CFG or SHELL.CFG; only those workstations that load Novell's ODI drivers are required to use NET.CFG. If both files are present on a single workstation, IPX and NETX will use NET.CFG and ignore SHELL.CFG.

Several entries that can be placed in these files affect printing:

```
LOCAL PRINTERS=0
IPX RETRIES=50
SPX ABORT TIMEOUT=1000
SPX CONNECTIONS=60
```

Use the first three entries at RPRINTER stations; the last entry should be used at the workstation running PSERVER.EXE.

We bought an inexpensive clone to use as our dedicated print server. According to its manufacturer, it has four COM ports and three parallel ports. However, we cannot get any printer attached to COM3 or COM4 to work (though they do work when attached to COM1 or COM2). We've tried to use COM3 and COM4 to support a modem and to print locally; nothing works. Is there any way to check to see if those ports are really there?

You can easily check to see if the machine's BIOS is recognizing the third and forth COM ports by running DOS's DEBUG program. Boot DOS at that computer, then type "DEBUG." At the "-" prompt, type "D 0:0400". You will see a display similar to the following:

```
0000:0400 F8 03 F8 02 00 00 00 00 ....
```

The "F8 03" represents COM1 (base I/O address 03F8; DEBUG shows byte pairs in reverse order). The "F8 02" represents COM2 (at address 02F8). If you see "00 00" as the next byte pair, your BIOS does not recognize the third and forth COM ports. If the next two bytes are "80 03" (or any other valid base address), then it does recognize these ports.

We recently bought some NE2000 boards for our file servers and print servers. (We use NE1000 boards in the workstations.) When we set up the NE2000s, we selected base I/O address 360, which should be clear. However, we now find that any printer attached to LPT1 fails to print. What's wrong?

The NE2000 (and the NE1000, for that matter) use a 32-byte range starting at the base address. For base address 360, that range extends to 37F, which overlaps the LPT1 parallel port range (378 to 37F). Just change the configuration of the LAN board to one of its other ranges (300 or 320 are usually available).

Our users are getting an error message that says "Network spooler error. Probably out of space on volume SYS:". However, when I run VOLINFO, it shows almost 20MB available. What's the real problem?

This error has two common causes. The first is that the supervisor has imposed a limit on user disk space, and this limit has been reached. To check this, have the user who first reported the problem log in, switch to SYS:PUBLIC, and type the DIR command. At the end of the directory listing will be a report on the number of bytes of free space. If it shows a small number or zero, you need to give the user more space on the SYS volume (use the DSPACE command).

The other frequent cause is when the job is deleted from the queue while it is still in "Adding" status. This is seen more often now that multitasking operating systems (such as Windows, DESQview, and Taskmax) are becoming more prevalent. The only solution here is to train your users on proper network printing procedures.

Is there any way to get NetWare to send data to a printer at 19,200 baud? Both core printing and PCONSOLE's print server options limit us to 9600 baud.

There are two ways to get around this limitation. The first way is to purchase Printer Assist from Fresh Technology (discussed in Chapter 13). This program allows printing at 19,200 baud to serial printers attached to workstations.

The other way is to print to a parallel port and buy a parallel-to-serial converter. A very popular, inexpensive brand is LONG-LINKS. This second option requires polled printing. The interrupts are never returned to the parallel port; they're lost in the conversion process.

Upgrade

> *We have two token ring cards in the file server, set to IRQ 7 (primary) and IRQ 2 (alternate). Before we upgraded from NetWare v2.15 to v2.20, both LANs worked and so did the printer attached to LPT1. Now we get nothing out of the printer, and sometimes when we print all of the workstations on the primary ring get network errors. What's going on, and what's the cure?*

You have an interrupt conflict. Both LPT1 and your primary token ring card are using IRQ 7. NetWare v2.15 used polling to print, ignoring the parallel port interrupt completely. NetWare v2.20 uses interrupt-driven printing if the port supports it.

The solution is to set either the card or the port to another interrupt, or to disable the interrupt on LPT1.

> *I've just upgraded from NetWare v2.15 to v3.11, and my old print queues don't work any more. PSERVER just doesn't seem to see them. Newly-created queues work okay, though. What do you suggest?*

To fix the problem, follow these steps:

1. In PCONSOLE, select "Print Queue Information" and delete all of old queues.

2. While still in PCONSOLE, select "Print Server Information" and delete the print servers.

3. Next, run FILER. Change the current directory to SYS:SYSTEM, and mark (with the <F5> key) all subdirectory names that consist of hexadecimal numbers. (These are the queues and print servers).

4. Press <Del>, and then choose to delete the entire directory structure. Confirm your choice when prompted. Exit FILER.

5. Change to the SYS:SYSTEM directory and run the NetWare BINDFIX program.

6. Go back into PCONSOLE and recreate the queues and print servers.

> *I'm running NetWare v2.2 with core printing enabled. I also have a dedicated print server running on an old IBM AT. When I first installed the new system, I used the console command "QUEUE name CREATE" to create some new queues. Those queues work for printers attached to the file server, but the print server can't handle them. How can I get them to work?*

Queues created via file server console commands only work at the server. Queues created through PCONSOLE work both places. To solve your problem, follow the steps listed in the answer to the previous question.

> *We recently upgraded from NetWare v2.15 to v2.2. Since we still have two printers attached to the file server, we included core printing in our new operating system. We also run PSERVER.VAP on the server. Are we headed for trouble?*

This setup is okay if you're careful. The main thing you must never do is have your print server manage a printer on the same port that core printing is managing. If both the print server and core printing try to manage LPT1, for example, you will eventually wind up with a "deadly embrace." This term describes a situation in which two tasks are each waiting for the other to go first. In other words, the file server and the print server are saying to each other, "No, you go ahead and print. I'll wait."

349

If you let the file server manage the local printers and have the VAP manage only remote ones, you'll be safe. But since you're running the VAP anyway, you should redo your operating system without core printing and add the local printers to the print server. You'll probably see a measurable improvement in file server performance.

> *We just upgraded from NetWare v2.15 to v2.2. We restored all our files from tape, except for those in SYS:SYSTEM, SYS:LOGIN, and SYS:PUBLIC. According to the documentation, the binderies should be okay. However, when we try to print, we get "Error 156." And, of course, nothing prints. What's the problem?*

Error 156 means that an invalid path was found. When you create a print queue or print server, NetWare creates a subdirectory under SYS:SYSTEM that corresponds to it. NetWare also creates two hidden files in each of those directories. Your upgrade process did not carry over those directories and their contents.

The solution is to delete all of the queues and print servers on your system, run BINDFIX, bring the file server down and reboot it, then create all your print queues and print servers again.

> *Is there any way to get a print job to enter a queue and be already on hold? There doesn't seem to be a parameter to accomplish it.*

Download the IQUEUE.ZIP file from NetWire (IQ is a shareware program and is described in Chapter 13). One of the files it contains is ONHOLD.COM. If you run this program before entering your application, any print files it sends will arrive in the queue with a user hold already in place.

> *After upgrading FS215-3 (NetWare v2.15) to FS311-3 (NetWare v3.11) we find that none of our PRINTCON job configurations work. Whenever we go into PRINTCON, we get the error message "Cannot attach to selected server as guest." How can we fix this?*

The problem is due to the server's name change. When you select an existing print job configuration in PRINTCON, it needs certain information (queue names and forms, among other things) from the target file server. If you're not already logged in to this server, PRINTCON tries to log in as GUEST. Since the name of the file server has changed, you cannot possibly log in; hence, the error message.

The solution is to go into PRINTCON.DAT with DEBUG (or a similar disk sector editor, such as the one from Norton Utilities). Scan for the old file server name and replace it with the new one. That will make the PRINTCON.DAT file usable. From there, you can document the configurations and regenerate them on the new file server.

PostScript Printing

We just got a new PostScript-based laser printer. To test it out, I attached it to my workstation and used the DOS PRINT command to print a test page supplied by the printer manufacturer. The test page printed as expected. Then I modified my word processor to use a PostScript driver, which also printed the test page as expected. Assuming that the setup was fine, I moved the printer to the print server and set up a queue for it. Now, it just blinks whenever we send a print job. Any suggestions?

First, look at the job in the queue (put the job on hold if you have to) and make sure that it is set for NO BANNERS. NetWare creates banner pages as the job begins to leave the queue, and the banner data does not include any PostScript control information. If it is set to print banners, check the CAPTURE or NPRINT command lines, or the default PRINTCON job configuration, and disable banner pages.

If banner pages are important to you, you can purchase Printer Assist by Fresh Technology (see the discussion of this product in Chapter 13.) Printer Assist has the ability to handle PostScript banners.

If banners are not the problem, complete the following steps:

1. Send a PostScript print job to a queue.

2. Use PCONSOLE to get the print queue ID and the job number of the print job you put into the queue.

3. Change your current directory to SYS:SYSTEM/queueid.

4. Use FILER to view the print job in that directory.

5. Look at the first few characters and the last few characters of the print job. If they are Escape characters or printer control codes, you will need to modify your PRINTCON definitions and select a PostScript printer. (See Chapter 7 for instructions.)

We use WordPerfect on our network. For small print jobs (1-5 pages), everything works fine. But as the jobs grow larger, printing takes much longer. As a test, I timed a five-page job at eight minutes. Then I appended the file to itself until it was a 20-page job. This file should have printed in about 32 minutes, but it took over an hour. What's wrong?

Contact WordPerfect Corporation and get the latest version of WordPerfect. Even if you're already using version 5.1, ask them to send the update diskette dated on or after 12/31/90. Also, get the updated PostScript driver (APLASIIN.PRS).

I have created some files with a database program. I'd like to send them to the laser printer, but the printer is set up for PostScript. My database has no PostScript ability. Is there anything I can do short of getting a new printer?

There are several alternatives. See Chapter 15 for special instructions on dealing with PostScript printers on a network.

Potpourri

We'd like to charge for printing, but Novell doesn't include that capability in their accounting function. Any ideas?

Printer Assist from Fresh Technology, LANSpool from Intel, and Mosaic from Insight all have an accounting feature. (These programs are discussed in Chapter 13.) You can use them to track printer usage.

However, be aware that it is not really possible to track the number of pages printed. One person might print just a few characters on a page, while another might print a 70KB graphic image. It might be fairer to charge by the byte, or by elapsed time.

We have an HP LaserJet Series III printer attached to our print server via the serial port. It worked when attached to a NetWare v2.15 file server, but we cannot seem to make it work with NetWare v2.2. Any ideas?

On both IBM and HP laser printers, serial printing requires the original IBM or HP cables, respectively (they're not interchangeable). Sometimes, when printers get moved or when a cable is already attached to the computer, the original cable is not used.

Get the original cable (it has a 25-pin connector at each end) and see if that fixes the problem. Here are the pinouts for a 9-to-25 pin converter if your computer has a 9-pin serial port:

```
      9 Pin                    25 Pin
        2  _____    2
        3  _____    3
        5  _____    7
        6  __
             |_____ 20
        8  __
```

Also, NetWare v2.15 polled the printer, while NetWare v2.2's print server uses interrupts. Make sure your printer is defined accordingly.

I'd like to have a serial printer about 50 feet away from the computer that manages it. I know we can do this with a standard serial cable, but we have to run it through an already crowded conduit. How can we get this to work?

There are two easy solutions here. If you're using Ethernet or token ring cabling, you can get a LANPort (from Intel) or LANPress (from Castelle) and attach that device to the LAN cable at the remote location. Both devices have serial ports for output and neither requires an attached PC. (These products are discussed in Chapter 14.)

The other solution is to get a pair of adapters that convert from serial cable to telephone wire. Run the telephone wire through the conduit (you might even find two free pairs already in the conduit). If you must have the adapters custom made, use the pinouts described in the previous answer.

We have a dot matrix printer that prints on tractor-fed special forms. From time to time, the printer goes off-line and we have to turn it off and back on again to get it to come back on-line. Occasionally, we have to down the server and turn it off and back on as well. Why is this happening?

Sometimes special forms (especially carbonless ones) generate a great deal of static electricity. Try grounding the printer. The static buildup is probably strongest along the paper path. If the printer has a metal paper guide, that is a good place to connect a lightweight, flexible chain that you could attach to ground.

Also, since the problem affects the server as well, make sure that the printer cable is grounded, too. (Pin 1 should be attached to the shield.)

We use NetWare Name Service. Capturing to a particular print queue usually works, but when users are logged into the new file server, named FS386-4, it always fails. What is the problem?

NetWare Name Service (NNS) handles printing as a domain-wide resource. Whenever you create a queue on any file server, it physically creates the queue as requested, then updates the binderies on all the other file servers in the domain with logical pointers to the physical queue. This allows NNS to seamlessly redirect print jobs to the proper locations.

Your new queue and the file server's bindery are out of synchronization. You need to run the NETCON program to resynchronize the servers. Here are the basic steps to follow:

1. Start NETCON.

2. Choose "Domain Administration."

3. Choose "Domain Synchronization."

4. Choose "Synchronize Domain."

5. Select the out-of-sync file server (FS386-4 in this example).

6. Select a template file server (one that you're sure is in sync).

7. Confirm the continuation request.

Current NetWare Printing Programs

This appendix contains information about the printing-related programs available for use with NetWare. (Version numbers are the most current as of this writing.)

It first lists printing-related programs distributed by Novell with its NetWare v2.20 and NetWare v3.11 products. The information shown was generated using the VERSION program, found in the SYS:PUBLIC directory.

Next, it presents a directory listing of these files, showing their date, time, and size.

At the end, it lists updates to these programs available from Novell or as downloadable files in the NOVLIB library on Novell's NetWire forum on CompuServe.

Current Version Numbers

CAPTURE.EXE:
    Version 3.50
        (c) Copyright 1983 - 1990 Novell, Inc. All rights reserved
    Checksum is 29D7D.

ENDCAP.EXE:
    Version EndCapture V1.00
    Checksum is FFFFD288.

NPRINT.EXE:
    Version 3.54
        (c) Copyright 1983 - 1991 Novell, Inc. All rights reserved
    Checksum is 3CE2C.

PCONSOLE.EXE:
>   Version 1.51
>   Requires Overlay Version 1.02
>   (c) Copyright 1983 - 1990 Novell, Inc. All rights reserved
>   Checksum is 6CEAB.

PRINTCON.EXE:
>   Version 1.52
>   Requires Overlay Version 1.02
>   (c) Copyright 1983 - 1991 Novell, Inc. All rights reserved
>   Checksum is 1FD30.

PRINTDEF.EXE:
>   Version 1.51
>   Requires Overlay Version 1.02
>   (c) Copyright 1983 - 1991 Novell, Inc. All rights reserved
>   Checksum is 115CA.

PSERVER.VAP:
>   Version PServer, Version 1.21
>   Checksum is 285FA.

PSTAT.EXE:
>   Version PStat V2.00
>   Checksum is 764F.

RPRINTER.EXE:
>   Version 1.21
>   Requires Overlay Version 1.02
>   Checksum is 3F0DC.

Date, Time, and Size

Directory of `A:\PRINT-2\PUBLIC`

```
CAPTURE   EXE     49505   1-28-91   4:21p
ENDCAP    EXF     13553   7-19-89  10:55a
NPRINT    EXE     85157   2-05-91   1:26p
PCONSOLE  EXE    233687   2-11-91   6:57a
PCONSOLE  HLP     40820   2-07-91   4:54p
PRINTCON  EXE    160823   1-26-91   7:58a
PRINTCON  HLP     14223   1-10-91   9:59a
PRINTDEF  EXE    192283   2-11-91   4:52p
PRINTDEF  HLP     34426   2-11-91   3:44p
PSTAT     EXE     28921   2-02-91  10:55a
```

Downloadable Files

This section describes files that are available on NetWire. Acquiring the latest version of the print server is recommended for users of NetWare v2.20 and v3.11. The PRINTCON update is only for NetWare v2.1x users (users of v2.20 and v3.11 already have an even newer version). The descriptions of these files are excerpted from their NOVLIB listings.

PKZ110.EXE is the program you can use to convert files with a .ZIP extension into a usable form. To save both space and charges for downloading time, and to make sure that related files are kept together, the PKZIP program is used to compress one or more programs into a single file. Its counterpart, PKUNZIP, is used to return them to their original form. If you do not already have a copy of this utility, you can download it from NOVLIB as well. Its description is presented here as the fourth file that you might want to download. Once you have the file, copy it to its own directory and type PKZ110. PKZ110.EXE is a self-extracting file (it has the PKUNZIP code built in). As a result, it will automatically extract the usable component files and place them in your current directory.

CAP-NT.ZIP   29-Mar-90   NOVLIB 6

This Beta version of the 286 and 386 CAPTURE has been modified so that the default setting is NO TABS. This will not override PRINTCON job settings. This modification was done at the request of end users.

PSV122.ZIP   04-Oct-91   NOVLIB 6

This file contains the following updated Print Server files v1.22:

PSERVER.VAP   PSERVER.EXE   PSERVER.NLM

This new VAP contains the auto load feature which allows an unattended load of the pserver.vap. The NLM and EXE address a problem with possible data corruption.

> **Note:** The NLM requires version 3.11. It will not work on a version 3.10 or lower server.

PRNTDF.ZIP   12-Jun-90   NOVLIB 6

This file contains the latest PRINTDEF v1.11 utility. This version correctly initializes the printer with the print header mode as defined in PRINTDEF and selected in PRINTCON.

> **Note:** To make use of this file, delete NET$PRN.DAT from SYS:PUBLIC and delete all copies of PRINTCON.DAT from the users' mailboxes. Then use this new PRINTDEF to create a new NET$PRN.DAT and your old PRINTCON to make new PRINTCON.DAT files. (You'll find instructions for using these programs in Chapter 7.)

PKZ110.EXE   13-Apr-90   NOVLIB 15

This file contains the newest version of PKZIP and PKUNZIP. It is self-extracting.

Network Printing Using Windows 3.0

This appendix gives some tips for making network printing work from within Microsoft Windows. It will cover both setup and performance enhancement. These descriptions assume that you have already installed Windows on your workstation or network, and that you have run IPX and NETX at your workstation before entering Windows.

There are three places within Windows where printing control information must be entered or edited:

1. The Control Panel's Network icon
2. The Control Panel's Printer icon
3. The Print Manager

We'll go into each of these in turn, and explain how to add or edit the information for network printing.

Accessing the Control Panel

To access Windows' control panel from within Program Manager, double-click on the Main Group (if necessary) and then double-click on the Control Panel Icon within that group. The control panel contains twelve icons; among them are the NetWork icon and the Printer icon.

The Control Panel's Network Icon

Double-click on the NetWork Icon from the control panel. If you are using the original NetWare Windows driver (the one included with Windows v3.0), you will see a menu that gives you the ability to attach to or detach from a file server and to enable or disable broadcast messages. We'll give instructions for users of this old driver, but a newer one is available from NetWire's NOVLIB (see Appendix A for information about downloading files from NOVLIB). The file name on NOVLIB is WINUPx.ZIP, where x represents the revision number. Currently, WINUP5.ZIP is the latest available. It is well worth the time and effort to download this driver and install it.

The next section is for users who have Version 1.00 of the Windows driver set. If you have Version 1.03, skip to that section. Discussion of the Control Panel's Printer Icon follows the second section.

Instructions for NetWare Driver Set v1.00

If you are using the old NetWare driver, you can edit the NETWARE.INI file to add some additional programs to the default ones. Look for the section of the INI file that resembles Figure B-1.

```
[MSW30-Utils]
Attach a File=<Attach
Detach a File=<Detach
Enable Broadcast Messages=<Messages
Disable Broadcast Messages=<No Messages
```

Figure B-1: Windows' NETWARE.INI file contains these lines for NetWare.

In this part of the file, add the lines shown in Figure B-2. (You may also add other NetWare programs, such as FCONSOLE, SYSCON, and FILER.)

```
Print Console=PCONSOLE
Printer Control=PRINTCON
```

Figure B-2: Insert these lines to add PCONSOLE and PRINTCON to the NetWare menu.

Instructions for NetWare Driver Set v1.03

Those users who have the new driver set (version 1.03 is the latest) will find a much larger list of selections, three of which apply to printing. They are "Max Jobs," "Buffer Size," and "Update Seconds." These parameters control how the Windows Print Manager will display its output at your workstation.

"Max Jobs" determines how many print jobs in any queue Windows will display. The default is 50, which is more jobs than most queues ever have at once. The range is from 1 to 250.

"Buffer Size" is the number of bytes of print output that will be buffered at your workstation before being sent to the print queue. The default of 3500 is also the minimum; this is the number you should use.

"Update Seconds" determines how often Windows will ask NetWare for an update of a given queue's status. The range is from 1 to 65 seconds. If you make the time too short, you'll significantly increase network traffic; if you make it too long, you'll be looking at jobs in the queue that have already been printed. The default value of 30 is usually an excellent choice.

The Control Panel's Printer Icon

To print from the Windows environment, you must first install a printer driver. Windows requires a separate driver for each port on your machine, whether the port is physical or logical. So, if your word processor is set up to send PostScript output to LPT1 and your label program expects a dot matrix printer on LPT2, you must install two printer drivers in Windows. Users who have their programs set up to expect the same kind of printer on all parallel ports still must install multiple drivers, even if it means installing the same driver more than once.

Here are the steps for installing a printer driver in Windows.

1. Double-click on the Control Panel Printer Icon to open it.

2. Click on "Add Printers." From the resulting list of printers shown, choose a printer and click on "Install."

3. Assign a logical port to the printer and make it active by clicking on it. There will probably be an "X" in the "Use Print Manager" box. Click on the box to remove the X. (This prevents double spooling, which occurs when you send jobs to the print manager's spool, and then print manager sends it to a NetWare queue. Double spooling increases network traffic and server overhead, and wastes disk space. It has no advantages.)

4. In addition to the usual COM and LPT choices, Windows also gives you two choices you may not be familiar with. One is called the "EPT Printer," for a special IBM Personal Page Printer that comes with its own controller card. The other is for LPT1.OS2. This was originally designed for people who used Windows in the OS/2 DOS box. Like NetWare, OS/2 spools printer output. In order for a DOS process to spool to OS/2, it had to use the slower DOS-based calls, rather than Window's normally faster use of direct BIOS calls. Normally, you will not need to use this setting. But if you are using RPRINTER at your workstation and your printer behaves strangely (continuously ejecting paper, or losing its connection to the print server), you might be able to fix the problem by selecting the LPT1.OS2 port.

5. Click on the "NetWork" button to assign a queue to service the selected port. First click on the file server name, then the queue name. Click on "Connect" to complete the assignment.

There is no option here to select banners, tabs, timeouts, and other parameters as you normally would in a CAPTURE statement. You should use PRINTCON to set up a default job configuration that makes the proper choices for you. If you are using version 1.03 of the NetWare driver set, you can open that program and choose the Printer icon from within it. Then select a queue and click on "Options." From there you'll have the ability to set most of the CAPTURE options.

Accessing the Print Manager

To access up the Print Manager, double-click on the Main group from within Program Manager, and then double-click on the Print Manger icon. That will start the Print Manager.

The Print Manager shows you the print jobs you have submitted to network queues. If you want to see all of the print jobs in the queue, pull down the View menu and choose "Selected Net Queue." To see other queues, choose "Other Net Queue" from the same menu. There is no browse facility; you'll have to name the other queue you wish to see. (You must name both the file server and the queue, using a slash "/" to separate them. If you just name the queue, you'll get an error message telling you that the queue no longer exists.)

To tell Windows that you don't want it to spool print jobs, click on the "Options" box and then on the "Network" menu item. Make sure the box labelled "Print Net Jobs Direct" has an "X" in it. The other item in this dialog box is "Update Network Display." If you remove the "X" here, it will stop Print Manager from updating the queue status display.

Printing with NetWare Lite

This appendix deals with NetWare Lite, Novell's peer-to-peer network product, only so far as printing is concerned. The following discussion assumes that you have already installed NetWare Lite at your site and that you are now ready to set up and use a shared printer.

Installing a Shared Printer

To share a printer on a NetWare Lite network, you must make that station a "Server." If you also want to use it as a workstation, you may do so by running the "Client" program at that same station. If not, you can run "Client" at any other workstations you want to participate in the NetWare Lite network.

After loading the "Client" software and logging in to the network as Supervisor, type the "NET" command. This command, without any parameters, brings up a main menu. From that menu, select "Supervise the network." The resulting options are shown in Figure C-1.

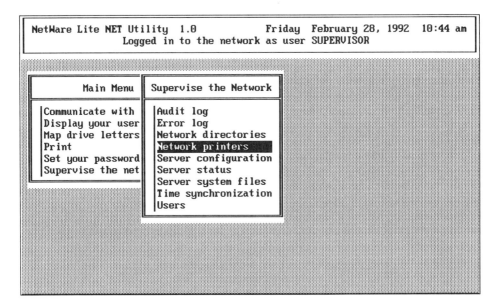

Figure C-1: You define NetWare Lite printers via the "Network printers" options.

Choose "Network printers" to bring up a list of printers that have already been defined. (At first, this list will be empty.) Press <Ins> to add a printer to the list. The program asks for the name of the server and the name of the printer. After you answer, it will ask you to select the port the printer is attached to, as shown in Figure C-2.

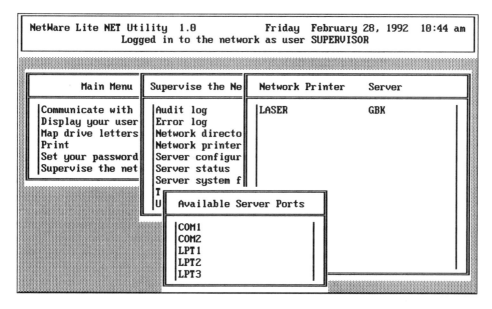

Figure C-2: You must select a port for the printer.

This completes the printer installation process. When you want to monitor the status of a printer, run NET and choose "Supervise the network" and "Network printers" again. The "Network Printer" list will display all of the printers that have been defined. Highlight the one you want to monitor and press <Enter>. You'll see a status screen similar to the one shown here in Figure C-3.

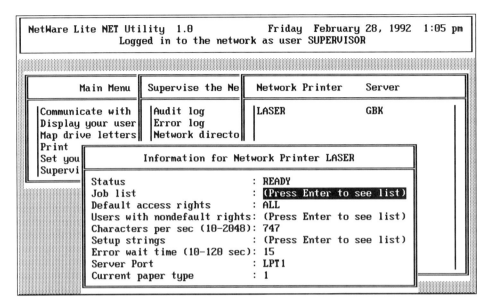

```
NetWare Lite NET Utility  1.0              Friday  February 28, 1992  1:05 pm
                        Logged in to the network as user SUPERVISOR

         Main Menu   ║ Supervise the Ne ║ Network Printer    Server

   Communicate with  ║ Audit log        ║ LASER              GBK
   Display your user ║ Error log        ║
   Map drive letters ║ Network directo  ║
   Print
   Set you ┌──────────────── Information for Network Printer LASER ──────────────┐
   Supervi │                                                                    │
           │  Status                       : READY                              │
           │  Job list                     : (Press Enter to see list)          │
           │  Default access rights        : ALL                                │
           │  Users with nondefault rights : (Press Enter to see list)          │
           │  Characters per sec (10-2048) : 747                                │
           │  Setup strings                : (Press Enter to see list)          │
           │  Error wait time (10-120 sec) : 15                                 │
           │  Server Port                  : LPT1                               │
           │  Current paper type           : 1                                  │
           └────────────────────────────────────────────────────────────────────┘
```

Figure C-3: You can monitor network printers from this Supervisor's printer management screen.

Using a Shared Printer

To use a printer that's not attached to your workstation, run the CAPTURE command. The syntax is "NET CAPTURE parameters." (All Netware Lite commands are built in to the NET program. You can access them via NET's main menu or by specifying the command as a parameter on the NET command line.)

If you need help with the CAPTURE parameters, you can display help information by typing "NET HELP CAPTURE." The help screen shown in Figure C-4 shows the additional parameters you can include.

```
┌──────────────────────────────────────────────────────────────────┐
│ Usage:    NET CAPTURE                                              │
│                                                                    │
│           NET CAPTURE DEL Port                                     │
│                                                                    │
│           NET CAPTURE Port      Printer  Server    Settings        │
│                       (optional)        (optional) (optional)      │
│ ──────────────────────────────────────────────────────────────────│
│ Meaning:  NET CAPTURE......Lists captured ports and settings.      │
│           NET CAPTURE DEL..Deletes capture of specified port.      │
│           Port............LPT1, LPT2, or LPT3.                     │
│           Printer.........Network Printer where you want jobs sent.│
│           Server..........Server that the Network Printer is connected to.│
│           Settings........Specify one or more of the following:    │
│             banner....b=y/n     formfeed....f=y/n    tabs.....t=0-32│
│             copies....c=1-250   notify......n=y/n    setup....s=string│
│             direct....d=y/n     paper type..p=1-10   wait.....w=0-3600│
│ ──────────────────────────────────────────────────────────────────│
│ Example:  c:\>net capture lpt1 laser                               │
│                                                                    │
│       Redirects jobs sent to the client's LPT1 port to Network Printer LASER.│
└──────────────────────────────────────────────────────────────────┘
```

Figure C-4: NET HELP CAPTURE displays information about the command line parameters.

Most of these parameters are the same as their counterparts in NetWare 286 or NetWare 386 (see the discussion of CAPTURE parameters in Chapter 6). The differences are listed below.

Papertype   Same as the NetWare "Form" parameter, except that it only allows form numbers (1-10)

Wait   Same as the NetWare "Timeout" parameter

Tabs   The default is zero (in NetWare it's 8)

Banner   You specify only "Y" or "N" (there is no "Name=" field)

Formfeed   Also "Y" or "N" (there isn't a "NoFormFeed" option)

Direct   This parameter has no NetWare counterpart. When it's set to "Y," print jobs will start printing at the printer before they have completely left the application program that's sending them. When set to "N," printing behaves as in regular NetWare: print jobs don't start printing until after the application releases them.

You can also set up a CAPTURE command in menu mode. Run the menu program "NET" and then select the "Print" option. You'll see a list of the three parallel ports (LPT1, LPT2, and LPT3). When you highlight the desired port and press <Enter>, you'll see the screen shown in Figure C-5.

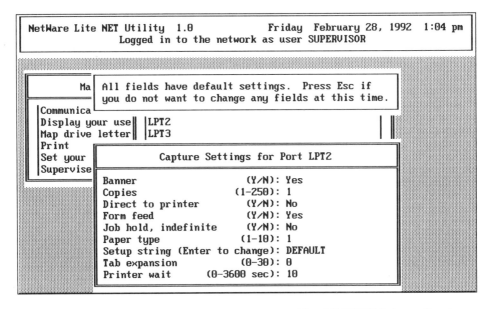

Figure C-5: You can use NET to enter the NetWare Lite CAPTURE information in menu mode.

To print an existing file, use the "NET PRINT filename" command. NET PRINT is not like NetWare's NPRINT command, where the parameters are nearly identical to the parameters for CAPTURE. Instead, NetWare Lite assumes that NET CAPTURE has already been issued, and uses the same settings. The only additional parameter (which is optional) is to specify the name of a network printer. Figure C-6 shows the help screen for NET PRINT.

```
Usage:    NET PRINT Filename NetworkPrinter
                           (optional)

Meaning:  PRINT............Prints a file on a Network Printer.
          Filename.........The name of the file to be printed.
          NetworkPrinter...The name of a Network Printer (first use
                           CAPTURE to assign the Network Printer to a
                           port at your workstation).  If you do not
                           specify a Network Printer, the job is sent
                           to the first available captured port.

Example:  c:\>net print memo.txt laserletter
```

Figure C-6: The NET PRINT help screen shows how to use the command.

Index

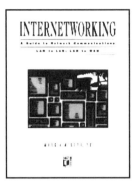

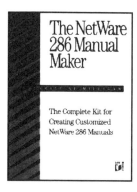

M&T BOOKS

ORDER FORM

To Order: Return this form with your payment to M&T Books, 411 Borel Avenue, Suite 100, San Mateo, CA 94402 or **call toll-free 1-800-533-4372 (in California, call 1-800-356-2002).**

ITEM #	DESCRIPTION	DISK	PRICE

Subtotal

CA residents add sales tax ___%

Add $4.50 per item for shipping and handling

TOTAL

Charge my:
- ☐ **Visa**
- ☐ **MasterCard**
- ☐ **AmExpress**

- ☐ **Check enclosed, payable to M&T Books.**

CARD NO.

SIGNATURE   EXP. DATE

NAME

ADDRESS

CITY

STATE   ZIP

M&T GUARANTEE: If your are not satisfied with your order for any reason, return it to us within 25 days of receipt for a full refund. Note: Refunds on disks apply only when returned with book within guarantee period. Disks damaged in transit or defective will be promptly replaced, but cannot be exchanged for a disk from a different title.

8041

This book belongs to:

Steve Whitaker

Tell us what you think and we'll send you a free M&T Books catalog

It is our goal at M&T Books to produce the best technical books available. But you can help us make our books even better by letting us know what you think about this particular title.Please take a moment to fill out this card and mail it to us. Your opinion is appreciated.

Tell us about yourself

Name_____

Company_____

Address_____

City_____

State/Zip_____

Title of this book?

_____

Where did you purchase this book?

☐ Bookstore
☐ Catalog
☐ Direct Mail
☐ Magazine Ad
☐ Postcard Pack
☐ Other

Why did you choose this book?

☐ Recommended
☐ Read book review
☐ Read ad/catalog copy
☐ Responded to a special offer
☐ M&T Books' reputation
☐ Price
☐ Nice Cover

How would you rate the overall content of this book?

☐ Excellent
☐ Good
☐ Fair
☐ Poor

Why?

_____

_____

What chapters did you find valuable?

_____

_____

_____

What did you find least useful?

_____

_____

_____

What topic(s) would you add to future editions of this book?

_____

_____

_____

What other titles would you like to see M&T Books publish?

_____

_____

_____

Which format do you prefer for the optional disk?

☐ 5.25"   ☐ 3.5"

Any other comments?

_____

_____

_____

☐ Check here for
M&T Books Catalog

M&T BOOKS

I.S.B.N. 2578

BUSINESS REPLY MAIL

FIRST CLASS MAIL PERMIT 2660 SAN MATEO, CA

POSTAGE WILL BE PAID BY ADDRESSEE

M&T BOOKS

411 Borel Avenue, Suite 100
San Mateo, CA 94402-9885

PLEASE FOLD ALONG LINE AND STAPLE OR TAPE CLOSED